ORIENTAL FASHIONS

Are the best things in life passing you by?

MAN MATE IN BRIEF

S-T-R-E-T-C-H

S-T-R-E-T-C-H

IT'S A MAN'S WORLD
MEN'S ADVENTURE MAGAZINES, THE POSTWAR PULPS

By Adam Parfrey

Design Editor: Hedi El Kholti

Contributors: Bruce Jay Friedman
Josh Alan Friedman
Mort Künstler
Norman Saunders
David Saunders
Bill Devine

ISBN: 0-922915-81-4

Feral House
PO Box 13067
Los Angeles, CA 90013
www.feralhouse.com

Printed in China

ACKNOWLEDGMENTS
The author wishes to express his thanks to:

Mort Künstler, the primary illustrator of the men's adventure genre, for unearthing hundreds of paintings from his attic, and the hours it took him and his staff (Jane, Paula and Lissette) to photograph a good number of them, and discovering, whenever possible, the magazines in which they appeared.

Josh Alan Friedman for contacts and interviews with Magazine Management personnel, including the late, great Mario Puzo.

Bruce Jay Friedman for his recollections and fine article on the Martin Goodman days.

David Saunders for the photographs, slides and article about—and from—his father's great career.

Jonathan Shaw and Greg Escalante for their collections of original Norm Eastman paintings, and Billy Shire, Joe Coleman, Dona Abuaf and Gary Pressman for their help.

Dian Hanson for her recommendations.

Bill Devine for being the original, devout collector of men's adventure magazines, and the ability to reproduce and enhance his checklist.

Bill Nelson, Edward Smith, Andrew Barbantini, Jeffrey Rich, Norm Stringer, Rich Pathos, Ira Meshbane, Glenn Dunn—and his new *Man's Story* take-off—for scans of magazines and illustrations.

Crispin, Jodi, Laura, Ween, Michael, Steve, Peter, Lance, and Allan for their ongoing support.

Marti and Alice for their love.

Hedi el Kholti for so much of his time, not to mention his collaborative brilliance.

CONTENTS

Our Navy

'The Gyp Joint'

Mid-April, 1945   Price 25 Cent

Adam Parfrey

FROM PULP TO POSTERITY:
THE ORIGINS OF MEN'S ADVENTURE MAGAZINES

SOON AFTER THE SMOOCHES OF VJ DAY, soldiers were brought home and thrown into civilian life. Despite labor battles and false starts, the American capitalist machine started to roar. Europe and Asia began rebuilding with Marshall Plan billions, and in the States, millions of servicemen took advantage of G.I. Bill perks and attended college, trained for jobs and took out cheap loans for homes, farms and businesses.

A societal expansion, unseen in world history since the Roman empire, hit America. This was a time of confidence and arrogance—of bigness. After decades of the Great Depression and wartime shortages and sacrifice, spending, consuming and reproducing became synonymous with patriotism.

You couldn't convince the postwar Fortune 500 that they could show off their cars, liquor, cigarettes and electric devices in publications synonymous with a depressed economy. These mags were even named after the raggy paper stock on which they were printed: *pulps*. Where in the past the blue-collar workers were content with their nickel and dime pulps, they now needed larger magazines to fit the larger furniture in their larger suburban homes. Though many of the themes remained the same—evil savages, Japs and Nazis torturing hussies in their scanties—the lure of wealth was dangled subliminally into the minds of readers, since large slicks were once a format reserved for an audience of Ivy League city slickers, as seen in the haughty *Harper's*, eggheaded *Esquire* and commodious Condé Nast publications.

This new era lacked its means of instruction for gray flannel and blue-collar foot soldiers. After vets returned home, battles were fought daily in the expanding corporate world. Instead of being sent to Boot Camp, given uniforms and meals and taught how to make camp and murder, corporate soldiers were expected to compete in the marketplace, where they were threatened by demotion and a variety of ridicule. It is not a coincidence that the word "fired" also means to discharge a firearm or explosive device. The humiliations of the working world and romance were more subtle and devious. Instead of losing your leg to a grenade, you lost your liver drinking off the stress, or your head in a traffic accident to another worker speeding past romantic defeats.

In wartime the Armed Services taught soldiers how to fight enemies, but in postwar America, working-class soldiers depended upon the mass-market magazines for their civilian life-lessons. Men's magazines. Men's adventure magazines. All of them had, among the lures of woman flesh and vicious bad guys, a lot of warnings, how-to's, and comforting memories of wartime, when decisions were black and white, the villains darker and victories sweeter.

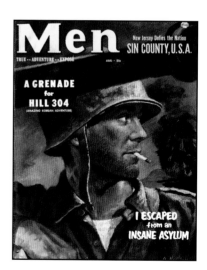

OUR NAVY, April 1945.

TRUE, December 1946. Illustration: Ralph Stein.

MEN, August 1952. Illustration: George Kanelous.

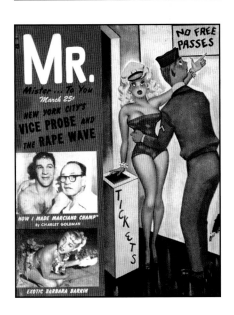

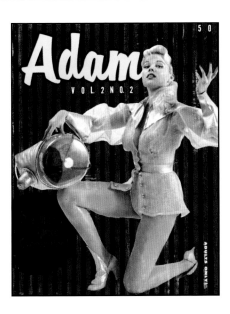

A selection of adventure mag-era girlie slicks for men:

SWAGGER, January 1951. **SATAN: DEVILISH ENTERTAINMENT FOR MEN**, June 1957.
TOMCAT, August 1958. **MR.: MISTER … TO YOU**, March 1953.
JEM: THE MAGAZINE FOR MASTERFUL MEN, March 1958. **ADAM**, Vol. 2 No. 2, 1958.

When the Age of Anxiety came to America at the height of the Cold War, a chaotic market scrambled to sell magazines, at whatever cost.

Everyone knew why Fawcett Publications' *True* commanded a massive two million copy circulation. Its inoffensive emphasis on mild recreation and dogs and sweaters made for family-sanctified barbershop reading and the safe and proper gift of wives, who could rely on *True* accommodating husbands without arousing them with photo-spreads of comely hoores or suggestive lip-smacking articles.

Publishers understood that the reason for *True*'s large circulation would not hold for impulsive newsstand purchases. Sensational illustrations, come-on headlines and barely-covered nymphos beckoned male readers. The trick was to tease coinage from pockets rather than intimidate buyers fearing humiliation at the sales register and later with the family at home.

For decades, with its Petty and Varga(s) spreads, as well as its consumerist manifestos, *Esquire* was seen as the prototype of the so-called men's magazine until December 1953, which brought in *Playboy* magazine and the girlie slicker imitations. But neither *Esquire*, nor *Playboy* or the copy publications hit the same audiences, really, of Fawcett's *True* magazine, the pulp era of *Argosy* and *Adventure* magazines. The wildest, greasiest subject matter of men's adventure magazines of the '50s, '60s and early '70s— the Nazi torture fiend—was first portrayed in wartime detective magazines. That evil Nazi, as a character, outperforms the sadism of DeSade, whose abridged books sold in the back of many torture-laden adventure mags.

Men's adventure magazines followed the pulp blueprint almost precisely. Mutant Chinks and Japs, vicious enemies of America, spear-chucking, head-collecting savages and damsels in distress saved at the last second by heroic white men. But unlike the majority of pulp publications, most adventure magazines began to purvey the "true story," whether or not their editorial staffs actually produced truthful articles, or even cared to do so.

Pulp art and Pulp Culture, which ended soon after the end of World War II and prior to the emergence of adventure magazines, have earned extravagant book-length investigations in recent years.

Though many of the best pulp illustrators had even more extraordinary careers in the postwar men's adventure slicks, this genre has not had its books, its public consideration. Perhaps this is due to a more limited audience and consequently, a narrower subject matter. Perhaps it's more difficult to accept extremities in race, gender, and sadistic sleaze in more recent publications. Whatever the cause of mass-market inattention, these magazines deserve our interest, as they tell us so much about American working-class fears, desires and wet dreams of the early '50s through the early '70s—a time when cover illustrations became smaller and smaller, replaced at first by text and later by photos of girls, when the nth sadistic Nazi torture scene failed to attract as many buyers as lower-rung softcore photographs.

Speaking to the several extant writers and editors of the men's adventure magazine genre, I was surprised by how little they were aware that their publications put across themes that might be interpreted as being racist, misogynist, imperialist, or any other postmodern academic construct today.

"That was the way things were," said Bruce Jay Friedman, editor of several Man's Management publications. "We didn't think twice about it."

Most scribes laboring for Martin Goodman's Magazine Management firm and other repositories of adventure magazines spoke of feeling like well-compensated slaves of a very particular style that was not their own. A July '64 issue of *Writer's Digest* encapsulated the style desired by *Saga* magazine, a less cheesy variety of men's adventure magazine:

> We are principally interested in strong-action picturestories on non-war adventure themes; man against nature, man against beast, man against man. We try to stress the "man triumphant" idea whenever possible.

This was not the style with which editor Bruce Jay Friedman felt most comfortable, and when editing publications for Martin Goodman he unsuccessfully tried to talk him out of running advertisements for trusses, an ad signaling the magazine's target audience: blue-collar yahoos. It would be years before he could raise his head at industry cocktail parties, when his acclaimed examples of "black humor fiction" were seen as appropriate material for a hipper, more monied crowd.

Men's adventure magazines, or the "sweat" or "armpit school," as exemplified by Martin Goodman with its "animal nibbler" "Sintown epics," "prison breakouts," "ingenious G.I. manufactured contraptions," "revenge trackdown," and "death trek" yarns, were by no means the "leg shackler" magazines, with their overt torture, Nazi/Jap/Commie/Cuban style.

It's the lowest of the low, the Nazi torture magazines that are the most sought-after today, due primarily to amazing cover paintings by Norm Eastman, Rafael DeSoto and Norman Saunders, former stars of the most extreme, violent, strange and torturous pre-Code pulps. Their leg shackler paintings are remarkable both for their sadistic extremity and genius of execution.

Looking at these magazines, and their perversity, you start to wonder what possessed those who drew, wrote, edited and published them. When you look at the biographies of certain responsible parties, the bulb brightens.

There's Norman Saunders, illustrator, King of the Pulps, and later, creator of the great tongue-in-cheek kiddie horror "Mars Attacks" cards, and if we believe his son David Saunders, he had his most fun with Wacky Packs, the beyond-*Mad* Magazine rip at advertising and corporatism. And Bruce Jay Friedman, later the author of *Steambath* and *Stern* and *The Lonely Man*, one of the first writers heralded for perpetrating diseased black humor on the the American public. Read Bruce Jay and son Josh Alan's articles about the genre, and look at the party pictures, and you begin to understand that the tongues were packed in cheek, and sometimes they spilled out. As long as buyers were roped in, publishers overlooked the dark "in" humor.

* * * * *

Most heterosexuals today would not be comfortable purchasing a magazine illustrating the adventures of manly men. Male interest in male things is no longer sanctioned for straight audiences, particularly in the form of a magazine, outside of professional sports. *Sports Illustrated*'s annual swimsuit issue is the signifier that allows men to become obsessed with male sports figures in the way women were once allowed to swoon over crooners and soap opera stars.

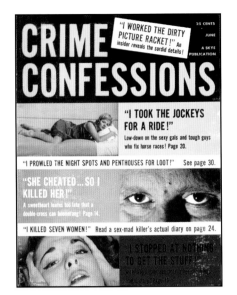

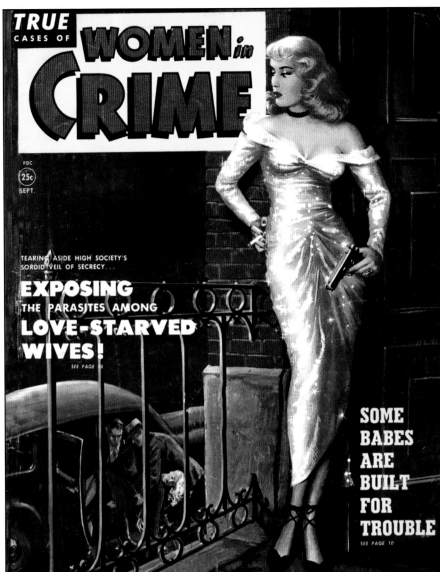

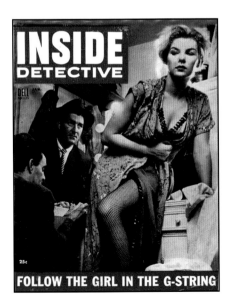

Adventure mag-period "true crime" slicks for men:

CRIME CONFESSIONS, June 1956. **PRIVATE EYE ILLUSTRATED**, November 1963.
TRUE CASES OF WOMEN IN CRIME, September 1950. **INSIDE DETECTIVE**, January 1955.
BEST TRUE FACT DETECTIVE, 1946. **UNDERWORLD DETECTIVE**, January 1950. Illustration: J. George Janes.

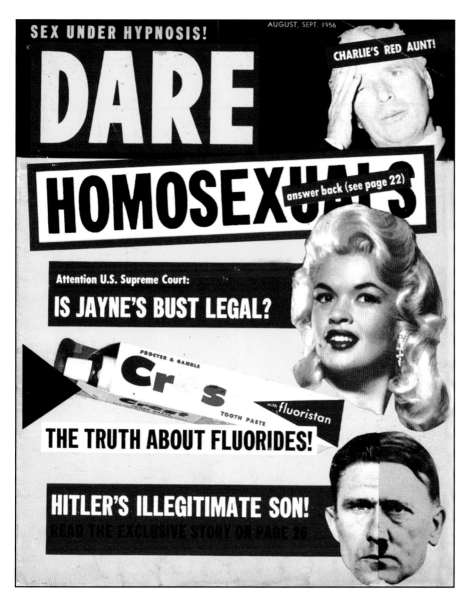

Period gossip magazines read by men:

DARE, August, September 1956. **UNCENSORED**, December 1954.
CONFIDENTIAL, July 1957. **BEHIND THE SCENE**, November 1956.
ON THE Q.T., August 1955. **EXPOSED: ALL THE FACTS … ALL THE NAMES**, June 1957.

Magazines with *Male* in their title are pitched to quite a different audience today than back in 1953. *Urban Male Magazine* uses the acronym *UMM* to avoid the confusion of hetero male readers who wish to purchase yet another magazine with a woman celebrity on its cover, but not be lumped in with buyers of *Bulk Male* magazine, for devout worshippers of "bear" gay daddies. *Male2Day* advertises itself as "the most informative free gay magazine." *Certified Male* is for Iron John/Robert Bly advocates.

For Men Only, Magazine Management's long-running adventure title, would not be seen today as being legitimately heterosexual. Gender exclusion is allowed gay and lesbians but not happy hetero couples fulfilling progressive notions of equality.

In their time, men's adventure magazines revealed an American dream distressed by fear. Among the combat heroes, early Korean War-era issues hinted of degeneration taking hold in "sinful cities," and an increasingly sissified American male. Readers were warned of a growing epidemic of lesbianism, one that could steal devoted wives and girlfriends. Fear of homosexuality was addressed several ways. A sociological approach, specific to Cold War paranoia, informed the reader that normal-looking men, the type that wear a wedding ring and cut your meat at the market, could be secretively undertaking a "gay life." A psychiatric approach reassured readers that abnormal homosexual impulses could be successfully turned back with therapy. Joe Weider's *American Manhood* magazine ignored the issue almost completely, but its cover illustrations featured unusually gay-looking bodybuilder type hunks. *Men in Adventure* warned buyers with an all-caps headline filling a third of the magazine: "YOU CAN BE FRAMED ON A HOMO RAP!" The "homo rap" was an extortion racket played by street-savvy juvies who could easily convince policemen that the innocent reader was some sort of bullying pedophile.

Adventure magazines really exploded onto the market during the Korean War, what Mario Puzo called "the non-fun war." And the genre ended in the early '70s, a period heavily soaked in, according to Puzo, "another non-fun war." The non-fun wars were never exploitable. According to Martin Goodman, whose Magazine Management company put out many of the bestselling PG-rated men's adventure magazines, "you can't *give away* the Vietnam War." But, says Puzo, World War II was totally "fun," totally exploitable.

The psychic confusion and indefinable enemies of the Cold War resulted in lower sales figures, and by result, fewer magazines exploited the fears of Red China, Soviet Union, North Korea and Vietnam and other Commie dominoes. For a couple years, though, Fidel Castro, so annoying close and demonstrably hateful to American soil, was often seen burning the feet and threatening the scantily-clad Miss America type. "Watch her die screaming, gringo dog!"

It was this latter stage of the Cold War conflict that also saw the explosion of the softcore girlie nudie, when men no longer pretended interest in the hoary patriotism of the past and a strange publishing revolution started to focus on beaver and pubic hair. Nothing to believe in except the desperate reality of pink.

RACKETS, June 1956. The consumer racket adventure.

REAL, February 1967. The "non-fun," no-circ war.

G.I. COMBAT, February 1959. Illustration: Joe Kubert. Adventure in comics.

FOR MEN ONLY, June 1972.

MALE, August 1972.

MEN, June 1972.

TRUE ACTION, June 1971.

MAN'S DARING, May 1965.

MAN'S LIFE, November 1974.

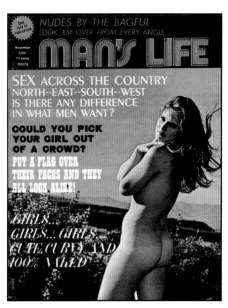

The transition from adventure illustration to photographed flesh.

Bruce Jay Friedman

EVEN THE RHINOS WERE NYMPHOS

IN 1954, AFTER SEVERAL RATHER PLEASANT, humdrum years of Korean War duty, I was employed as an assistant editor of *Focus* magazine, one of the many publications of a medium-vast company called Magazine Management. Editorial jobs were difficult to come by the early '50s. (Have they ever been easy to come by?) A job at *F.Y.I.*, the house organ of Time-Life, had been dangled in my direction and mysteriously withdrawn. I was quite nervous before the final interview series and trotted around the block several times, turning up in a heavy sweat, which may have counted against me. My disappointment was great, since I had been assured that although I would not actually be working on any of the esteemed Luce publications, I would "get to visit every floor" of the building. I had tried *Collier's*, where I was instructed to start a file on myself and house it in the personnel department, tossing in items of interest that might come about in my everyday life. At the end of the year, "the three most interesting files" were to be called down and hired. I was given an upcoming issue of *Collier's* and instructed to study it in an attempt to worm out the secret of the magazine's prominence. The lead story was a photo essay on airports at night, transport planes slumbering peacefully in hangars. The following piece offered readers a history of garlic. On my own initiative, I created a photo essay on Bronx playground bullies which failed to impress Dan Mich, the powerful editor of *Look* magazine. However, I was invited to a party at which male and female *Look* staffers went into a little room and then popped out, wearing each others' underwear.

I am not entirely clear on how I got to the Magazine Management Company, but somewhere in the picture is a chance encounter involving my mother and a furrier at the House of Chan restaurant. I believe the furrier's son-in-law worked for the company and helped me to get a foot in the door. My editor at *Focus* was a towering fellow named James A. "Big Jim" Bryans, whose view it was that in order to succeed at newsstand publishing, one had to hammer away at what he called the Big Emotions—that is, Hunger, Sex, Death, Jobs, etc. This advice has held up. I was introduced to Martin Goodman, the owner of the company, a congenial silver-haired gentleman who looked a bit like Hopalong Cassidy. Although I was under the impression that I had already been hired, he looked me over, nonetheless, and said, "Alright, let's give him a try." I worked for the company for eleven years, and I am still not quite certain I ever pinned down the job. Through the time of our association, I found Martin Goodman to be a supportive

Bruce Jay Friedman in his office at Magazine Management, 1950s.

Martin Goodman, Magazine Management's boss. A photo he used in the masthead of *Men* for a couple of years.

MEN ONLY, March 1952. Hopalong Cassidy, a lookalike for Martin Goodman.

SWANK, March 1958.

SWANK, March 1958. Photo: Mario Casilli.

friend, but at no time was I unaware of a chilling side to him, one that had sent scores of editors writhing into clinics with colitis symptoms. He was at his most quietly fearsome when some unfortunate new editor made the mistake of showing him a photo layout on logrolling. Part of the Martin Goodman legend is that his brothers called him Mr. Goodman. It was said that he was called Mr. Goodman as a little boy. Once, flushed with confidence, having written a well-received novel, I attempted to call him Martin. I thought I had done well until I realized my voice had been an octave too high.

Focus was a peppier and saltier version of a magazine phenomenon called *Quick* which was virtually bite-sized and flourished in the early '50s. Most of the Magazine Management publications were peppier and saltier versions of other successful publishing ventures. That might have served as a motto for the company: A bit late, but peppier and saltier. We played Jayne Mansfield to the various Marilyn Monroes of publishing.

New magazines were created and done away with as casually as quarters are popped into Vegas slot machines. No sooner had I settled in as *Focus* staffer than I was switched off to another bite-sizer called *Picture Life*. I believe that Martin Goodman began this venture because of his affection for the word "life." A genius at divining the buying habits of magazine shoppers, he had great faith in the pulling power of key words. I always felt he came a cropper in the case of *True Action*. Both "true" and "action" are clearly splendid words individually; when combined, however, they seemed to represent a stinging rebuke to a magazine called *False Action*, which, of course, did not exist.

Picture Life, alas, did not flourish. It predicted correctly that Floyd Patterson would win the heavyweight title and received exactly one letter—from a dying man who was confident he would be able to eke out an extra month of life if only we were to run a six-page picture layout featuring Mitzi Gaynor sniffing gloves. No matter. A series of waggish freelance captions I did for a Magazine Management cheesecaker called *Tab* attracted the attention of Martin Goodman. I was pried away from my position beneath the thumb of "Big Jim" Bryans, given a secretary, an assistant, and the reins of a new entry called *Swank*. My three-man team was considered a large staff in MM terms; years later, when I visited the *Saturday Evening Post* and saw entire floors of people thrown over to the publication of one (skinny) magazine, I felt like Lemuel Gulliver on some weird and wasteful new island. (We were terribly arrogant at Magazine Management and always felt—much in the style of late-night drinkers who are convinced they can take over Haiti—that a handful of us could have "saved" *Life*, *Look*, *Collier's*, etc.) *Swank* had once belonged to Arnold Gingrich of *Esquire* and had published Hemingway stories in the '20s—but had never quite caught fire. I was instructed to "take off after *Esquire* and be classy, but not too classy." The advertising people refused to drop their truss ads, which were a trademark of Martin Goodman publications; I argued that you could not kick off each issue with a giant truss ad and then turn around and be urbane and classy (I now feel otherwise) but I was voted down. My first call to a literary agent—heady stuff—was to the distinguished James Oliver Brown. My goal—acquisition of the rights to a Boileau-Narcejac suspense novel, for condensation in *Swank*.

"I don't like your price, Friedman," said Brown.

"I'm not too crazy about it either," I said.

Actually, the fee of one thousand dollars for a twenty-thousand-word selection may have been an all-time Martin Goodman record breaker. In declining my offer, Brown said he accepted one from Alfred Hitchcock for $150,000. (The novel was turned into the film *Vertigo*.) To this day, I think of Brown's name as being James Oliver I-don't-like-your-price-Friedman Brown.

Swank published new stories by William Saroyan and Graham Greene, and God alone knows who read them. Truss ads and all, the magazine attempted to be classy and risqué. I assigned the late A.C. Spectorsky to do an article on girl pinching. He did one on girl bumping which I rejected. He did a second version on girl shoving; I sent it back. He countered with a third, on girl tickling. I returned it and paid him half his fee. Years later, he asked me to join him at *Playboy*.

"I am making this offer," he said, "because of your quite proper refusal to accept anything but girl pinching."

Swank failed to set the world on fire. I could tell its sales were feeble because Martin Goodman would walk into my office each month, smack the current issue, and leave. *Playboy* and its legion of imitators in the lit-clit field were beginning to throw their weight around. Risqué was not enough. Though dismissed by some as an "armpit" publisher, Martin Goodman, tapping some strange vein of propriety, refused to "go all the way" and *Swank* faded out of the picture, eventually be sold to someone down the street. In an ironic rendezvous with destiny, the magazine was subsequently published by Martin Goodman's son, Charles, quite properly, as a class tits-and-asser.

In my early years at Magazine Management, I had shown some flashy moves in the backcourt, but my shots were simply not going in. I was Mr. Around-the-Rim-and-Out. Despite my disappointing stats, Martin Goodman decided I was the man to take over *Male*, which, along with *Stag*, was a cornerstone of the Goodman chain, a hot seller in the burgeoning men's adventure field. There was a clear-cut hierarchy in this chamber of publishing. High above all others, at a lonely, nosebleed-producing altitude, stood the mighty *True*, which had achieved its status through newsbreaking revelations about hanky-panky in the conduct of World War II. Several notches below, but sturdy nonetheless, was a slick-looking Western cuspidor of a magazine called *Argosy*. There followed, at least in terms of "classiness"— if not circulation—*Saga*; and then, after a leap and a bound, one reached the nether world of the Goodman books (as our magazines were referred to at the time), *Male*, *Stag*, *For Men Only*, *Man's World*, *Action for Men*, *True Action*, and so on. By no means did Magazine Management represent the end of the line. There were legions of other titles that generally featured Gestapo women prancing around captive Yanks in leg shackles. When the men's field met local opposition, the broom used was generally a large one and we were miffed at being swept off the newsstands along with the leg shacklers. Standing off to the side, refusing categorization, was a publication called *Man's Magazine*, which both fascinated and disturbed Martin Goodman. It had a modest circulation, was quite unflashy, and seemed to be morosely going its own way. It was nonetheless, the only competitive magazine

that Martin Goodman would smack. I think he was peeved that despite its sluggish appearance it had any circulation at all. And it wasn't his.

A regular activity at Magazine Management was the examination of current issues of *True* and *Argosy*—and perhaps some renegade magazine that had shown a flurry of sales—and the attempt to ferret out the secret of their various achievements.

"Do you think they have our books spread out in front of them?" someone would ask. (Do girls like it, too?)

"You're damned right," would be someone's brave answer—although it seemed unlikely that Fawcett's lordly Ralph Daigh would invest time in cutting his way through the underbrush of truss ads to peek at a *Male* lead story. This was an era of great snobbishness. A *Male* editor would grow pale at a cocktail party when confronted by a *True* staffer. A *True* person, on the other hand, would be unable to meet the eyes of a Time-Lifer, who in turn was made uncomfortable by an Alfred Knopfer. There was no end to this, of course, and I'm sure that even Knopfers would feel one-upped by *Times Literary Supplement* people, and so on up to God—that is, until the era of camp and the put-on, when it became a strong social advantage to identify yourself as the managing editor of *Forced Enema*.

I became involved with *Male* at a time when both *Stag* and *Male* had built circulations in excess of a million copies on the strength of stories about people who had been nibbled half to death by ferocious little animals. The titles were terrifying cries of anguish. "A Grysbok Sucked my Bones"; "Give Me Back My

15

Mel Shestack (left) presents Bruce Jay Friedman mock cover of *Male* at same party, 1966.

Seated: Chip Goodman, Martin Goodman (both with cigars) and Jo Eno (BJF's secretary).

Leg"; they seemed to have even more power when couched in the present continuous tense. "A Boar is Grabbing My Brain."

Salted in among these animal nibblers were backup yarns about third-rail executions. All this in the supposedly halcyon Eisenhower years. I would have been only too happy to sail in and begin cranking out more of these—but there had been a sudden, unexplainable cessation of interest in these accounts of leg-nibbling ordeals. The men's adventure books had been holding the line with Sintown, or what I always thought of as "scratch the surface" yarns. (Outwardly, Winkleton, Illinois, is a quiet, tree-lined little community… But scratch the surface of this supposedly God-fearing little town and you will find that not since Sodom and Gomorrah and blah blah blah.) Any town with a bar and a hooker would do—but somehow the unmasking of fleshpots did not quite do as a total diet for "our guys." We never did find out with any precision exactly who "our guys" were. They seemed to be multiple men's magazine readers who would buy *Argosy* and *True* and then return, with a certain petulance, and buy one or two of ours. Much in the style of someone who had eaten dinner, but requires a cup of chile to be put properly over the top. We were reasonably sure our readers drank beer and had some affiliation with Iwo. There may have been some migrant workers mixed in among them. My brother-in-law was the only reader I was able to pinpoint with any certainty.

We failed, finally, to come up with a concise formula, one that could be as crisply stated as that of, say, the confession magazines: "Sin, confess, repent." With a bit of tap dancing and some Nielsen-type research, we discovered what "our guys," whoever they were, liked and didn't. There were some surprises. Sports, for example,

were of little interest. Fiction was weak. Forget about Westerns. There seemed, at the time, to be no appetite whatever for nostalgia. Perhaps there was a realization that the '50s were the past, even though they were going in. The Civil War could be slipped through as a theme so long as the writer concentrated on life in a vermin-infested cell. What we did find was a ferocious craving for what was actual and real (although, ironically, *Real*, as a title, did not work, a trusted employee of Martin Goodman's treacherously slipping off to try it and, with great embarrassment, failing instantly). Our staple product became the verifiably true story of some fellow who had survived a Japanese "rat cage," made a record-breaking Death Trek through Borneo, raided Schveinfurt, or helped to storm the Remagen Bridge. Dutifully, we served these up to "our guys," who were appreciative. There were, however, just so many Borneo death trekkers to be gotten hold of. Rather swiftly, *Man's World*, *Men*, and inevitably, *True Action* had been assigned to my group. This meant I had to purchase some fifty stories each month, an awesome number of death treks. (Most magazine publishers feel that if an editor comes up with one or two strong stories per issue, he is in good shape; not so with Martin Goodman, who required no fewer than twelve. If the last story in *True Action* was a bit shaky, he would smack it.)

It was at this point that there arose the notion of simply making up "true" stories and providing them with full documentation. What a giddy and bracing sensation as we set about falsifying our first "true" jungle trek. No doubt Goebbels, W.R. Hearst, and various CIA operatives before us had experienced that same lift to the spirits. *Above left*: The wallet dropped by Howard "Copter" Gibbons as he was searched by Customs at Manila

Mario Puzo (left), Bruce Jay Friedman at Bruce's party leaving
Magazine Management, 1966.

Airport in 1943; *top right*, Aita, the jungle girl who assisted
Gibbons on the first 35-mile leg of his 1,000-mile Borneo "Trek to
Glory." There was, of course, no Howard "Copter" Gibbons. His
photograph was that of a Hungarian gymnast, provided to us by
Sovfoto, under the impression that we were doing UNESCO cov-
erage. The agency finally got wind of what we were up to and
threatened to sue if we did not stop using their gymnasts as Yank
death trekkers. Secretaries around the office pitched in and
helped us along with photographs of their boyfriends.

Once we had made our little "adjustment," we began with
great verve to make up entirely new bombing raids, indeed, to
create new World War II battles, ones that had turned the tide
against the Axis and brought Hitler to his knees. The master of
the latter technique was Mario Puzo, who would create giant
mythical armies, lock them in combat in Central Europe, and
have casualties coming in by the hundreds of thousands.
Although our mail was heavy, I don't recall a single letter cast-
ing doubt on any of these epic conflicts. Many correspondents,
however, scolded us for incorrectly identifying a tank tread or
rifle designation in our documentation. It required minimal
effort on our part to begin making up brilliant reviews for our
Action Book Bonuses. These in turn were culled from mythical
journals of criticism. "Absolutely stunning in its impact…"—
Record. (Well, a few of us around the office loved it and we had
sort of gone on record as feeling that way.) Since it was so simple and pure an idea, I would guess that the idea of inventing
"true" stories first occurred to Martin Goodman. Nonetheless, a
certain ritual had to be carried out—one in which he would
appear in my office holding the layout of a fabricated GI land-

ing "a bit north of Anzio, and hitherto unrevealed, but a thousand times more critical to the Allied fortunes."

"This one true?" he would ask.

"Well, sort of," I would say.

"Mm hmm."

He would then give the layout a light tap, not quite a smack, and
disappear.

We were not so much altering tapes as creating new ones; mon-
keying around with existing tapes could be a tricky business. On
one occasion, we ran a fully documented piece about a
Canadian who died after a valiant death trek through
Indochina. To spruce things up a bit, and to add a bit of salt to
the illustration, we sent along a few jungle nymphos as com-
panions for our man. When the magazine was on the stands,
we learned that the heroic Canadian was alive, after all—the
most popular minister in the Toronto area. A surefire lawsuit if
ever there was one—once our Canadian edition crossed the
border. With the entire staff gathered round, I called a reporter
on a Toronto newspaper and casually inquired about the fellow,
learning that he had, indeed, been a popular minister, but had
gone off to hunt bear and was believed to have perished in the
wilderness. Covering the receiver, I hollered out: "He went bear
hunting and he's dead."

A great cheer rang out and everyone returned happily to
work.

In preparing our fabricated true adventures, it was important
to maintain a degree of geographical balance. One day I
glanced at the dummy of an issue that had gone to press and
noted, with horror, that no fewer than three of our Yank "rat
cage" survivals took place in Japan-dominated territories.
George Fox, who was to share the screen credit on *Earthquake*
with Mario Puzo, was dispatched by limo (the only limo dis-
patch in MM history) to the printer with instructions to reset
the type, putting one rat cage in Germany and another in
contemporary Rio.

Along with death trek and survival stories, yarns about tough
cops who had embarked on country cleanups were surefire; also
guaranteed to please were pieces that had anything to do with
islands—storming them, hiding out on them, buying them at
bargain rates, becoming GI king of them. (My favorite, written
by the great Walter Kaylin, had to do with a seaman who took
charge of one and went about ruling it while sitting on the
shoulders of a weird little chum with whom he had washed
ashore.) "Breakouts" were another highly successful feature.
Any story called "We Go at Dawn" or "No Prison Bars Can Hold
Me" would be read with satisfaction. It was preferable that the
escape be from some death camp or other, but San Quentin did
nicely and our readers enjoyed it immensely when people had to
burrow their way out of mile-long tunnels. Another source of
delight was the account of some GI who had attacked the
enemy with an ingeniously devised contraption. For years,
Glenn Infield heroes went after the enemy with everything from
lethal flying scooters to grenade-bearing chickens. Also popular
was the revenge or "trackdown" yarn, one in which the hero
caught up with someone who had behaved unattractively to
him in a hell camp (Remember me, Kraus?) and gunned him
down in a postwar Ankara café. Additionally, our readers had a

Godfather illustration by Mort Künstler, published prior to the movie deal.

fine time with any story in which the author was in a lather about something, be it Furnace Repair Vultures Who Are Cheating You Blind or those So-Called Soviet Tuna Boats off Fire Island Which Are Stealing All Our Secrets. Our best men in this department was Joseph Millard, who could get himself into a snit on any subject, and, indeed, did so some ten times a month. If America wasted too many of our hard-earned dollars on missiles, it got him hot under the collar. If not enough was spent, it got his dander up all the same. There was no pleasing this fellow.

As to the physical makeup of the "books," our readers seemed to prefer illustrations in which each hair follicle shone through with brilliance. Attempts at nonrepresentational Chagall-like drawings brought out the worst in Martin Goodman. Illustrations were generally gotten up before the true adventures were created. No writer has ever been left quite so shaken as Mario Puzo, his first week on the job, when the author-to-be of *The Godfather* was shown a finished illustration for a thirty-thousand-word nympho jungle trek yarn he had not yet begun to write. Martin Goodman considered the "feel" of each magazine to be terribly important to its success and, like a newsstand alchemist, would brew up a different paper mixture each month—pulp, slick, semi-slick, four-color, duotone—giving each new issue a certain pimpmobile look to it.

Although Magazine Management had the reputation of being something of a "sin pit," the Goodman magazines, at root, were outrageously pristine, almost conventlike. Never before has there been a case in which the name triumphed so resoundingly over the game. Although "nymphos" abounded in the pages of *Male* and *Stag* (even the rhinos were nymphos) and girls were mentioned frequently who would do "anything and everything," one would have to look elsewhere to discover exactly what that anything and everything was. Would-be masturbators were made to settle for a few lubricious crumbs. "Throw 'em a few hot words," was Martin Goodman's edict when a nervous editor suggested heating things up a bit for sales. These were along the lines of "heaving breasts," "long shapely legs," "a flash of pink panties." It may be that a "dark triangle" or two slipped by, but I rather doubt it. In the pictorial division, each magazine ran a set of pictures of young women in bathing suits throwing haughty looks over their shoulders. The famed Magazine Management retoucher was Murray Shapiro, whose coveted job it was to airbrush out nipple areolas and pubic hair strands on photos of cheesecake models who had been careless during shooting sessions. There is no record that a single areola or strand ever slipped past his eagle eye and made its way to the newsstand. (From the look *Stag* took on in the late '70s, one gathers that Shapiro had undergone a wild career change, spending his hours dabbing back in strands quite similar to the ones he spent so much time erasing.)

Despite his essential innocence of heart, the Magazine Management editor tended to walk about with a heavy sense of insecurity and the feeling of being up to something a bit shady. The cocktail party could be an unnerving experience, loaded with booby traps. Inevitably, the question would be posed.

"What kind of work do you do?"

"I'm in publishing."

"What type?"

"Magazines."

"Really. Which ones?"

"Men's adventure."

"You don't say." (And here the trap would start to close.) "That *True* magazine stuff?"

"Sort of."

"What do you mean by 'sort of'?" (Rare was the Inquisitor who failed to pick up the scent at this point.) "What are the magazines called?"

"Well, they're sort of called *Male*, *Men*, you know…"

"Oh, those. Haw haw haw. What'd you just call them? Men's adventure. That's funny. Listen, tell me something truthfully, I've always wanted to know… Do you get to screw those girls or not?"

Time has a way of adding a cosmetic touch to past love affairs, old marriages, uneasy situations. I think of my years at Magazine Management as being carefree ones spent in a happy environment. I can also recall that MM editors had, perhaps, the highest divorce rate in publishing. I believe we came in at 3.7 per editor at one point, nosing out *Newsweek*. Quite regularly, one of our people, beset by domestic woes, would run his head at full speed into the watercooler. I remember giving it a hard tap or two with my own forehead. Still, there were compensations—money seemed to fly around in small gusts if not great blizzards. While salaries were kept low, Christmas bonuses were often substantial and it was possible to supplement one's income by staying awake all night and doing freelance assignments for the legions of MM publications. Though I gave the impression of being skilled as a death trek writer, I never actually wrote one of them and remained the coach who had never actually played the game. I did, on the other hand, create a column of short newsy items called Stag Confidential, which told drivers how to rotate their tires effectively, encouraged job seekers to "hotfoot it" up to Vancouver, and advised rascally types on how to spot "joydolls" at a glance. This was a time of great and disciplined production for me. As editor of five magazines, and an annual or two, I was able to commute two and a half hours each day, write three novels and dozens of short stories and magazines articles, work out at Vic Tanny's gym, play games with my sons, and, to a degree, continue on with my marriage. I don't recall actually working on the magazines. They seemed to come trotting out by themselves. This may have been attributable to my one useful insight as an administrator, which was to hire the gifted and the guilty. It got back to me that I was considered a decent fellow who hired people and bought material on a compassionate basis. Let me correct the record and state that not a single decision was made on the basis of anything but total self-interest. The more brilliant the employee, the less I had to do. I recall spending most of my time ordering up cheese danishes and taking strolls through MM corridors, looking in on Bessie Little

of movie, confession and TV; the great Stan Lee, whose empire of comic artists, which at first fanned out into the distance, was to shrink to a single desk (and no secretary), then blossom forth into an empire once again when college students made cult figures of the Fantastic Four. Afternoons, I might allow myself to be worked over by the legendary "gentle con artist," Melvin B. Shestack, whose ingenious cons never once redoubted to his own enrichment. (On one occasion he had me convinced that J.D. Salinger had ended his retirement and was about to go entirely the other way, with appearances on the Johnny Carson show—and that his first planned visit was to meet the team of *Male*, a magazine he had admired while living in seclusion. Shestack managed his con by including that one perfect, seemingly unfakable detail. All his information had been passed along by Salinger's tree pruner.)

It took me a good year and a half to gather up the courage to say goodbye to MM, and about ten seconds to adjust to my new life as a gypsy. Magazine Management was great fun, but it was just one of those eleven-year things. I had occasion, recently, to look over the current men's adventure field only to find that there was no field left to speak of. The once mighty *True* had been purchased by a California company, whose policy, as enunciated in its first issue, seemed to be one of dealing with the New Sophistication facing East and breaking wind. "What this country needs is … a magazine fearlessly dedicated to men, and men's pursuits. Without apologies to anyone… We're not anti-women, we're pro-men. And if that's male chauvinism, then snort! Oink! Snort." With cover stories on Bob Hope, Johnny Cash, and Woody Hayes, *Argosy*, that once sleek, dangerous gunfighter of a monthly, would seem to be pegged toward retired police chiefs. *Stag* and *Male* appear to be beating an orderly retreat in the face of the *Gallery-Oui-Genesis-Game* onslaught [editor's note: this article was written in 1975], begrudgingly giving ground in the form of four-color "beaver" photos and articles calming masturbatory fears.

What happened to the men's adventure field? In terms of reader interest, the Korean War proved to be a bore. Long before Abbie Hoffman and Daniel Ellsberg, the prescient Martin Goodman was able to point out that you could not "give Vietnam away" on the newsstands. World War II receded, finally, too far into the distance and became parodistic by its nature. "Iwo" somehow became a laugh line, a Brooklyn joke. Mix in the power of Columbo, the appeal of the instant replay, *The Towering Inferno*, the stampede of chic newsstand porn and you begin to get some answers. There is also the elevation-of-Falstaff (Dustin Hoffman)-to-hero argument for those who care to fiddle with such notions.

Recently, I walked into a handsomely appointed Madison Avenue cigar and magazine store in search of some of my old adventure books. The stalls were lined with row upon row of paperbacks such as *Anal Hatcheck Girl*—and racks of chic British import magazines, featuring color photographs of the labia minora of Victorian factory wenches.

I asked for *Male* and *Men*. Looking me over carefully, the owner led me to a back shelf, glanced about furtively and slipped my two purchases into a brown paper bag. Taking my money quickly, he returned to the cash register and refused to meet my eyes.

We never did make it into the club, and I must say I was pleased to find that out.

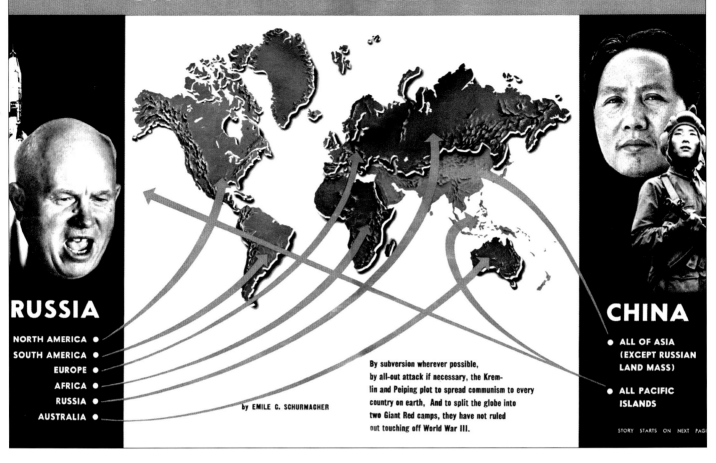

RUSSIA

- NORTH AMERICA
- SOUTH AMERICA
- EUROPE
- AFRICA
- RUSSIA
- AUSTRALIA

by EMILE C. SCHURMACHER

By subversion wherever possible, by all-out attack if necessary, the Kremlin and Peiping plot to spread communism to every country on earth, And to split the globe into two Giant Red camps, they have not ruled out touching off World War III.

CHINA

- ALL OF ASIA (EXCEPT RUSSIAN LAND MASS)
- ALL PACIFIC ISLANDS

STORY STARTS ON NEXT PAGE

FIDEL CASTRO: MARKED FOR DEATH BY GANGLAND

Meyer Lansky (above) ran pre-Castro Cuban gambling empire. Lucky Luciano (below) was linked to drug traffic.

Cuba's leader has stepped on a lot of important toes. But his biggest mistake was to double-cross the U.S. mob syndicate. Now the word is out: "Gun down the big guy with the beard!"

By JUAN ROBLES

At 5 p.m. on a broiling hot day last July, a crowd of reporters and cameramen was milling about in the air-conditioned press room of Havana's new Ministry of Information building. They were waiting for Premier Fidel Castro to appear for a press conference which had been scheduled for 4:30. Castro — delayed as usual — was still upstairs, presiding over a meeting of ministry officials.

At exactly 5:10 a side door in the conference room opened and two bearded Cuban army officers stepped out, submachine guns held at the ready. Seconds later, Castro followed, his husky frame towering over those around him as he walked toward a staircase leading to the press room.

Suddenly, a shower of shattered glass cascaded from a large window in the corridor wall. Three bullets ripped into the plaster just above Castro's head. With a shout, the bodyguards grabbed the Premier and unceremoniously pushed him to the floor. As they did so, a second volley of silent bullets blasted a row of holes where he had been standing. Then a single shot was heard.

Within minutes, squads of armed police and troops blocked off the area around the Ministry of Information building. Others fanned out through the buildings and rooftops on the side facing the corridor where Castro had escaped death by inches.   *(continued on page 36)*

Josh Alan Friedman

THROW 'EM A FEW HOT WORDS

HE NEVER SPOKE ABOUT THE MAGAZINES outside the office and rarely brought them home. As a tyke in the late 1950s, I couldn't fathom what my dad did up at Magazine Management—but it looked profoundly fun. Manual typewriters banged away above my head from partitioned bunkers, the fatherly aroma of cigar smoke everywhere. I grabbed handfuls of rubber bands, paper clips and pencils with pyramid-shaped erasers to bite. Cork boards dripped with clippings and memos. It was a bustling New York newsroom, a fraternity of hard-typing men and muscle-bound illustrators at easels. The moment I learned to hunt and peck on a typewriter, by first or second grade, I banged out a page, thrust it into my father's lap and demanded, "Publish it!"

By the time I did enter the game, the men's adventure genre was gone. Magazine Management itself dissolved in 1975. Unlike millions of World War II vets, whose life-long romance with the noble war was *always* an industry, those of us raised during the '60s saw nothing adventurous about Vietnam. Nobody wanted to revel in stories about napalm vs. gooks or Cong hell camps in a war where *we* were the bad guys and the losers. For the generations to follow, the market slid ever crotchward; mankind was more intent on skipping over text and cutting to the chase—vaginas and nothing but vaginas. After *Playboy* sold its sibling *Oui*, it degenerated yearly, until the day it was sold to notorious publisher Murray Traub in the '80s. (Traub's magazines operated from the same building as Show World on 8th Avenue.) *Oui*, like most others in its genre, bottomed out with typo-laden smeary ink, triple-ghost, out-of-focus photos and dirt-cheap printing. Writers became nearly obsolete… strokebook packagers need only apply.

All of which makes the distant era of men's adventure magazines seem fiercely literary by comparison. The feisty lower ranks of the newsstand spawned dozens of pulp empires. There was Pyramid, Stanley, Star Editions, Candar, Jalart, Hanro, Volitant, Rostam, EmTee, even Fawcett and Macfadden. All had editorial offices in midtown Manhattan. Hundreds of butch titles came and went: *Man's Daring Adventure*, *Man's Action*, *Men in Adventure*, *Man's Illustrated*, *Challenge For Men*, *Man's Magazine*, *Real Men*, *Man To Man*, *Man's Book*, *Man's Epic*, *Men Today*; *Climax*, *Sir!*, *Dude*, *Nugget* and *Cavalier*.

"Excellent Publications," anxious for credibility denied to the pulps, generously offered its resources on each masthead: "Permission is hereby granted to quote from this issue of this magazine on radio or TV, provided a total of not more than 1,000 words is quoted."

STAG, December 1960. "How Russia and China Plan to Divide the World."

FURY, November 1960. "Fidel Castro Marked for Death by Gangland."

Real, the short-lived title created by a former Mag Management editor, ran an article in 1964 called "That Dirty Mess in Vietnam!: Is The U.S. Fighting For A Rotten Cause?" The lead: "Somewhere in the stinking jungles of Vietnam an American GI was dying with a Communist bullet in his belly." Even anti-war pieces had the political attitude of John Wayne.

Mario Puzo's piece on sharks (*Men*, April 1966) predated *Jaws* by a decade in its aquatic paranoia. It detailed all manner of questionable shark attacks at our nation's beaches. What would today draw ire for wrong thinking, it suggested readers "go out and kill sharks" to vent anger, as sharks are the most evil monsters on earth. Even more against wildlife was "great white hunter" T. Murray Smith's "The Monster Every Hunter Enjoys Killing," an anti-crocodile polemic in Pyramid's *Bluebook* from 1965. "I Was Lion Bait..." from a 1966 issue of *Guy*, recounts the moment-by-moment dismemberment of the arrogant Barranco—King of the Lion Tamers—with real photos. Finally, in a 1968 *For Men Only*, the tide changed with a sympathetic portrait of "nature's unloved children," with ample warnings to call off the heartless slaughter of the American wolf.

Thinning out wildlife was but one recurring theme. If all the fatalities listed in men's adventure magazines were tabulated, the human race might have been wiped out. Though sex became the dominant subject after war played out, a stubborn resurgence of The Good War is still upon us. Historian (plagiarist) Stephen Ambrose's reglamorization of WWII in the 1990s, spawned a new battlefield of movies, documentaries and novels depicting the glory of brotherhood in battle. So nothing much has changed after all.

The illustrators who provided the fabulous covers of soldiers with anacondas wrapped around their necks surrounded by nymphos—now seen as classic period art—were a breed apart. Many were serious bodybuilders, actually resembling the action heroes on their covers. Art director Mel Blum, for one, was a huge, deaf weightlifter, though he remained terrified of publisher Martin Goodman. "Did *Guh-man* like it? Is it all right with Guh-man?" he would often ask Bruce Jay. Mort Künstler was another top-dollar freelance artist, who could command about a thousand bucks for a detailed painting of a civil war death camp. He was the only one who could take Blum at arm-wrestling, in which they often engaged.

James Bama, a first-string artist, was yet another weightlifter. Bruce Jay recalls visiting his studio, where he worked upon a dozen canvasses at once—adding brushstrokes to Mag Management covers, advertisements, other magazines' covers and back. Finally, there was Al Hollingsworth, possibly the first Black cartoonist in men's adventure, whom Bruce Jay brought in early on. Hollingsworth was an exceedingly jolly fellow who later became a distinguished painter and—needless to say—was also a massive weightlifter.

The following interviews, which I conducted on behalf of *Swank's* 30th anniversary in 1984, were an anachronistic rebuke to tits 'n' ass mags of that moment. *Swank* was an "impulse buy"—the newsstand choice, you might say, for a customer who had already tired of that month's *Playboy*, *Penthouse* or *Hustler*. Its pages were strictly gyno, all accompanying text exclamations of orgasmic frenzy. *Swank* and *Stag*, then published by Martin's son, Chip Goodman, were the only two titles extant with direct lineage to Magazine Management. Chip, who passed away not long after, seemed quietly satisfied to publish this last hurrah in honor of his heritage. The layout included space-age bachelor pad *Swank* covers and vintage cheesecake. God only knows who read it.

Bruce Jay Friedman

(Novels include *Stern*, *About Harry Towns* and *Violencia!* Plays and screenplays include *Scuba Duba*, *Steambath*, *Stir Crazy* and *Splash*.)

When did you begin at the company?

Friedman: I first joined Magazine Management in 1954, and worked for "Big Jim" Bryans, who was editor of *Focus* and *Picture Life*. It was a valuable experience because he was the best "title" guy, or packager.

Do you recall any of his titles?

"What's Worse Than Sex?" He'd send me back to sharpen up titles and blurbs, literally a hundred times, like a Marine drill instructor. But when you become a Marine, you're really proud of it. Martin Goodman was also a very good title man. They believed in Big Emotions selling magazines, and they were right. I began as assistant editor of *Focus*, a small-format magazine, a quarter the size of ,say, the *New Yorker*. It was a sensationalized version of a successful one that *Look* had introduced called *Quick*, which you could also stick in your pocket.

What's an approximate chronology of the Mag Management titles you edited?

There was *Swank* in the '50s—it couldn't make up its mind what it was. Stroke books were beginning to come in. The first one that went the distance, so to speak, and was seriously sexy, was *Nugget*. *Swank* petered out at the end of the '50s; Martin Goodman wasn't prepared to make it sexy. It was put on ice for a while. He didn't want to be associated with the kind of magazines which led to the real strokers.

So he said, "I'm *throwing* you another magazine," which was *Male*, one of his banner publications. And then he threw me another, which was *Men*, and then he threw me *Man's World* and then *True Action*.

Was there a distinction between Male, Men *and* Man's World*?*

It's like today—when I write a hero, he's never as good as the sidekick. I had four magazines at once. *Male* was supposed to be the mainline publication. I would try to put my "best stuff" into *Male*, so *Men* became the sidekick. As a result, somehow, *Men* would have the real stuff. To make a quick reference to *Splash*, the John Candy role had to be better, because the pressure was off. To spin that out further, *True Action*, which was supposed to be the junkyard—after all, you're doing four titles, you gotta come up with 40 adventure stories a month—*True Action*, the ashcan one, was a sly favorite of mine. Because there was no pressure. The heat was on when it came to *Male* magazine, 'cause it had a record of good sales.

Mario Puzo said he only wrote for Male *and* Men*.*

He was one of our big guns, we would never put him into *True Action*. Imagine trying to get 40 stories, and I had to believe in each one. There was just a small group of guys.

I heard you kept about 50 writers out there swimming in assignments.

It's an inflated number, because they kept *me* working. I never did any favors. The only thing I did that was of any value, which made me seem heroic, is that once every couple of weeks, I would go in to Martin Goodman and say you really gotta pay these guys. He *really* didn't like to sign checks. The checks weren't for me, but it's

MAN'S MAGAZINE, August 1960. "The Plot to Kill Nixon."
FOR MEN ONLY, August 1964. "Malcolm X—Will He become America's Black Hitler?"

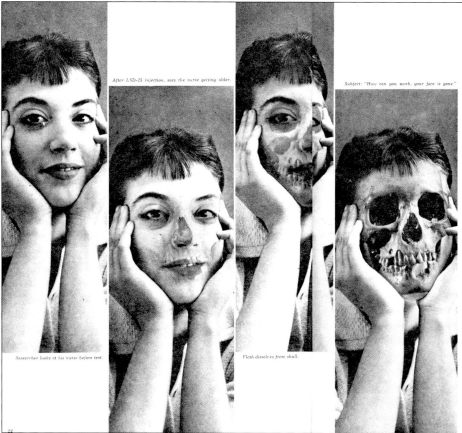

After LSD-25 injection, sees the nurse getting older.

Subject: "How can you work, your face is gone."

Researcher looks at his nurse before test.

Flesh dissolves from skull.

PHOTOGRAPHY BY DAVID LINTON

THE WORLD OF

Madness

D URING A normal lifespan, one family in five in the United States, has one of its members in a mental institution. The most common mental disorder—schizophrenia. Half of the people now committed to mental institutions have schizophrenia—a total of 350,000 victims.

Up to now, the schizophrenic has been the problem of the psychiatrist. Latest medical evidence leads us to believe that it might be the biochemist who will solve this disturbing ailment.

What is schizophrenia? The American Psychiatric Association says: ". . . The disorders are marked by a strong tendency to retreat from reality, by emotional disharmony, unpredictable disturbances in stream of thought, regressive behaviour, and in some, by a tendency to deterioration of personal habits and moral controls."

A noted psychiatrist explains it this way: "The symptoms of a schizophrenic develop slowly. They follow no set pattern of growth which makes the disease apparent at once to the psychiatrist.

"To the average person, there is the world of reality and the world of imagination. To him reality holds the upper hand and dominates his experiences in everyday life. To the schizophrenic, depending upon how great his disturbance is, the imaginary world holds the upper hand affecting reality. Thus he imagines the whole world of reality corresponds with his image of it. His emotions suggest the image and his senses actually believe the hallucination."

Because his feelings have almost no relation to what is taking place, he is given to daydreams. In the early stages of schizophrenia, the slightest gesture on the part of another person may have a very

---

LOOKING FOR A NEW JOB? SALARY PLUS GIRLS!

By ARTHUR STANDISH

A FEW MONTHS BACK the newspapers in Westchester County, N. Y., carried the story of a milkman who knocked on the back door of a dwelling in an upper-class housing development and was answered by a golf club bouncing solidly off the top of his noggin. It was a No. 4 Iron and there was some question among local golfers as to whether or not it was the proper club for the shot. There was little question among them—since most of them were married men—that the blow had been deserved. It was common gossip in the neighborhood that the wife of the man who tee'd off on the milkman had been cuckolding her hubby with him for some months.

However, later events seemed to prove the golfer-husband a caddy and his blow a misplaced stroke in the rough. When he was hauled into court on an assault-and-battery charge, the milkman produced company records to prove that this was the first time he'd ever delivered moo-juice on that particular route; he'd simply been filling in for the regular milkman who'd been ill that day. Thus the shot was disallowed and the golfer had to pay damages and received a suspended sentence on the criminal charge.

Was he sorry? Heck, no! His comment when it was all over seemed to echo the sentiments of many a suburban husband who goes off to work all day and leaves his wife behind as fair prey to the hanky-panky and cottage cheese cuddling of the neighborhood milkman. Said the outraged golf-

er: "Naturally, I'm sorry I clubbed the wrong man; but, hell, these milkmen are all alike; you can't trust any of them!"

In a backstroke way, the observation was kind of a compliment to the Casanova potential of all milkmen. To follow through on it raises the question of why milkmen land on the kancddling green more often than other men. Is it that milkmen are just naturally sexier, more appealing, have a better technique? Not at all. The fact is that their amorous successes are directly related to the sex potential of their jobs—which is high.

Certain jobs offer more erotic possibilities than others do. The milkman rates high in this category. The reasons are simple.

Firstly, he arrives at many of his customers' houses in the mid-morning hours. The frequent breakfast argument between spouses still edgy over their first cup of coffee works in his favor. The woman of the house has gotten her husband off to work, her children off to school and now faces the drudgery of housework. She's feeling harried and more like a housemaid than an attractive woman. In short, she's ripe for a man's attention.

Secondly, the milkman delivers to the back door and his presence isn't apt to cause comments among the neighbors. Often he lets himself into the house. He may find a lonely woman just waiting for a sympathetic ear, to bend.

Thirdly, many housewives, just past the hectic breakfast hour, still haven't dressed. So he finds a distraught female in a negligee, or a housecoat, apt

to fall open at his first admiring glance.

Fourthly, the milkman's time, in most cases, is his own. His route has a great deal of leeway timewise. Nobody will question an hour or so spent in pleasant dalliance.

Y ES, THE MILKMAN'S JOB affords him two of the most necessary ingredients to any love affair: timing and intimacy. Also, he's given the advantage of a place to conduct it since he's alone with the lady in a house which is sure to have at least one bedroom. Is it any wonder that the title "Milkman" has become a joking synonym for roue?

But the milkman isn't alone in this professional advantage. Many jobs, for a variety of reasons, offer a high degree of amorous opportunity. For the man who believes in combining business with pleasure, some of the top ones may bear consideration before he embarks on a career.

Higher on the list than even the milkman, is the masseur. It would be hard to beat the advantage of coming into physical contact with a lady in a private situation as a gambit to initiate further intimacies. And, unlike the milkman, the masseur's clientele is as apt to be unmarried as married. One ladies' masseur, interviewed for this article, had this to say about the romantic side of his work:

"Don't ever get the idea that these women are taken advantage of by the men in my profession. On the contrary, as a general rule, it works the other way around. Even the 'strictly-work-rubber-downer' is hard put to resist the constant seduction these women put him through. Somehow, they get the idea that a massage parlor is like a house of male prostitution. I'd say at least 50% of our customers come to us with sex in mind. After awhile, you just say 'What-the-hell' and give them what they want. And when vacation time rolls around you get as far away from women as you can. That's why so many masseurs are bachelors. Not many wives would put up with what goes on."

It's the physical contact that does it and, to a greater, or lesser degree, this is what places hairdressers, male nurses, ladies' tailors and even shoe salesmen high up on the list of sex-scoring jobholders. It all relates, in a way, to the epitome of the type: the obstetrician.

I T'S LONG BEEN KNOWN that the most faithful wives show strong evidence of falling in love with their obstetrician. However, the man who walks like a stork is not to be envied for this. Considering the circumstances dictated by his profession, sex is pretty much out for him. And, once his function has been fulfilled, most women are too embarrassed to seek him out for a romantic follow-up.

Other doctors, however, rate very high on Cupid's job list. This is because their relationship with women places them in the role of giving advice—quite often intimate advice. In Freudian terms, they appeal tremendously. This may apply to anyone who gives advice to women in the course of his job. Thus such diverse *(Continued on page 50)*

Every red-blooded male knows that a job should be something more than just a way to make a living. If you're looking for real fringe benefits, check your job for sex potential.

Consciously or otherwise, working women compete for the favors of the men in charge. And when women compete, it's inevitable that sex is one of the weapons they use.

REAL ADVENTURE, November 1956. "The World of Madness."
MAN'S ACTION, March 1964. "Looking for a New Job?"

DIAL "S" FOR SEX

This new game of dialing a stranger for titilation and dates is fantastically dangerous and often leads to murder and rape!

By Algernon R. Case

THE POLICE LIEUTENANT took me with him to the apartment in lower Manhattan where the young girl's body was found.

"My God!" he cried when we went through the door and saw the pool of blood on the carpet beside the hall closet. The girl was lying on her face, with her black hair in the edge of the pool.

The carpet was soft gray, neatly wall-to-wall throughout the apartment. I was shocked. I had seen some blood in my time as a crime reporter and free lance journalist, but never this much!

"Her jugulars were slashed, Lieutenant," said the sergeant who admitted us. "Both of them."

"I didn't know humans had that much blood!" the lieutenant said.

"Four or five quarts, according to the coroner. Slashed with a razor blade, he thinks. She'd been knocked out by a blow on the back of her neck. Somebody knew anatomy. In each leg was slashed also. Look." The sergeant pointed into the closet. The walls literally dripped blood above the body.

"The killer must have shoved her in there as soon as he slashed her," the lieutenant said. "Blood seems to have been spurting. He pointed to a splash five feet high on the closet wall.

"Here's where he wiped his hands," the sergeant said, holding open a blood-smeared housecoat that hung from the closet pole.

We backed away from the sight of it, instinctively shielding ourselves from the horror.

"The place was wrecked pretty good," said the lieutenant, looking around.

"She fought, all right. There were at least two girls here. A blonde, and the brunette who was killed. They both fought. We found tufts of blonde hair in two different rooms."

I watched the body was photographed and then taken to the city morgue. Not much was known about the case for a couple of days. Then my friend, the police lieutenant, phoned me after they had found the other girl. The blonde.

"They always seem to do this fool thing in pairs," he

said. "Brace yourself, Al. This was one of your dial-for-sex cases."

"So that's what it was!" I said with a shudder.

"One of the most dangerous bits of sex business known to the department. I've told you that before." He certainly had!

SEVERAL WEEKS EARLIER I had received one of those fantastic calls myself. My phone rang late at night, and I was naturally startled.

I climbed out of bed and half stumbled toward the phone.

"Hello," said a girl's voice. "Is this Al?"

"Yes, it is," I said.

The girl giggled, and then a muffled sound told me that she had put her hand over the mouthpiece.

"Hello . . ." I said. "Who is this?"

"This is Doris," she said.

"Doris who?" I asked, very puzzled. I could not immediately recall anyone named Doris who might be calling me at such an hour, and giggling. It was 1:30 a.m. I was clear-headed by now, wondering if it might be one of those calls I had discussed with my lieutenant friend so many times. "Hello," I said again.

"Hello," said another girl's voice—obviously a different one. I knew, because it was lower, huskier than the first, and more confident. "I hope we didn't wake you up, Al."

"You didn't," I said positively.

"Do you mean you were not asleep?"

"No, I wasn't," I said with a friendly chuckle. "Who is this?"

"Marie," she said. "Doris was too bashful to talk to you."

(Let me call attention right here to the obviously young and unworldly quality of these girls. Older females, who are really familiar with vice, would bring off their solicitations more adroitly—indeed, professionally. No wonder I hadn't been as alarmed as the lieutenant thought I should have been!)

"We couldn't sleep," Marie went on, "and we thought we'd see if anyone (Continued on page 57)

She pops acid-drenched sugar cube, will give herself to him until reaction sets in. He then acts as GCM (Ground Control Man), talks soothingly, assures her she's not going mad on "trip." Below, Detective Robert Owens, Covington, Kentucky, surveys underground laboratory after raid. Police said lab was "one of the most sophisticated" in country, had more than $250,000 worth of drugs on premises. Enormous profits prompt pushers to produce speed and acid. Said one dealer, "It's a seller's market. We can't keep up with the demands of acid heads and meth monsters who come looking for us."

20 MILLION ACID HEADS
On A One Way Trip— America's Coming Crisis

They'll try anything from grass to skag in their need to satisfy a lust for the ultimate high—which is a slab in the morgue.

by Dave Graham

IF ANYBODY had any doubt about the seriousness of the drug problem in this country, he saw it dispelled at the Woodstock Music and Art Fair held at White Lake, N.Y. one recent August.

The grim statistics tell their own story:

Nearly 400 youngsters had freaked out on LSD. One youth died from an overdose. Another, reportedly stoned on the acid, climbed a sound tower near the stage and fell 60 feet to the ground, breaking his back.

A spot check among the estimated 400,000 rock music fans indicated that 99 per cent were smoking marijuana. "There was so much grass being smoked last night," said a 19-year-old student from Ohio, "that you could get stoned just sitting there breathing. It got so you didn't even want another drag of anything."

The so-called music drugs were popular—pot, hashish, methamphetamines (speed), mescalin and peyote. All produce euphoria and permit the user to "groove" on the music. Said a 22-year-old mathematics major from Boston, "You can hear every sound, every click of the guitar pick. When you get a really heavy group (one using hard bass notes and intricate percussion rhythms) you can feel the music actually hitting you. Most of the rock music nowadays is played by stoned people for stoned people."

While the rock groups played on and on, six ambulances were kept busy rushing young people to Horton Memorial Hospital in Middletown to be treated for drug overdose. About 80 arrests were made among those who were hawking drugs or in possession of LSD, but according to police it would have been ridiculous to "bust" pot smokers. "There isn't enough space in Sullivan or the next three counties to put them in," said a state police sergeant.

(Continued on page 48)

Research on marijuana smoking indicates that Allen Ginsberg's message is false. Medical men give five reasons why pot is dangerous.

Grass, acid and skag turned on audience at Woodstock Music & Art Fair, opened eyes of over-30 crowd who'd played down drug role.

WILDCAT, June 1960. "Dial "S" for Sex."
BLUEBOOK, November 1972. "20 Million Acid Heads."

MAN'S SMASHING STORIES, June 1959. Model: Jane Logan.
EXOTIC, Volume 1, 4. Model: Tanya Murrietta.
MEN TODAY, April 1961. Model: Scarlet Rebel .
BATTLE CRY, June 1964. Model: June Wilkinson.

as if they were. So he'd piss and moan and finally do me a *favor*—do *me* a favor, by signing these checks.

You always said that's 80 percent of being a good editor.

Getting the guys the money.

You never did tune Swank *to your liking?*

Well, this was about the time *Playboy* had been introduced. But Martin Goodman marched in with *Nugget*, which had the first real tits and ass, along with ribald classics. He threw the copy of *Nugget* down on my desk and smacked it, saying, "This is what I mean." So I asked, "Where's *Esquire*?" And he said, "This is what we're really trying to achieve." I said, "Well I don't see any truss ads in this book. Every page has color, and you have nips in here." It was an impossible situation. I kept publishing *Swank* as some weird bastardization of *Male* and *Esquire*. It was some weird hybrid of classiness and adventure, and I wasn't ever comfortable with it.

How about the girls? There was a monthly feature called "Swank Dines Out With." Sophia Loren, Jayne Mansfield, Anita Ekberg. Was that for real?

Well, I dined out with them.

You really dined out with them?!

Well, not each one. But I did dine out with Jayne Mansfield, Cleo Moore, Tina Louise, I actually dined out with a half dozen. Others that *Swank* dined out with were pieces written for us by a Hollywood reporter, like Brigitte Bardot, which I kind of sharpened up.

Didn't that help the job along?

Oh, yeah.

Who was the most striking one?

I still feel the impact of seeing Tina Louise when she was 18. She was one of the most astonishing looking people I've ever seen.

Do you remember where you dined with her?

Well, I don't know if I actually dined—I know she came up to the office. It wasn't always a question of *dining* out in a restaurant, I saw them in different places.

Then it wasn't actually over candlelight and champagne, like the logo cartoon?

Maybe once. Although when I was dining out with Jayne Mansfield, a pilot came in during the interview and started to roll around with her, but she never missed a beat.

These days, editors often preside over porn photo shoots for their magazines. Did the editors of Mag Management ever do that with girlie shoots?

I never did; or maybe once, to come up with an early cover of *Swank*. Mel Blum was the art director, and I showed up at one shoot. One where the girls are on safari, and he was giving them little pinches and winking at me. It was a little hot, actually.

You bought a lot of shoots from Russ Meyer?

Well, you call them "shoots," we called them "sets." There would be a picture agent, usually a Viennese guy, who would come up with a briefcase full of "sets." They were contact pictures of an individual girl, shot by one of his photographers. You'd circle the contacts you wanted; he would then blow them up, and you'd bring them in to Martin Goodman who would pick the final selection. He spent a lot of time laboriously eliminating nipples, or outer areolas with a red pencil. There were conflicts, because he would have certain fetishistic inclinations different from mine. I thought his taste was really coarse, and I'm sure he felt the same about mine. He always prevailed since he was the publisher.

How did you pick the cartoons?

They came in two different ways. There were a few cartoon agents, a guy named Art Paul, an old Broadway character who stuttered, and he would come up stuttering with a pile of cartoons. He was like [Broadway composer] Jules Styne, the least likely guy to have great cartoons, but he had great ones. Then we had a Cartoon Day, where individual cartoonists would come up, and I would see them and make selections on the spot. Some of these guys were distinguished cartoonists. On the back of each cartoon was a coded box where you could see crosses—sometimes there were eight crosses. I would know I was the ninth person they were seeing, so a less secure man would have been offended. But I like to think my judgment was better than the first eight guys who passed. It was a simple matter of the *New Yorker* paying the most, so Herb Goldberg would want to publish his stuff there first. I would sit and chat with these guys, many of who were exceptional men who did brilliant work. We used a lot of cartoons.

But earlier, *Swank* had a different approach, since it was "classier." The *Swank* cartoons were picked more for their appearance than wit, to go opposite the truss ads. Guys who could do sexy broads had an edge. Then there were cartoons that came in through the mail. I was careful to pick my own cartoons, I was very proud of that, something I jealously guarded. The highest honor I ever conferred on anybody was when I trusted Mario [Puzo] to pick out cartoons. I think his eyes would moisten if he remembered—it really was a matter of conferring supreme trust in somebody to let them choose your cartoons.

"I don't think a girl should accept gifts from strange men . . . but then, I suppose by tomorrow morning, you won't be a strange man anymore."

STAG, January 1969.

27

Walter Wager

(A number of W.W.'s spy-thriller novels have become movies, including *Die Hard II*, *Twilight's Last Gleaming* and *Telefon*.)

What year did you join the club?

Wager: I never worked there, I was a writer for them and wrote about a hundred pieces. In 1952 I started doing research memos for other writers to use for articles in their little news magazine, *Focus*. Then the memos got good enough for them to run. It was the beginning of a brilliant career writing fake true adventure stories. Later on, when I was working with Bruce, a whole genre of stories developed in which Allied pilots or spies, in various parts of the world, were hidden by the underground in secret headquarters which were always brothels, cathouses. Bruce said they were doing so well, let's do another. I said, "For God's sake, Bruce, we've done everything except an underwater cathouse."

He said, "I love it, do that."

Someone else ended up writing it: an underwater whorehouse which was used to train Italian scuba divers.

Was this in a submarine?

An underwater building. The Allies infiltrated the whorehouse and wiped out the scuba divers.

Your staple was the spy-espionage story?

Yes. I went to work at the United Nations as an editor for two years. When I came back in '56, I continued doing stuff for Magazine Management. I did some genteel sex stories, also. You found out what part of each city was the red light district, then you wrote a vigorously indignant article about the hookers. The first article I did for *Swank* in '56 was called "Build A Better Monster"—a picture story on Hollywood monsters which advised readers on how to get ahead in life by building one. *Swank* had a sense of humor. Then I did a piece of fiction for *Swank* which was later reprinted in an Australian magazine, so *Swank* was obviously being read around the world.

Did you get paid for the reprint?

I got a big $25 from the Australians. I would do an article every week for Bruce. I would bring it in on Thursday and have a check in my mailbox Saturday. The most attractive thing about *Swank* was the sort of freewheeling atmosphere there. But it was a time of very cautious writing about sex. *Swank* was the baby of all the men's magazines there.

How do you mean?

It never got as big as the others and it didn't live as long. [*Swank* ceased publication several times.] It was always an experimental venture. Martin Goodman's effort to compete with *Esquire*, but a little saucier. It had the advantage of working on a modest budget, so it needed an inventive editor.

Do you recall a favorite story you wrote for Swank?

A piece of fiction that preceded *The Stepford Wives*. A story about an engineer whose wife dies, and he builds a new wife ["The Second Mrs. Gilbert," Aug. 1956]. Every night was perfect, he'd come home, she'd be waiting with martinis, she never bothered him to have a baby. Then he comes home one evening and can't find her. He goes down to the basement and there she is in his workshop building a perfect new husband.

Were any of your Mag Management stories developed later into novels?

Oh, yes! I did a double-length piece of fiction for *Men* which developed into the novel *Viper Three*, very successful here and abroad, and later became the film *Twilight's Last Gleaming* [starring Burt Lancaster]. You wanna hear something funny? Not only did it first appear in a Magazine Management book, but after the novel was successful and the paperback came out years later, Chip Goodman [heir to Martin Goodman's empire] didn't know it had come from an original story in his father's company—he bought the condensation rights again.

Mario Puzo

[World War II veteran. M.P.'s novels include *The Dark Arena*, *The Fortunate Pilgrim*, *Fools Die*; non-fiction books include *The Godfather Papers*, *Inside Las Vegas*; screenplays include all the *Godfather* films, *Earthquake* and *Superman*. Puzo passed away in 1999 at the age of 78.]

When did you arrive and which titles did you work on?

Puzo: When I got to Magazine Management, I think it was '60. I worked on *Male* and *Men*.

Did you save any of your issues?

I had some, but I don't know where the hell they are now.

Did you ever meet any authentic readers of the magazines back then?

Naw. But I got letters, the magazines got letters. They would correct factual details, which was very funny, 'cause the whole piece was usually made up.

How did it feel when you ran out of real battles and started making up new World War II battles?

Oh, it was a lot of fun. I wrote "A Bridge Too Far," that story of the Arnhem invasion. After you got through reading *my* story, you thought the Allies won the battle, not the Germans.

Weren't there any letters doubting this version?

Never. I got the airborne division wrong and received a letter about that. The funniest time was when the FBI came up to investigate us on a story made up about Russia. We printed some photos from Russia of people on the beach, and identified them as a group from the underground, or one of those bullshit things, and the FBI came up to ask us to really identify them. They talked mostly to [associate editor] Bernie Garfinkel, but he wouldn't spill the beans. Finally, just to get rid of them, he told 'em, hey, the story was all made up.

Did you use any of your own World War II experiences in those stories?

I used to love to do research—like when I wrote an adventure story about the Arctic, I would read all the Arctic books. I became an expert on the Arctic. Then I did an article on sharks, which was fascinating. It never occurred to me that sharks would make a novel or a movie. Doing research, I came across the story of *The Sting* in an old book, which I remember because it was such a good scam. But again, it never occurred to me it would make a movie.

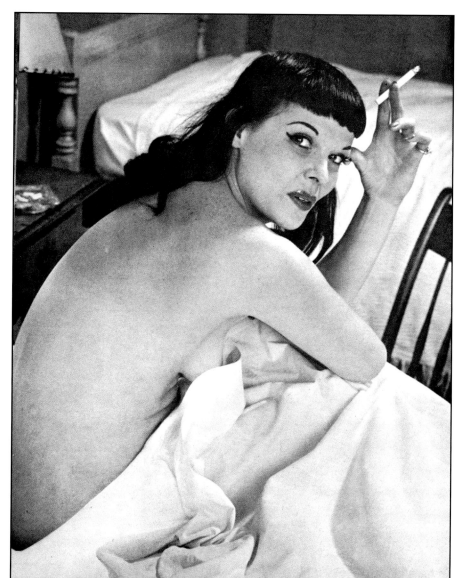

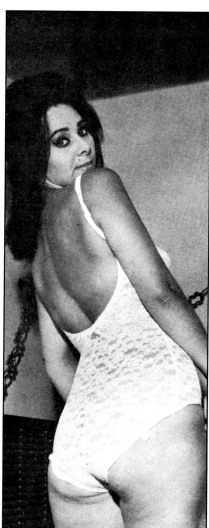

Covered strategically: girls in adventure magazines.

MAN'S ADVENTURE, July 1964. Model: Jinx. **ESCAPE**, September 1961. Model: Dolores Del Raye.
MEN IN CONFLICT, December 1967. Model: Tana Rexi. **MALE**, December 1967. Model: Vicki.
NEW MAN, September 1965. Model: Eva.

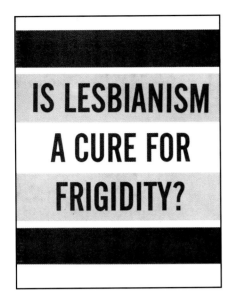

IS LESBIANISM A CURE FOR FRIGIDITY?

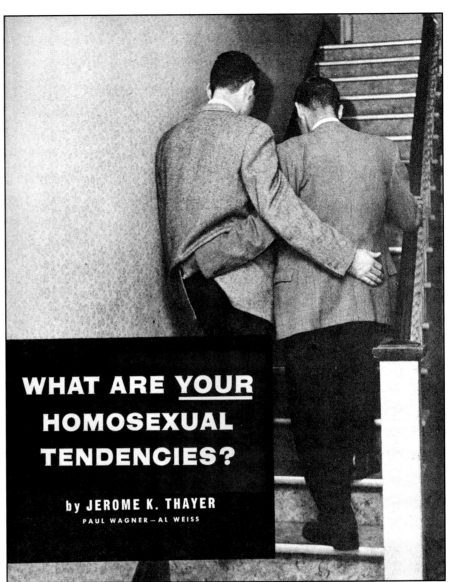

WHAT ARE YOUR HOMOSEXUAL TENDENCIES?

by JEROME K. THAYER
PAUL WAGNER — AL WEISS

IS SPACE A CURE FOR FRIGIDITY?

A report on the love reactions of men and women under space conditions!

by DR. DMITRI TREBOYAN
Illustrated by VIC PREZIO

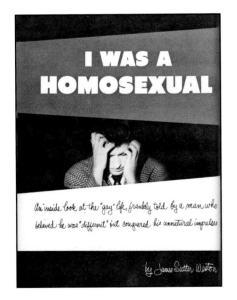

I WAS A HOMOSEXUAL

An inside look at the "gay" life, frankly told by a man who believed he was "different" but conquered his unnatural impulses

by James Sutter Weston

THE QUEER RING THAT ROCKED N.Y.

The limp-wristed set is putting a not-too-dainty squeeze on lonely and naive tourists.

By Kingston E. Worth

HOW TO TELL IF YOUR GIRL FRIEND IS A Lesbian
By Caswell Stuart

REAL MEN, April 1964. "Is lesbianism a cure for frigid women?" **MAN'S LOOK**, February 1962. "Is space..."
TRUE ADVENTURES, March 1957. "What are your homosexual tendencies?" **REAL**, December 1953. "I was a homosexual."
BOLD MEN, March 1961. "The queer ring..." **MEN IN ADVENTURE**, March 1964. "How to tell if your girlfriend is a lesbian"

30

You used to have a lot of books around your desk.

Yeah, well, remember, I had to turn out three stories a month, and by doing all that research, it wasn't that hard. I'll tell ya, sometimes I would read 10 or 20 books to do one article. I'd go to the library and get 'em. I loved to read and I'm a very fast reader. I could read two books a day, so I just used to eat 'em up. I used to read them on company time and at home. We were always looking for stuff we could take off on, so part of our job was reading a lot.

In recent years they've been digging out your old Mag Management stories and making what seem to be illegitimate movies out of them.

Yeah, well, the book bonuses, which were long stories, were very much like movie scripts. When I came to do movie scripts, essentially what I did was write a book bonus, which was broken up into dialog and description of scenes. You had to be economical, you had to cram as much action and plot as possible into a short space.

Did you sense 25 years ago that it was so close to writing a movie script?

No, because at that time, I was never interested in writing for the movies. It never occurred to me that someday I would be a guy who wrote movies. I didn't think of those stories in movie terms.

I remember a paperback with the "Mario Cleri" pseudonym.

That was called "Seven Graves to Munich" in the magazine. Then I wrote it as a movie script, *Seven Graves for Rogen*. I made a lot of money on it, because I had it optioned about four times, and then finally it was made into a terrible movie. I had my name taken off the screenplay, but I got credit, you know, story by Mario Puzo.

Don't you have to keep a close eye on that today, if producers go scouring through old magazines for stories with your pen name?

Yeah, but they're so similar. Like, *The A-Team* on TV today. I wrote a story called "The Lorch Team." I turned that into a movie script that's been optioned. But they got the idea, I think, from that story I wrote.

When did these stories start to get optioned?

After *The Godfather*.

Did you ever write a story at Magazine Management which was a direct predecessor to The Godfather?

The funny thing is, I don't think I ever wrote anything about gangsters. They were usually pure adventure stories dealing with the war or some exotic locale. The magazines didn't print gangster stuff, that wasn't part of our repertoire, as they say.

Did you ever write a story on Vietnam?

Yeah, I did one or two, but they were absolute poison. The readers didn't like to read about it. That was very early on in Vietnam. We used to emphasize that Vietnam only had poison sticks. How the Poison Stick Army Beat America's Ultra-Modern Weapons, shit like that.

But it never went over?

Nah, they hated it. Also we weren't the heroes. Just like the Korean War—we used to call that The No Fun War. World War II was The Fun War. And you could get some mileage out of the Civil War and World War I. World War II was a bonanza. But Korea and Vietnam were losers.

Did you ever write a story about animals nibbling people apart?

No, that wasn't part of my repertoire. Just a shark story. We had specialists. I was the big specialist for adventure and war stories. John Bowers was the specialist on hot love stories, another guy was a factual reporter.

How about the legendary, though untraceable, Walter Kaylin?

He was great! He wrote these great adventures, but he couldn't turn them out that fast. He was outrageous, he just carried it off. He'd have this one guy killing a thousand other guys. Then they beat him into the ground, you think he's dead, but he rises up again and kills another thousand guys.

Remember the illustrations of huge armies that accompanied your stories?

Bruce used to scare me to death and say we got the illos, and I hadn't even started the story yet. Sometimes you had to write a story because they had a good illustration, you'd build a story around it. You'd stray off a bit, but you wrote a scene that would correspond exactly with the action in the illo.

They never ran abstract illustrations?

They were literal. Bruce showed me an illo of American paratroopers dropping on the roof of a German prison camp. I wrote that scene, and worked the rest of the story around it.

How many pages of a book bonus could you write in a typical day?

I used to do a book bonus on the weekends, which was at least 60 pages. I never could write in the office, I had to work at home. When I was working on *The Godfather*, I was doing three stories a month, I was writing book reviews for *The New York Times*, *Book World*, *Time* magazine, and I wrote a children's book [*The Runaway Summer of Davie Shaw*]. All at one time. And I was publishing other articles. I had four years where I must have knocked out millions of words.

I tell ya, it's absolutely the best training a writer could get, to work on those magazines. You did everything.

There's no equivalent today.

It's a shame. If I had a son who wanted to be a writer, I wouldn't even bother to send him to college. I'd get him a job up there as an assistant editor, leave him there for five years and he'd know everything. You've got to turn out a lot of copy.

Now that men's magazines have all gone the route of pornography, when you look back, do the Magazine Management books seem more special?

They were innocent in a funny kind of way. We had cheesecake and the stories themselves were innocent. They were like *Doc Savage* and *The Shadow* brought up to date.

Like comic books for grown-ups?

Righ ... Walter Kaylin, come back!

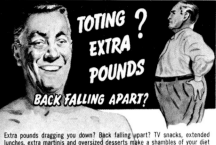

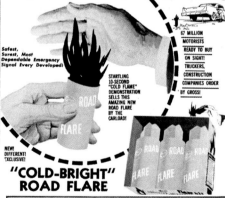

John Bowers

[Non-fiction books include *In the Land of NYX: Night and its Inhabitants*, *The Golden Bowers*; novels include *The Colony*, *No More Reunions*, *Helene*.]

How does Magazine Management stick to your bones?

BOWERS: If you worked there even a year, you were inoculated for life. You were doing freelance stuff later, you knew people who went on to other magazines where you got assignments, or you gave them work. Symbiotic relationships. Nine-to-five, I worked there only two years.

What titles did you write for?

Male, *Men*, *True Action* and all the specials we did.

Wasn't your specialty in the romantic vein?

Well, that's putting it gently. I did the Rock Around Dolls of New Orleans, the Promiscuous Women of D.C., I did the hotsie-totsies in all their forms.

Hotsie-totsies?

Girlie copy.

Did you write copy for the models?

We didn't do that so much then. But I did everything, as we all did—blurbs, captions, picture selections, book cutting. I did at least one original article each month. And if I had to pay for a suit or if a girlfriend cost me a lot of money, I could always get another assignment.

Since you were restricted to phrases like "dark triangle" and "heaving chest," did you feel held back?

No, in a way it was an art form. It was like Kabuki theater—you had a certain ritual, a certain type of lead, certain characters, you meshed them into a beginning, middle and end, and it worked. I couldn't have done it if I'd used my full range of imagination. It was suggestive, and women were vehicles for pleasure, they weren't full-rounded characters. They were always ready, gripping, sexed-up. It'd wear you down if this were in actuality, you'd be fucking morning, noon and night.

How did you come by this formula?

I may have invented it. Bruce had a genius for figuring out where guys' talents went, what their interests were, how they would operate best. He figured out that Mario was an adventurer, he could spin a yarn and was partial to *Moby Dick* or *War and Peace*. He knew I was interested in women and the things that make sexy copy. I came from a fairly repressed, puritanical background, that's always been a breeding ground for lurid writing.

Where are you from?

I grew up in Tennessee. I worked in the State Department previous to Magazine Management. I jumped from a buttoned-down world—which was far crazier than the ostensibly wild and woolly Magazine Management—into working at the magazine. It was the only place I ever felt total *simpatico* with everyone, no one seemed like an out-and-out boss. We were all writing novels or screenplays, and had our sights on something else.

Did you improve at writing while working there?

Oh, yeah. I learned how to cut copy, which is the main thing to learn as a professional—least copy makes the best copy, and don't overwrite, learn to cut out adjectives. At Magazine Management we learned to make things move, action, a terrific lesson. That's why *The Godfather* and *Gorky Park* worked so well. They have characters that are involved in action, they're not cerebral people wondering whether they're going to have a cup of tea for 20 chapters, like in Henry James.

Does any piece you wrote stand out best?

You know, they all sort of mesh together. The first one I remember was on the women of Washington. I'd throw in little touches of my own to keep it fun.

For instance?

An in-joke, like giving the name of my old high school coach for a villain.

How specific, in the early '60s, could you write about sex in Male*? Could you list the address of a whorehouse?*

You'd just say these women were available and leave it to the readers—you could find them in government offices, bars, on the street, horny and ready to go. Here was what happened at a diplomatic party, and it never came out in the press.

How factual was this?

It was total entertainment, we made everything up. The funny thing was, a lot of people out there believed us. We'd make up a battle in World War II where they had a counter attack on roller skates against a giant tank armada. Readers who I met in Tennessee, where a lot of copies sold at train and bus stations, said what they liked about the magazines was they were real, factual.

Any particular sources of inspiration for your hotsie-totsie stories?

Just my own natural horniness. You had to be a little horny, you had to like women. I was not married, I was gallivanting around, the '60s were made for me.

Did you go to model shoots back then?

Yeah. It was exciting. I'd never seen anything like it. The guy that shot the pictures did work for Magazine Management, but in this case he wasn't.

You mean they were shooting real nudity for Nugget*, as opposed to the bikini pix of* Swank*?*

Yeah, he never knew, he would take a set and hustle them as a freelancer, same as today.

What do you recall about out an early '60s photo shoot, compared to today? What's the difference between a nude model of 1962 and one from 1984?

The women were dolled up, their hair lacquered, even though nude, and you wouldn't recognize them off the set. The women were narcissistic, and after they appeared they lost interest in it. They were exhibitionists and they wanted people to look, but once they'd done it, the thrill was gone, they went on to other ways of being narcissistic. It's taken more for granted now, there's no inhibition, everyone connected with it now is more self-assured. Back than it was done sneakily, and as a result, it was more exciting, because it was hidden and outrageous.

What was your reaction the first time seeing a naked broad on a set?

Nearly fainting. I almost keeled over. To introduce myself, the photographer let me hold a camera to pretend I was part of the team, not just a voyeur.

How do you see the men's magazine fantasy machine differing from that time to now, having stayed close to the business?

It always fits in with the climate of the times. Back then, we skirted around the issue, but it was a more puritanical society. Bruce always said, and he said he heard it from Jim Bryans, give them *Big Emotions*. If someone steals money in a story, don't have them steal $15 off a cab driver, have him steal millions off a company. If someone parachutes out of a plane, don't have them do it from a Piper Cub at 500 feet, have him parachute out of a supersonic jet 30,000 miles in space. And that's what today's magazines do, they try to go the limit. Given the culture of the time, Magazine Management went to the limit.

Where is the progression of men's magazines headed?

We may now be seeing the last of girlie magazines. How many nude women can you see? This era will die, and all you'll have to do is go to some back issues of *Screw* or *Playboy*, which we'll have as a record, just as Victorian porn is always available. Magazine Management was not an outgrowth of *Playboy* at all, they were never true girlie magazines. They were in the tradition of the old pulps. Yarns and stories, heroes people could identify with. It was so wonderful that other things don't quite live up to it. Like your first girl who was perfect, but you left her, then you keep romanticizing her. Some guys are still lost back there, expecting a rebirth, not able to move forward. They're still writing about the Second World War, locked in that time warp. I think the world for the pulps died, and when it did, Magazine Management folded.

"*The first thing I noticed about you was your terrific sense of humor.*"

REAL

Mel Shestack

[Author of the *Encyclopedia of Country Music*, co-author of *Secrets of Success*, and editor extraordinaire at dozens of publications.]

What was your specialty at Mag Management?

SHESTACK: The Adventure Jobs. I made them all up. That was a real problem because people used to call and ask, "Where do I get a job milking snakes?" There was big money, you got $50 every snake you milked the venom out of in Ocala, Florida. I came up with another great job: keeping the whores in good shape in Las Vegas by being their masseur. The best one of all was a job where you make $50,000 marrying hookers to save them, through a foundation out West that I made up.

Did readers call in on that one?

One day there was a man, nine feet tall, all neck, hands big as tennis rackets—a California State Trooper. He said, "I wanna marry one of them *hoores*." He had the clipping. He said, "You G.G. Burke?" We all had pseudonyms, that was mine. He said, "I'm ready, I don't even care about the money. Fella I know married a *hoore* and she's a great wife."

I looked at him and said, off the top of my head: "God, ya know, *hundreds* and *hundreds* of men have called—you're late, when did you read the issue? Our office has been besieged, I'm here weekends lining them up and we've run out of whores." I said, "Give me your address, there's a list of 326 guys before you. When your name comes, believe me, I'll call."

And he fell for it?

Yeah, of course he fell for it, they're dorks.

Did the publisher, Martin Goodman, know these were fake jobs?

I assume he did not.

In which mag were the fake jobs described?

True Action. It was my favorite. It was a magazine of phenomenal unimportance, that's what I liked about it. Nobody would ever check facts. Bruce eventually turned it over to me entirely.

So the nature of your articles was to con the readership? Did that carry over to the staff?

I would say to some extent.

Could you recall a few? How about the time you had Puzo waiting on some dock at three a.m. for a shipment of silk shirts for 50 cents?

About 80 percent of the time I came through. I had an uncle in the shirt business. It started out real, like all of them, and then something happened in the middle—I either can't do it, or it doesn't work.

But you never warned the recipient once the deal fell through?

No … I can't for the life of me remember things I did, but I only did it to people I had a great affection for. People who should really be angry still invite me to dinner. Everybody was so damned tolerant. It was a company of flawed geniuses. Everybody had his idiosyncratic behavior, yet it worked together like a team. Everybody liked his fellows for what they were and didn't dislike them for what they were not. A great deal of affection.

How was the money there?

Our salaries were low, but you could make a hell of a lot freelancing. You got paid for everything you wrote, above your salary. It doesn't happen anywhere like that today. That's why everyone was so happy there. You learned to write fast. We went out to great restaurants on Fridays. I remember I wanted to go to Montreal for a weekend—I knew if I stayed up that night and wrote some stupid story—I said, Bruce, I need a story. He knew what I could do and said you take this one. In the morning I'd turn it in, he'd look at it, write $350. Friday I'd have $350, which was more than enough in 1962 to take a plane to Montreal and have money left over. You could plan your life. It was magnificent.

This was no Mary Tyler Moore newsroom, it was a large organization.

There were about 60 people. And then a constant stream of artists and writers and schleps and friends came through. Gloria Steinem used to come up, she thought it was quite wonderful. It was at the pre-liberation days, maybe '63, she was new people. I think she wanted to write for it; she also looked outasight. Wallace Markfield came up to do a story on Magazine Management for some literary-type magazine. Markfield loved it so much, he stayed a second week. It was Good Friday and I remember him saying, "God, *we'll* be off tomorrow," as if he became part of the thing.

Do you recall Fellini's visit?

One day Fellini came into the office with, I believe, Mr. Rizzoli [Rizzoli Books and Films], to see Marvel Comics. There was a secretary who worked for Stan Lee named Fabulous Flo Steinberg. She said, "Stan, there's a Mr. Fellini on the phone, you wanna talk to him?"

Stan said, "Who's he with?"

She said, "Rizzoli Films, can he come up, he's a comic book fan?" There stood Alain Cluny, Mr. Rizzoli and Fellini, wearing white socks, his shirt was open. Whoever was at the front desk wouldn't let them in. I remember walking out and saying, "Don't you know who this is?"

Fellini said, "I'm just a guy who likes comic books."

He used to do *fumettis* and I think Mr. Goodman sat down with him and made some kind of deal to distribute magazines from Italy. It was the height of Fellini's fame. He met with Stan Lee for a few minutes, but he got more interested in us—he spent some time with us because we were more interesting. We were living comic books, those were just on paper.

What kind of photo sessions did you arrange for True Action?

I never was involved with girlie pictures, not once. I set up pictures of people robbing, pickpocketing, breaking into apartments. They were all posed by friends. Once [*Playboy* Executive Editor] Arthur Kretchmer posed breaking into my Mercury in a parking lot for a Beware-of-Guys-Who-Break-Into-Cars story.

I was into making the impossible believable. One minute, we'd be dealing with World War II, then we'd be doing T.S. Eliot imitations. These were very witty guys, well-educated, and everybody had great ambitions. Ernest Tidyman, who won an Oscar for *The French Connection*, Martin Cruz Smith did *Gorky Park*, George Penty, who wrote the first book on the Kennedys in the '50s, he edited *For Men Only*, and of course, Bruce and Mario.

Even Mickey Spillane and Elizabeth Hardwick were nine-to-fivers at Mag Management in a previous era. Would you like to see the old team back together again, Mel?

I don't think it ever could happen. Hollywood, maybe. They were looking for Bruce to go into the *Saturday Evening Post* as editor-in-chief, but he never wanted to be an editor—if he had brought us, the magazine would not have died. It was the best group of imaginative minds that I have ever seen. Mario once told me—or maybe I just think he told me—if you want to write about Eskimos, study the customs of the Samoan islanders, then say it's what Eskimos do, it works. It's credibility, not reality, credibility. He was the C.B. DeMille of men's mags. I think he was the only one there who'd really been in World War II, but it didn't matter, it became *Mario's* World War II. He could take his imagination and make it credible. My God, I think he created the mafia, I don't think the mafia was ever like that, but it is today, because he did it. *The Dirty Dozen* and *The A-Team* are absolute direct rip-offs of Mario's Magazine Management stuff, everything they do, the way they carry their guns.

Glen Infield wrote great stories about aircraft that were created specially to be used in World War II—these planes could pick cotton and blow your nose. George Fox had Nazis boiled in chocolate, they'd fall in a vat and go down eating to their death.

Men's adventure mags were a large genre by the early '60s, before Vietnam spoiled our enjoyment of war. How did yours rate in the pantheon?

Ours were the best, the diamonds, the platinum. We had these wonderful illustrations of women in the Aleutians, and there'd be Japs in heavy furs with icicles coming out of their nose. But she'd be wearing a new mini-skirt with high heels, carrying a submachine gun, her parka open with no brassiere, popping out. And yet it seemed real, you believed that it happened. There'd be a ragtag band of guerrillas in the fiction, and there was always a sergeant or a mechanic who ran things, never an officer. He'd meet the boss' daughter who was visiting from Vassar and she'd be a real bitch. He'd screw her in the back of a car, always in a garage where the car'd be on a lift, and she'd get no pleasure out of it.

Always written in symbolic, not graphic language?

Oh, yeah. She found a real man, and boy, her life changed, then she went off her way.

You loved everything you read?

I edited that stuff, I read it all. I went from that to the *Saturday Evening Post*. The very first day at the *Post* I edited a piece by John O'Hara and Hannah Arendt. She said, "Come on, vat are you *doink*?"

I said, "You're okay Arendt, but you're no Walter Kaylin."

HOW MASCULINE ARE YOU?

by A. J. Smith

MASCULINITY RATING TEST

To figure out your score, turn to page 75

To figure out your score, turn to page 75

1. **Which sports appeal to you most?**
   (a) golf, tennis
   (b) fishing, hunting
   (c) croquet, shuffleboard
   (d) hiking, boating
   (e) hockey, football
   (f) nothing

2. **Which of the following groups do you prefer to read?**
   (a) Newspapers and news magazines
   (b) Comics, sex books
   (c) Religious books, poetry
   (d) Don't like to read

3. **What is your chief sexual outlet?**
   (a) Women (non-prostitutes)
   (b) Prostitutes
   (c) Masturbation
   (d) Other men

4. **What is your average number of intercourses per week?**
   (a) Three or more
   (b) One or two
   (c) Less than one

5. **How long are you able to continue intercourse?**
   (a) Two minutes or less
   (b) two to five minutes
   (c) more than five

6. **How much hair do you have on your body and chest?**
   (a) None
   (b) Small amount
   (c) A great deal

7. **How much hair is there on your head?**
   (a) Full head
   (b) It's thinning
   (c) Completely bald

8. **In which group is the career you would most like to have if it were possible?**
   (a) athlete, engineer, doctor, lawyer, architect
   (b) editor, politician
   (c) business man, military officer
   (d) writer
   (e) musician, artist, clergyman

9. **Do you usually enjoy your meals?**

10. **In which group do your hobby interests lie?**
    (a) gardening, carpentry, automobiles
    (b) photography, poker
    (c) cooking, bridge
    (d) music, painting
    (e) none

11. **At what age did you begin sexual activity?**
    (a) 11-13 years
    (b) 14 or over

12. **Do you use depilatories or cosmetics?**

13. **What are your drinking habits?**
    (a) Never imbibe
    (b) Drink moderately
    (c) Heavy drinking

14. **If married, how many extra-marital affairs have you had with non-prostitutes?**
    (a) one or less
    (b) two
    (c) three or more
    or
    If single, do you visit prostitutes
    (a) Occasionally
    (b) Often
    (c) Never

15. **Do you like most people you know?**

16. **How do you make decisions?**
    (a) Try to get someone else to assume the responsibility
    (b) Try to figure all the angles
    (c) Act on impulse

17. **Would you like to wear expensive clothes?**

18. **Do you feel like jumping off when you are in a high place?**

19. **Is your wife or girl-friend**
    (a) Faithful
    (b) Flirtatious
    (c) Unfaithful

20. **Which of the two choices do the following words make you think of?**
    TRAIN (a) travel (A) engine
    DEVIL (b) tempt (B) Hell
    DESPISE (c) dirt (C) coward
    MACHINE (d) sew (D) engine
    FRESH (e) flirt (E) meat

Adam Parfrey

THE ILLUSTRATORS

MEN'S ADVENTURE MAGAZINES are not known for their writing. The howling head-lines, perhaps. They're best remembered for their sensational, figurative illustrations executed in a style not unlike Socialist Realism or even the Fascist aesthetic that slav-ishly depicted the Communist and Nazi leaders, their programs and wars.

The difference is this: adventure magazines of the '50s and '60s knew their audience of war vets had already been gorged with American nationalist propa-ganda, and so needed to another way to attract attention on crowded news-stands. The spur to a consumerist solution? Fear. And the pleasure that comes from fighting and overcoming that fear.

As Bruce Jay Friedman tells us in "Even the Rhinos Were Nymphos," Martin Goodman pushed his editors and illustrators to unceasingly play to "The Big Emotions"—namely Hunger, Sex, Employment—to sell magazines. And as Friedman admitted in a recent conversation, "The covers sold the books." "You get just a couple of seconds to pull in the reader," says Mort Künstler, the prima-ry illustrator for Goodman's magazines. "To do this I used the same techniques as Michelangelo and DaVinci. Color, shade, dominant mass."

The way Magazine Management worked, the illustrations usually came first. Künstler tells me that editors like Friedman provided him a short typed apercu which he took to "The Bunker" (nickname for the room for Magazine Management illustrators) and instantly sketched ideas for cover illustrations. When the sketch was approved, he'd bring it home and work on the painting for at least several days, after which he would bring in the completed painting(s) to headquarters (625 Madison Avenue), and pick up the ones already pho-tographed. "I did at least five pictures a month," says Künstler. "Now they're all up in the attic gathering dust. Hundreds of them, four thick, floor to the ceiling."

The illustrator began his career in the early '50s painting for the adventure mag-azines a kind of heroic realism that built upon Korean War-era portraits of the noble soldier. "I never copied the style of other illustrators," says Künstler. "It was all my own. I got called on to do the covers with bigger scenes because other illus-trators had a hard time doing them. Since I had to put more time and attention into those paintings, I was also paid better." The covers were usually thematical-ly based on editorial demand, which were usually loose enough to bear illustra-tive suggestion. "True magazine always wanted to have illustrations reflect what really happened, but things were a bit different at Magazine Management. Once in a while I'd get a direction from Bruce [Friedman] to go a bit overboard. Like

Magazine Management illustrators Mort Künstler (left) and James Bama in Mexico, 1961.

MALE, October 1959. Illustration: Mort Künstler.

MEN, January 1957. Illustration: James Bama.

and an illustration for an Aurora Jerry West plastic model box also appear online.

An introductory animation to www.mortkunstler.com says: "America's Roots, America's Growth, America's Challenges, America's Triumphs: Mort Künstler is America's Artist." As Armand Hammer, the late billionaire and owner of a New York City gallery that shows Künstler's work, put it: "His paintings have continually confirmed his talent, and the caliber of Künstler's overall artistic output has now placed him at the forefront of contemporary realism." (Hammer's biographer, Edward Jay Epstein, regards the billionaire's art dealings as a means to cover up speculatively traitorous deals with the Soviet Union. It's interesting to note that in 1977 Hammer Galleries was the first to exhibit Künstler's illustrations, that so often sell a heroic patriotism.)

The "contemporary realism" of Mort Künstler is decidedly not the Fine Art world-friendly and unsettlingly zit-specific Photo-Realism or Super-Realism of Chuck Close and Duane Hanson, but a cinematic realism with larger-than-life perspectives. Subordinating personal belief to professional conduct is a liability as far as Fine Art critics are concerned, though a number of artists, like Jeff Koons, have lampooned that notion, in the way they've made "Fine Art" the basis of their careerism. Many critics have even begun to hail the better results of Socialist Realism, not to mention the work of artists like Komar and Melamid, who'd be nothing without Socialist Realism and capitalist iconography providing context for their "Sots" irony. When consumerist capitalism becomes a memory of the past, technically acute work, like that of Mort Künstler, will likely be acknowledged by critics who now lavish praise on the ironic but technically incompetent. Künstler has a Hallmark card explanation for the style of his work: "The three H's. Hand, head, heart. These are what helped me create all my paintings. People who say it's just technique have no idea that it's just a small part of the story."

What distinguishes Künstler's work from the Nazi and Jap torture found in lower-circ magazines that are currently the most fetishistically collected, is that the severest damsel-in-distress illustrations originated with pre-Code pulps of the '30s. The most notable illustrators of this style, Norm Eastman and Norman Saunders (who is portrayed later in this chapter by his son, David) began their careers in the pulps and so were able to track down former pulp art directors who found new jobs with adventure magazines, and for a while in the '60s and early '70s, torture found a means to bypass the Comics Code and become accepted on a certain level in both magazines and movies.

Consumerism, the specifically American style of propaganda, best promoted by the work of Mort Künstler in the '50s and beyond, is an aesthetic limited by little beyond the ability to sell a magazine, though it rhetorically promoted the idea that America, no matter its behavior, was always morally superior. Other political beliefs, Nazism and Communism particularly, were by the conduct of their soldiers always portrayed as being perverse, ruthless and vicious. The racial component and sadistic misogyny of men's magazines from the '50s, the '60s and even the '70s is today astounding.

What's also astonishing is the imagination of the illustrations, all tractioned by the ability to depict fear. Fear of enemies, fear of animals, fear of women, fear of any loaded attack on the buyer's manliness.

once he asked me to do this cover where he asked me to portray several German tanks going off a bridge, and showing one in the midst of going over. Maybe one, but two or three? I argued against the believability of that." But in the end, he relented and painted what editor Friedman wished to see.

Still painting practically every day, including Civil War paintings as "official artist" for the movie *Gods and Generals*, a Robert Duvall-starring movie, Künstler illustrated many adventure magazines, including the top-sellers *True* and *Argosy*, as well as a number of the second tier including *Saga*, *Cavalier*, *True Adventure* and "five pictures a month for *Male*, *Stag*, *For Men Only* and other Magazine Management magazines." The *MKünstler* signature appeared more frequently than the pseudonym Emmett Kaye. Künstler's website doesn't mention his extensive experience with Magazine Management ("that was unintentional … Magazine Management was so long ago, but like Mario Puzo said, it was an incredible training ground"). In its "Art Gallery," the website revisits some of the illustrator's history in an area called "Documenting America," featuring his work for advertising agencies, movie studios, book publishers, and high-level operations like *National Geographic*, *Newsweek* and *Boys Life*. Illustrations of an SLA-enraptured Patty Hearst for *Newsweek*, posters for *The Poseidon Adventure* and a Moms Mabley movie, an advertisement for Bacchus after-shave lotion

Left, and above: similarities of war propaganda and Soviet Socialist realism to adventure magazine illustration.

Left: Poster illustration: H.R. Hopps, circa 1917.

Above: illustration: Khmelko, "Triumph of our fatherland," circa 1953 (detail).

STAG, May 1965. Illustration: Mort Künstler.

Illustration: Mort Künstler.

MAN'S ILLUSTRATED, August 1957. Illustration: Mort Künstler.

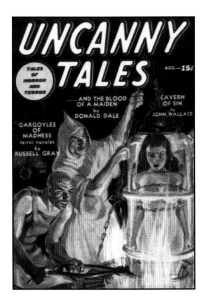

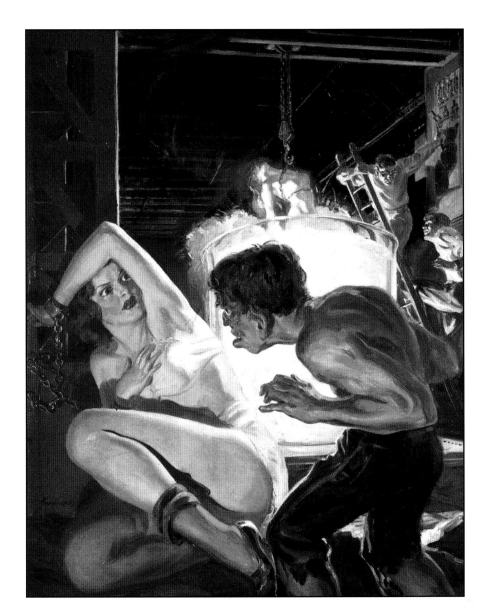

Reminiscent of adventure mags' "sadistic burlesque" 25 years later.

UNCANNY TALES, August 1939. (*The Classic Era of American Pulp Magazines*, Peter Haining, p. 149.) **EERIE STORIES**, August 1937. (*Pulp Culture*, Frank M. Robinson and Lawrence Davidson, p. 104.) The Grand Guignol visits the "shudder pulps" in Norman Saunders' cover for **MYSTERY TALES**, June 1938. (*Pulp Art* by Robert Lesser, p. 116.) Two cards from Saunders' visions for *Mars Attacks*, © Topps Chewing Gum Inc.

David Saunders

NORMAN SAUNDERS
AND THE EVOLUTION OF MEN'S MAGAZINE ILLUSTRATION

MY FATHER, Norman Blaine Saunders (1907–1989), actually lived a blood-and-guts hell-raising life which informed his painted covers of pulps and men's adventure magazines. Fighting, drinking, shooting, boxcars, tramp steamers, jail cells, silver mines, Muslim snipers, opium-smoking loose women and lost souls, Nazi prison camps and "Jap" patrols. While other illustrators struggled through art school, Norm Saunders' rough-and-tumble life brought truth and reality into *True* and *Real*.

His career began in 1926 when, at age 19, Norm started selling freelance cartoons to *Captain Billy's Whiz Bang*, a spicy joke-book from Fawcett Publications. His natural drawing talent also won him a full scholarship at the Chicago Art Institute, but when Fawcett asked him to become a staff artist, Norm preferred to be a professional artist than study how.

Over the next 14 years Norm painted his way into the major leagues of illustration, as a cover artist for dozens of pulp magazines like *Eerie Mysteries*, *Ten Detective Aces*, *Wild West Weekly*, *Jungle Stories* and *Saucy Movie Tales*. The public was drawn to his sexy women and dynamic compositions, while art directors appreciated his unpretentious manner and ability to work fast. Dad's pulp career was as big and successful as any artist could hope for. "Before the war, I sold a hundred paintings a year for 75 to 150 bucks apiece, which was quite a chunk of change in those days. I was riding in style, through the Great Depression." Although times were hard, cheap thrills were in demand. Black and white movies and radio dramas had a magical power of suggestion, but only the pulp magazines produced a hand-held combination of the written word with fantastic colorful paintings to literally and visually substantiate the magic of radio and movies.

When the 38-year-old Army Master Sergeant returned in 1945, his war experiences had confirmed his humorously skeptical view of the human condition. Norm resumed his career illustrating scenes of adventure with an informed confidence that millions of postwar readers could relive vicariously.

When the circulation of pulps fizzled out, Dad continued painting covers for them until the last one folded in 1958. Titles were terminated or merged and reformatted as paperbacks, comic books and men's magazines. Norm followed his pulp art directors into these new formats, but the boom years were over. Although he got steady work from the men's magazines, the income was just enough to keep our family hungry, ill-clothed and in fear of the bank foreclosing our mortgage. Dad's adventure magazines paid $150 for color covers and $100 for a two-page spread, painted in black & white casein, which also required a second "carry-over" spot illustration for use after the story resumed in the back pages.

"Battle Cards" illustrated by Norman Saunders.

Norman Saunders is his own model for his *Man's Story*, November 1962 illustration.

During this transitional period, Norm tried using an agent to sell work, hopefully to a wider range of magazines. He signed with Sophie and Sidney Mendelssohn, a brother-sister act called American Artist Agency, who gouged off one-quarter of their artist's declining prices, but Norm ended this association because the only jobs they could find him were with the same art directors he had always worked for.

One pulp publisher who tried several new formats was Henry "Harry" Steeger of Popular Publications. After folding his pulps, he started Avon Comics and the Popular Library line of paperback books. Steeger also bought the venerable *Argosy* from Munsey Publications in 1943 and reformatted it as a men's magazine, along with *Adventure* and *See*, which provided Norm with hundreds of illustration jobs. There had been a strict pecking order among pulp illustrators with cover artists at the top. They were better paid and more prestigious than mere interior story illustrators, but Norm, like most cover artists, was now happy to paint black & white casein "spreads" and "spots" or to even do a pen & ink job.

MacFadden made its name with the slick, *Liberty*, and pulps like *Detective Magazine*. In the 1950s they put out the men's magazines *Climax* and *Saga*, which was a big seller, just behind Fawcett's *True* and Popular's *Argosy*.

Norm produced a large body of work for *True* and *Real*—manly action adventures, of the type featured in Hollywood films like *Fort Apache*, *The Big Sky* and *The Guns of Navarone*.

Dad told me that he felt adventure magazines were geared towards men who had served in the war but had seen no action, which describes about 85% of our 16 million returning servicemen. He felt that men who saw action never wanted to think about it again, while most servicemen who never reached a front line were doomed to a life of wondering about their manhood in the face of battle. That huge audience wanted to read about heroic battles to vicariously satisfy their frustrated and unfulfilled expectations. By 1962 a number of these magazines had evolved into a whole new genre that vicariously satisfied another sort of frustrated manhood: unfulfilled sexual expectations. The illustrations as well as the pin-up photo-spreads adhered to a strict censorship on nipples, bottoms and crotches, so the public could openly buy these magazines from displays at most newsstands and drug stores throughout the country, while constantly straining against these limits of decency in fascinating ways.

After 1960, mass-market publications reflected the "high fashion" look of graphic design, so very few magazines even used painted covers. Norm accepted lower fees for covers as well as any other freelance painting jobs he could find that weren't taken over by color photography. By 1965 *Saturday Evening Post*, *Cosmopolitan* and *Good Housekeeping* had fired all of their Rockwellesque illustrators. Realistic illustration was finally a thing of the past, with the only remaining exception being the outlandish fantasies of men's magazines, which looked better as

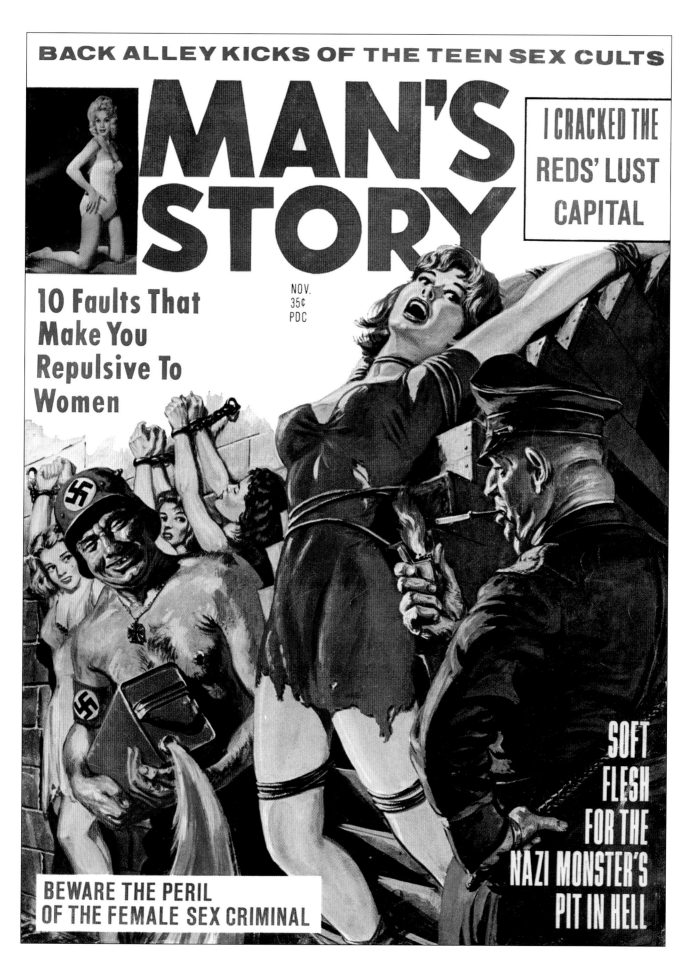

BACK ALLEY KICKS OF THE TEEN SEX CULTS

MAN'S STORY

NOV.
35¢
PDC

I CRACKED THE REDS' LUST CAPITAL

10 Faults That Make You Repulsive To Women

SOFT FLESH FOR THE NAZI MONSTER'S PIT IN HELL

BEWARE THE PERIL OF THE FEMALE SEX CRIMINAL

paintings than as photos or graphic design. Dad's prewar dream of becoming a "slick" illustrator evolved into doing society portraits or covers for the *New Yorker*. He started showing as a Western painter at the Grand Central Gallery and Kennedy Galleries. He guardedly tested all of these avenues, but his lifelong distrust of anything that smacked of the "high and mighty" kept him apart from high society.

Once Norm accepted the fact that his art career would never regain its prewar glory, he actually preferred to paint interior story illustrations rather than the higher-profile covers, where his lost prestige was more likely to be mocked or pitied by his old competitors and compatriots. Another rationale for preferring to paint interior story illustrations to covers was that each issue could run multiple story assignments that earned him slightly more money than the single full-color cover, which required more preparation and finishing time than the monochromatic interior story illustrations.

I asked Dad in 1966 why he left his work unsigned. He answered, "What's the use? I'm not doing my best work for these low-paying outfits, and anyway, everyone in the profession already knows my work by sight. Who am I supposed to impress? Some art director? What's a men's magazine job gonna prove to anyone? The only guy who's gonna sign this stuff is just some greenhorn who wants to see his name in print. I've already seen that!"

I never once heard my father talk about showing his portfolio to any new publisher, so I presume that he worked for just three or four of his old pulp publishers who had a men's magazine division. The names of Fawcett and Popular, MacFadden and Martin Goodman were repeated frequently. [Editor's note: see Bruce Jay and Josh Alan Friedman's articles and the material about Mort Künstler in this chapter for more on Goodman and his Magazine Management corp.]

Most of Norm's illustrations for *New Man*, *World of Men* and *Bluebook* have a combination of the same two names, "Reese" and "Shay's" written on their backs in red grease pencil. One reads, "*New Man* July, 'Darlings of Lust' — RITEWAY — pick up—from REESE." Another says, "Pick up for REESE—SHAY'S, 1180 6th Avenue, 19th floor." This address happens to be the one listed for editorial offices of EmTee Publications, QMG Publications, PDC Publications, Sterling Publications, Riteway Publications, Crestwood Publishing Company as well as the ubiquitous Harold Hammond of Hammond Associates, which is listed in the masthead on the contents pages as *Man's Life*, *Man's Story*, *Man's Illustrated*, *New Man*, *World of Men* and *Bluebook*. Was Harold Hammond the kingpin of this phantom empire or was he just a distribution and advertising partner? Norm's art directors for these titles were Ben Harvey and Louis Queralt, who were employed by someone named Reese at an outfit called Shay's.

One story Dad laughed to retell was a cover he brought in to the art director, Louis Queralt, for *New Man*. Norm was asked to make the "bosoms bigger." He proudly returned the next day with a sensationally endowed modification, but the director hesitated thoughtfully. "Can't you make them any bigger than that?" Norm was astounded. "Holy Shit, Louie, they don't get any bigger than that! They're already the size of watermelons! They don't make 'em as big as washtubs!" The art director's eyes lit up. "Yeah! That's IT! Make 'em as big as

washtubs!" Norm took the cover home and waited for the art director's addled mind to settle down, and the next day the unretouched job was approved.

Dad's daily work started at 9 a.m. and lasted to 3 p.m.; his evening hours were 9 p.m. to midnight. I would usually peek at his painting every night before bed and sometimes he would point out some detail that was a "lucky piece of business. Lots of artists get lucky breaks, but only a smart one knows when to leave 'em alone!" But I also knew to leave him alone if he didn't initiate the conversation. It was better not to interrupt his concentration during his late-night shift. Dad would take a deep drag on his cigarette and get to work. The cigarette burned down to the filter, dangling in his heavy glass ashtray for the next hour, until he'd "come up for air." Although he was a lifelong chain smoker, who always needed a lit cigarette, whenever he painted he could go for hours without a smoke. This phenomenon amused him. His adjustable drafting table was set at the height of a lectern and he sat on a swiveling barstool. He gracefully brushed in the tiniest details with a sweep of microscopic sable-hair brushes. He knew a million tricks using frenchcurves and triangles, producing slickly controlled effects. Dad preferred to paint from observation of actual objects, so he would arrange elaborately staged setups for his models and shoot Polaroid snapshots to refer to while he painted. He always used dramatic theatrical lighting, with colored filters for their illusive effects. Many paintings featured a "hot light" (red, orange or yellow) glowing on one side of the object and a "cold light" (purple, blue or green) shining on the other side. This "hot-to-cold" color scheme was a traditional technique for adding dimensional depth to a painting. "Cool" colors seem to move away from the viewer, while "hot" colors appear to confront the viewer's eye, but Norm intensified this principle to make his illustrations more eye-catching. I loved to watch Dad work. He'd start by splashing around some "blocked-in colors" to get focused, and then he'd make a seemingly reckless splotch of some unexpected color that appeared like a mistake at first. If I squealed, "Dad! What are you doing!?! You're gonna ruin it with that dirty color!" he'd mutter, "Wait a minute. See where I'm going with this." His paintings would magically resolve themselves before my eyes into realistic illusions. Dad used two white porcelain palettes, each with a grid of 64 wells. Before painting, he'd remove the Saran Wrap that kept the paint moist from the last session, and squeeze out tubes of casein and watercolor, adjusting consistency by squirting water from a turkey-baster. He kept a stack of typewriter paper handy for grooming the paint-laden brush tip, and wiping it off after each stroke. Once the top sheet of this stack was filled with slops and drips and splats, he would remove it—but rather than crumple it, he'd place it in another pile. Once every month or so, he would inspect this pile—holding up each page to appreciate the abstract beauty he had unconsciously created. "Hmm! This one's as good as any Pollock!" After selecting his favorites, he filed them away as respectfully as any of his artworks.

Dad said he could close his eyes and *see* anything he demanded to see. He could then open his eyes and still retain that image as he looked at a blank illustration board to mentally project the entire scene from his imagination. When he first confided this psychic ability to me, I asked him to demonstrate it. I requested a topic while Dad closed his eyes for a moment. Then he stared at a blank paper and instantly drew an elaborate scene as though he were tracing a vision before his eyes. This weird talent made Norm's compositions come alive in a personalized signature style that reflects his own temperament, so that his work appears "realistic" without being confined to the mechanical accuracy of a photograph.

Underlying Norm's illustrations is a vivid drawing style so personalized that it is best described as a cartoon. In fact, an under-drawing is technically a cartoon in the academic painting tradition, but these cartoons were accomplished by great draftsmen like Gustave Dore, Winsor McCay or Hal Foster, all of whom Norm revered.

One of the oddball jobs Dad took in the late '50s was at Topps Bubblegum Company, doing a dozen corrections on color photographs of baseball players who had been traded to new teams after their cards were ready to go to press. Without time to re-photograph the players, Topps needed someone to paint the uniforms and caps of the new teams over the former team's photos. Eventually Topps got the idea to make better use of Norm by doing a non-sports series. There was a big hubbub in 1961 about the centennial of the Civil War. The Civil Rights movement gave everyone a morbid curiosity about "The War To Free The Slaves," so Topps gave Dad a pile of rough sketches to get things rolling. He pasted tracing papers on them to redraw more dynamic compositions or he suggested other more dramatic scenes based on Matthew Brady's infamous battlefield photos which gruesomely detailed the astronomical waste of human lives. Norm was paid $25 for each finished card.

The Civil War cards depicted battle scenes of such bloody realism that Topps was flooded with letters of parental complaint. They decided to halt further distribution and to produce an "educational" series instead: Flags of All Nations. Although the United Nations was a hot topic in those Cold War years, no kids actually bought flag cards, but Topps never expected them to. It was just a crafty legal defense, in case they wound up in court and needed to show some edifying product to redeem their public image.

The "Mars Attacks" series was Dad's big sensation of 1962. It showed all the worst nightmares that kids could imagine about the worldwide mayhem of a Martian invasion. Millions of kids squealed as they opened each new pack to discover the Martians' ever-more fiendish ways to plague the human race. In 1965, Topps made *BATTLE!*—a 55-card set that blended men's magazines and bubblegum cards into a shocking mutant. With scant pretense of "historic education," this series was unique in its intention to show the horrors of children caught in World War II. Nazi planes bomb the school as shards of glass stab the teacher in the back. A Messerschmidt strafes two first-graders biking down a road. Nazis attack Mommy in the kitchen as her tiny son feebly defends her. Every scene was designed to terrify an elementary school student with enough morbid curiosity and five cents to buy another pack.

Topps and Norm Saunders continued to collaborate on an incredible variety of gum-selling products, most of which reflected popular trends on kiddie TV: Batman! Monster Valentines! Ugly Stickers! Nutty Initials! Rat Fink! Mad Foldees! Insult Cards! Monster Alphabet! Groovy Names! Flower Power Alphabet! I can't remember them all, but

Topps usually had a new project every few months, throughout the '60s. But as Norm reached retirement age, there came one final project, that proved to be the most popular of his lifetime: The Wacky Pack.

The Wacky Pack's popular success was very satisfying to Norm, especially after a long career of storing up resentment for dishonest media men. He had a soapbox to preach with creative freedom to an immense audience for twelve years of Wacky Packs. The Topps office was a no-frills filthy old factory building, all smudged up with printer's ink and the stench of snubbed-out cigars, spittoons and pencil shavings, a perfect reflection of their penny-pinching low-overhead approach to business. One day in 1977, when Dad delivered some of the last Wackies, he was stunned to see they'd redone the whole place with polished conference tables, hardwood paneling and lavish interior decorations. When Dad asked, "What the hell happened here?" they said, "I hope you like it, because you paid for all this!" That finally brought it home for him. He calculated that Wacky Packages made Topps millions of dollars, but his only benefit, beyond the $50 freelance fee for each artwork, was the pride in knowing his work was so popular. He longed for recognition, just as all artists do, but in his case these were no delusions of grandeur—for those "fifteen minutes" his Wacky Packs really were as famous as the Beatles. Topps must be strictly possessive, because even Tim Burton's 1996 movie, *Mars Attacks*, gave Norm no credit. When *New York Magazine* ran a cover article on the Wacky Packs on Oct. 1, 1973, Norm said, "Well, after 50 years in the business, I finally made it to the SLICKS!"

The era of men's adventure magazines was the height of American fantasy illustration that subsequently influenced our entire culture. These artists may one day be regarded as the 20th century's version of Hieronymus Bosch, for the sadism and horrific infernos they invented. Oddly enough, there is also a moral parallel with Bosch, because both were cloaked in implied moral outrage and served the same social function as cautionary lessons for viewers to behave themselves ... or else! Instead of serving the church as did Bosch's work, the men's magazines served their own righteous patriotic conformity. They exude disgust for depraved Nazis and Commies, juvenile delinquents, cannibals, nudists and sexually deviant behavior. Judgmental tyrants like Joseph McCarthy and J. Edgar Hoover read the men's magazines with an ambiguous passion that approximates the zeal of Cardinal Richelieu and Torquemada. I hear Strom Thurmond still has his own massive collection, which he refuses to leave to the Library of Congress.

Dad never made good money from the men's magazines, but, as he said, "That's okay, kiddo! I wouldn't know what to do with it anyway! And as far as the fame goes, I won't care about posterity when I'm dead, which should be about any minute now! That's for you to worry about, David! I had a lot of good clean fun! I could do whatever I wanted. I could stay home and paint outrageous things and not have some goddamned front office man breathing down my neck!" From 1950 until 1972, Dad painted at least 50 men's adventure illustrations a year, suggesting a final tally of over 1000 paintings. He's gone now, but he left behind a thrilling legacy of artwork, filled with his irreverent spirit, his hard work, and his humorously skeptical affection for mankind which is evident in every single painting.

Norman Saunders

ILLUSTRATING FOR MEN'S MAGAZINES

[In this brief how-to article, Norman Saunders reveals his process for creating action illustrations suited to the adventure magazine genre. The illustration spoken about here was used in *Man's Illustrated*. The artist bio, excerpted here, did not mention that Saunders was best known for the "weird menace" variety pulps.]

THE WHACK-'EM, WHAM-'EM AND WOW-'EM magazine market is at the moment a lucrative field for the young illustrator. The editors of these virile, he-man periodicals are always on the alert for fresh talent. The artist who can render a tight, contrasty, convincing illustration replete with a handsome, muscle-bound hero, lush saronged native girls, and a dash of authentic local color is their man—and for good hard cash, too.

The ruggedly handsome young man in your neighborhood can become an adventure-bound hero (if you can manage to keep him quiet long enough to take his photograph). Girls are native to every locale, so wrap one up in a gaudy cotton print or clinging black chiffon, give her doe-eyes with an eyebrow pencil, let her hair down, and you're on your way to a successful career in the He-man magazine market. (Any good travel magazine is crammed with backgrounds and local color—a file of them is indispensable in this market.)

One or two other things are necessary, the first of which is a good camera. For my own purposes, the Polaroid camera, model 95 or 110, is the least expensive and turns out the most satisfactory end product. One of these cameras with a couple of No. 2 photo flood lamps (with reflectors) can turn out any illustration. Because you get a finished, contrasty print in just 60 seconds, you can reshoot half-a-dozen times in as many minutes to get exactly the information you need. Number 44 film gives the best definition—and is inexpensive: for less than three dollars you will have raw material for a 300-dollar painting.

You will soon be able to turn out photographs that can be laid out on a tracing board and transferred directly to your illustration board. A 40-watt frosted lightbulb in an empty box covered with ordinary windowpane glass will serve the purpose nicely. Make a fine ink tracing with a crowquill pen on tracing paper or thin bond paper, then enlarge the tracing to about one-and-a-half times the page size of the magazine.

Norman Saunders at the easel, and close-up on his model for **MALE**, August 1955.

THE ILLUSTRATOR, Fall 1959. Illustration: Norman Saunders.

Picture of Saunders from that issue.

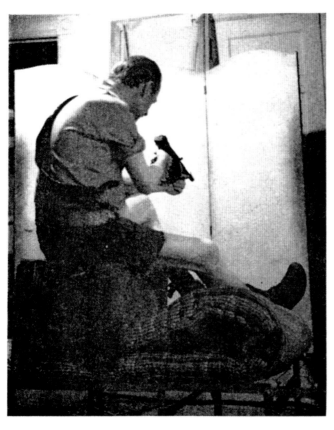

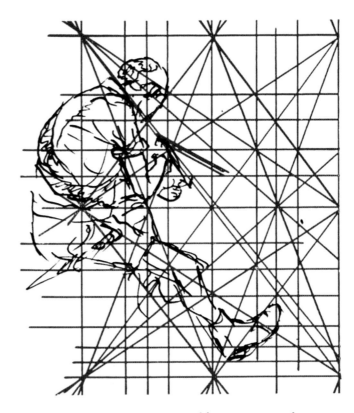

Sketch No. 5 Showing how machine gunner and girl were worked up in pen outline for enlarging.

Above and below are shown photos of models taken with Polaroid camera.

These tracings can be enlarged in any of the usual ways—a pantograph, lucied up with a prism, projected, or Photostatted. I prefer to enlarge them freehand. This is not only the cheapest, but also has the advantage of developing discipline and drawing ability, and allows me to make whatever slight changes I wish. It gives the finished product the stamp of personality.

Personality and individuality is the password to success in this field as in all others where creative ability, taste, and artistic judgment are involved. Editors and art directors tend to catalogue artists, utilizing their talents in specialized fields. As a result, individuality is a valuable asset in this profession.

In the double spread shown here, the Art Director of *Man's Illustrated*, Bernard Gordon, was particularly anxious to get a hunter's duck-blind effect, with the handsome G.I. hidden behind the foliage, native girls for decoys, and Japanese soldiers on the losing end.

Sketches No. 1 and No. 2 were my first attempt along this line. The small sketches [shown on pages 4 and 5 of the original magazine] are "spot sketches," to be used to brighten up the carry-over in the back of the magazine. Sketch No. 3 did not point up the situation sufficiently, so we finally settled on Sketch No. 4. This arrangement made the G.I. the dominant factor and clarified the idea. A photograph of the machine-gunner was made, and its tracing is Sketch No. 5. No. 6 is a series of tracings direct from the Polaroid photos of the "native girls" and the "Japanese soldiers." (These individual photos were juggled and shifted around to make room for the enemy in the background and to avoid losing one of the girls in the gutter—of the magazine, that is.)

The initial sketching on No. 7 was done in red or blue pencil to eliminate overworking or smudging, resulting in clear and distinct final black pencil lines. Sketch No. 8 is an enlargement of the photo of the hero with the girls and soldiers in the preceding sketch traced in the background. The back of this sketch was scumbled in black pencil for the final tracing on the illustration board. The halftone reproduction [above] shows the painting at this stage.

The final step was to organize the foliage so it would discreetly—and partially—hide the native girls, conceal the G.I. from the enemy, and still allow the reader to see what was going on. This was worked out in Sketch No. 9 on tracing paper directly over the illustration.

The reproduction above shows the final illustration as it was delivered to Mr. Gordon and accepted for publication, with only a few minor revisions. Getting out my old machete and chopping down some of the foliage took care of most of them!

Norman Saunders, who wrote the foregoing article, has a long and successful career as artist and illustrator. He came to Minneapolis from Roseau, Minnesota, to take his first art position as illustrator for Fawcett Modern Mechanics magazine. In the middle '30s, Fawcett Publications moved to New York and Saunders moved to New York to open a freelance studio, doing cover designs for magazines and later, for little pocket books.

Saunders exhibits his paintings regularly in New York and keeps busy doing illustrations and cover designs for magazines. Over 30 years have passed since he took that first art position in Minneapolis and his star has risen steadily ever since. There is a good reason for this. He worked very hard at being an artist when he was an art student and he is still working very hard at it today.

— Editor, *The Illustrator*

RUGGED MEN

THE VIRGIN GROOM
a young bride's worst enem

ENJOY THAT CIGARETT
...AND LIVE LONGE

"I ESCAPED FROM SIBERIA!

JANUARY   PDC   3

JAIL FOR
BEANBALL
ARTISTS?

COUR
OF TH
SHARK

AMERICAN HISTORY

SCALPING INDIANS, High Noon showdowns in the Wild West, the Civil War, Pancho Villa, the Alamo and Mexican conflicts. All were fitting material for adventure magazines, as well as publications that specialized in Western culture but are included here because of their adventure magazine influences, particularly in their illustrations.

It's all high school textbook and Hollywood-style American history, the kind written by the winner of the battles. The adventure magazine buyers, those benefiting from American expansion and the expulsion and reservation encampments of the land's original residents, are able to look back at the wars and colonialization tenderly, with a longing undoubtedly absent from American Indian and Mexican readers if they came across the same magazines with their portrayal as sadistic savages. Maybe I'm wrong, here. Perhaps these people enjoyed reflecting on their momentary victories against white devils.

One gets the sense that American history was a more obligatory than sales-worthy subject, since far fewer magazines portrayed American history than vicious animals, exotic scenes and episodes from World War II. But every issue of the American past easily brought back the gendered ideal of the manly man, a situation lost to urban convenience and its coddled demasculinized men.

Adventure magazines only came into their own purveying more recent and less psychically confusing victories against the Japs and Huns.

Turn of the century Dime Readers and a five-cent silent movie serial magazine show savagery of American Indians against white women, and the "masked hunter," fond of amputating innocents.

THE MASKED HUNTER by Capt. Frederick Whittaker, Beadle's Frontier Series, issue #43, © 1908.

WILD JIM, The Traitor Spy by W.J. Hamilton, Beadle's Frontier Series, issue #3, © 1908.

WILD WEST WEEKLY, "Young Wild West Cornered by Apaches and Other Stories, or Arietta and the Poisoned Arrow" by An Old Scout, Issue #507, July 5, 1912.

IND.

ESCAPE
TO ADVENTURE

NOV.
35¢

DIANE O'BRIEN

TROPIC OF CANCER
ALL-TIME SEX NOVEL

"JOY GIRL" PRISONERS OF THE APACHES

SHORES

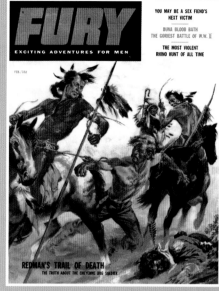

RUGGED MEN, January 1958. Illustration: Clarence Doore.

ESCAPE TO ADVENTURE, November 1961. Illustration: Shores.

REAL, May 1953. Illustration: George Mayers.

FURY, February 1958. Uncredited.

ESCAPE TO ADVENTURE, July 1962. Illustration: Shores.

MAN TO MAN, February 1958. Uncredited.

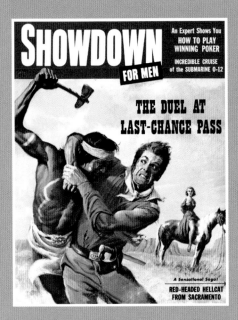

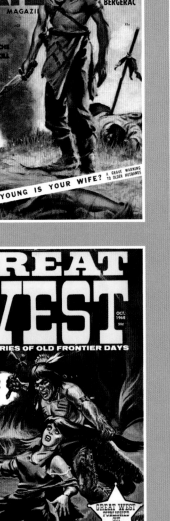

SHOWDOWN FOR MEN, April 1958. Uncredited.

PERIL, March 1960. Uncredited.

REAL, May 1953. Illustration: George Mayers.

GREAT WEST, October 1968. Uncredited.

AMERICAN MANHOOD, July 1953. Illustration: Peter Poulton.

TRUE WEST, June 1958. Illustration: Brummett Echohawk.

TRUE WEST

ALL TRUE — ALL FACT — STORIES OF THE REAL WEST

June, 1958 - 25c

BIG FOOT WALLACE
and the Little Author
Raw, Hilarious, Authentic Frontier Humor

FRONTIERLAND
DEATH ON THE NORTH PLAINS
I Knew Rose of the Cimarron
Last Hanging in Arizona
"The Heck You Say, Dr. Harrington!"
Comanche Captive

ECHOHAWK

TRUE WEST

NON-FICTION

TRUE WEST
Frontier Times
OLD WEST

PUBLISHED IN THE WEST

December, 1967

TREASURE IN A SYRUP CAN

N. C. WYETH — PAINTER OF ME... IN ACTION

BUGLER, SOUND THE ADVANCE

HOW A GREAT LAWMAN DIE

—TILGHMAN'S LAST ASSIGNMENT—

TERLINGUA FLAPDOODLE

LOST GOLD of the LAVAS
PIRATE'S COVE
CACHE OF THE THUNDERING HORSES

T. Oughton

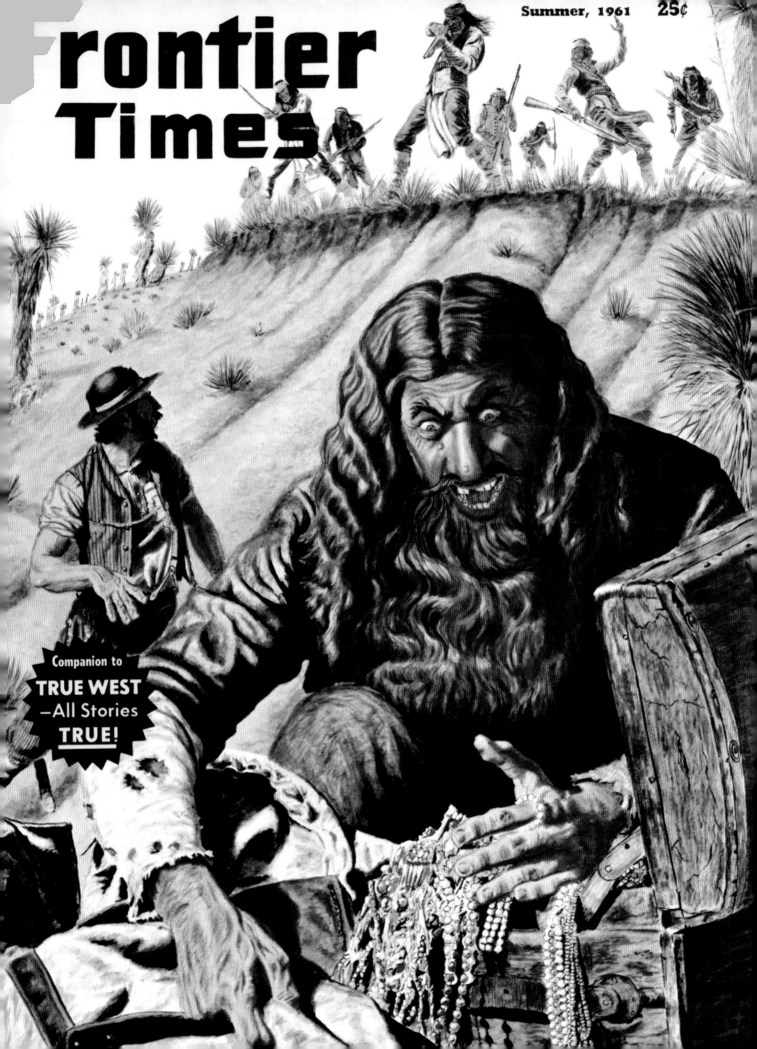

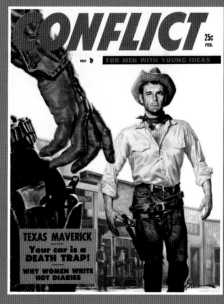

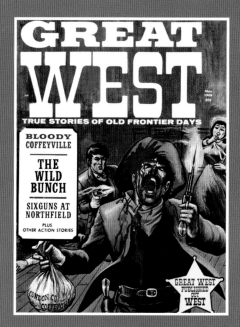

previous page: **TRUE WEST**, December 1967. Illustration: Taylor Oughton.

previous page: **FRONTIER TIMES**, Summer 1961. Illustration: Joe Grandee.

Illustration: Mort Künstler.

"Shootout with Holster," 1958. Magazine Management Illustration: Mort Künstler.

CONFLICT, February 1958. Illustration: George Gross.

REAL ADVENTURE, February 1958. Uncredited.

GREAT WEST, May 1968. Uncredited.

REAL MEN, October 1958. Illustration: Vic Prezio.

"Naked Came the Cowboy," 1957. Magazine Management Illustration: Mort Künstler.

TRUE ADVENTURE, June 1958. Illustration: John Styga.

True ADVENTURES

June, 25c

THE TREASURE OF MUNGO'S LANDING

THIS STORY WILL SHOCK YOU

THEY CALL ME MR. DEATH

CLIMAX

EXCITING STORIES FOR MEN

FEB.

ONLY 25¢

PRIVATE LIFE and LOVES of ARISTOTLE ONASSIS

H.G. WELLS: PLAYBOY and PROPHET

SLICKEST GAMBLER on the MISSISSIPPI

CLIMAX, February 1961. Uncredited.

TRUE ADVENTURES, October 1959. Illustration: Joe Little.

Illustration: Norman Saunders.

PERIL, December 1957. Illustration: Schulz.

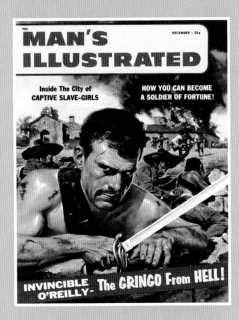

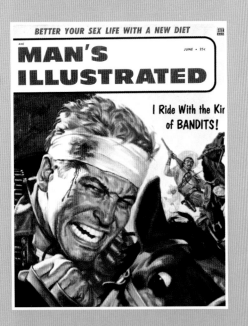

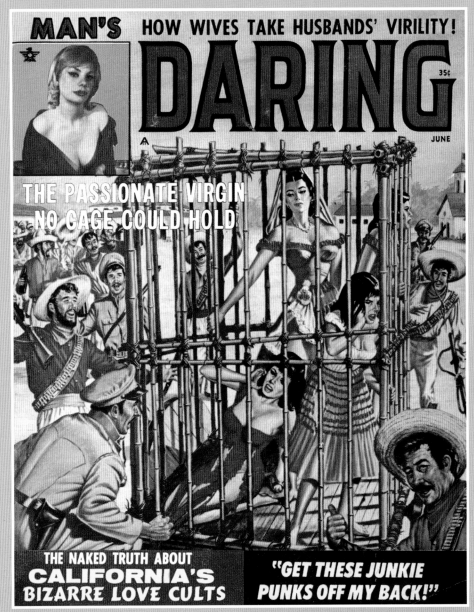

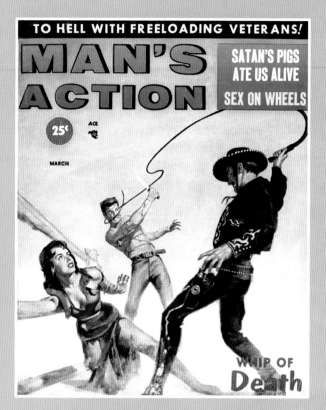

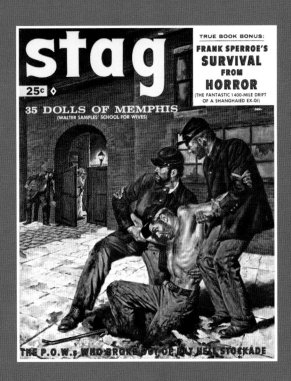

SAGA, January 1959. Uncredited.

Illustration: Norman Saunders.

SAGA, December 1959. Illustration: Charles McBarron.

SAGA

ADVENTURE STORIES FOR MEN

DEC.

STILL 25¢

WASHINGTON'S BOY CRUSADER

THE STORY BEHIND BOB KENNEDY'S STRUGGLE TO NAB JIMMY HOFFA

OO FAST WITH A GUN
THE BLOODY TRAIL F JOHN WESLEY HARDIN

GRAND OLE OPRY

HE DAY THE KIDS WENT TO WAR

WAR AGAINST NATURE

IF IT ISN'T A HEADHUNTER, it's a shark; if it isn't a Jap, it's a Komodo dragon; if it isn't a savage, it's a gorilla; if it isn't an Arab, it's a killer crab. It's The Enemy.

In the mid-to-late '50s, following the Korean conflict, Americans must have tired of the common war story, so the adventure magazines turned to a different sort of foe. Covers started featuring new rivals — not of nation, race or gender, but of species that harbored terrorist-style antipathy for the American male.

Every month produced a surprising new breed of threat, four-legged, winged and finned. From out of nowhere, creatures would unleash mob violence, a kind unknown in zoology's annals, on a lone white male and, at times, his shocked mate. Chewing, scratching, clawing, the critters seemed inspired to invert genetic fate by ganging up on a potential taxidermist or weekend hunter. The illustrated assaults would range from the life-threatening to the disgusting, but they were always peculiar, and often hilarious. This is the direct inspiration for Neon Park and Frank Zappa's famous *Weasels Ripped My Flesh* cover (see page 77).

Did the animal attack issues satirize Cold War paranoia, or did they provoke more of it? This distrust of nature was tailor-made for suburbanites who viewed nature from within the luxuriously appointed shells of Airstream trailers. Illustrators went through most of Noah's ark before new human enemies in Cuba and overseas replaced the animal threat. In the mid-'60s, mutant varieties of *Homo sapiens*, tattooed and long-haired, attacked Joe Normal in America itself. In adventure magazines, the war against nature became a fight against the unnatural, a fight waged on city streets.

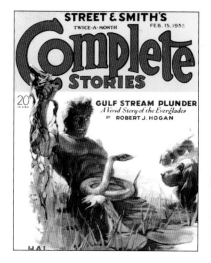

Adventure slicks are not the first time men are depicted as being attacked by animals, but perhaps the first time by crabs. The pulps pictured on this page reveal this primeval fear as seen earlier in the twentieth century, pulp style.

MALE, March 1969. Illustration: Mort Künstler.

COMPLETE STORIES, February 15, 1933. Illustration: H.W. Scott.

THE POPULAR MAGAZINE, September 2, 1930. Illustration: Howard V. Brown.

WILD GAME STORIES, November 1926. Uncredited.

MALE

25 RUGGED FEATURES

OKLAHOMA CITY:
HOT TOWN, U.S.A.

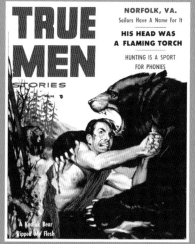

MALE, December 1952. Illustration: Robert Doares.

TRUE MEN, June 1959. Uncredited.

MEN, December 1952. Uncredited.

MAN'S DARING ADVENTURES, August 1956. Illustration: L.B. Cole.

TRUE MEN, June 1957. Uncredited.

PERIL, May 1958. Uncredited.

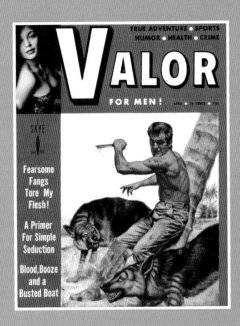

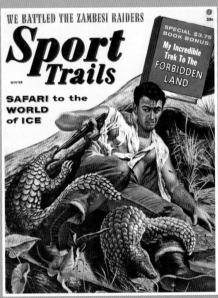

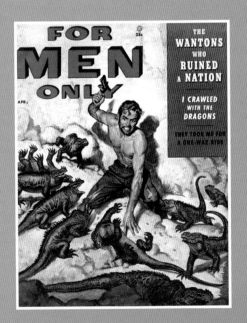

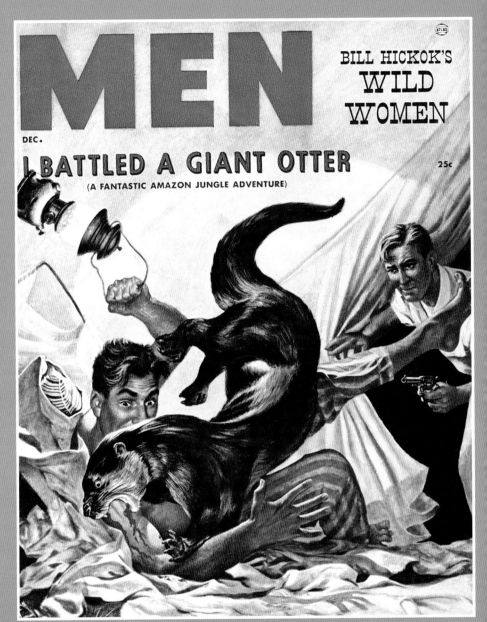

VALOR, April 1968. Uncredited.

SPORT TRAILS, Winter 1956–1957. Illustration: Mort Künstler.

FOR MEN ONLY, April 1955. Uncredited.

MEN, December 1953. Illustration: Robert Doares.

MAN'S LIFE, September 1956. Illustration: "American Art Agency."

LET'S **GIVE** DOPE TO DRUG ADDICTS!

MAN'S
MAGAZINE

SECRET LOVE LIFE
of JUAN PERON

BASEBALL'S BIGGEST
SCREWBALLS

MARCH 25¢

**THE MOOSE
WENT MAD!**

K

MALE

JOURNEY
INTO
TERROR
(An Incredible ARCTIC Adventure)

JAN • 25¢

NUDISM
EXPOSED
(AMERICA'S STRANGEST CULT)

JULY • 25 CENTS

Champ
ACTION-PACKED FOR MEN OF ACTION

Marquis de Sade's
EVIL SEX

THE MAN
WHO BETRAYED
IRELAND

A HILLMAN PUBLICATION

Drunken Hunter vs.
Battle-Scarred Grizzly:
**THE DEVIL WEIGHS
A THOUSAND POUNDS**

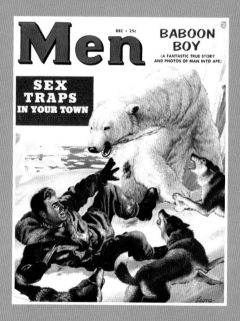

Men
DEC • 25¢

BABOON
BOY
(A FANTASTIC TRUE STORY
AND PHOTOS OF MAN INTO APE)

**SEX
TRAPS
IN YOUR TOWN**

STAG, December 1972. Original Illustration: Mort Künstler.

MAN'S MAGAZINE, March 1956. Illustration: Frank Cozzarelli.

MALE, January 1954. Illustration: Simon Greco.

CHAMP, July 1957. Uncredited.

MEN, December 1953. Illustration: Leone.

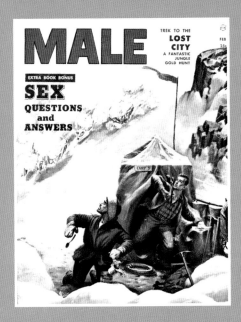

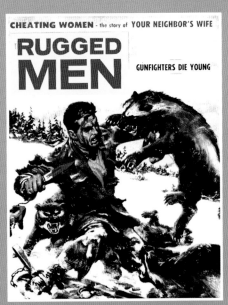

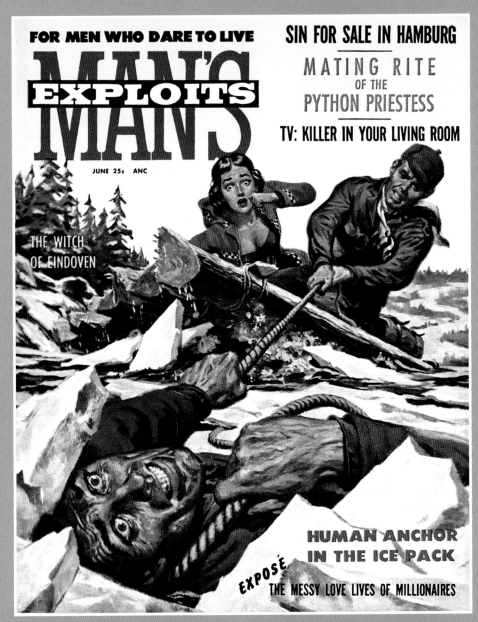

MALE, February 1954. Uncredited.

CAVALIER, September 1961. Uncredited.

RUGGED MEN, November 1957. Illustration: Clarence Doore.

MAN'S EXPLOITS, June 1957. Uncredited.

FURY, November 1960. Illustration: Philip Ronfor.

FURY

XCITING ADVENTURES FOR MEN

VEMBER 35c

SLAUGHTER IN THE SKY
The facts on the Air Force's biggest foul-up

GANGLAND'S SECRET PLOT TO
KILL FIDEL CASTRO

THE CORPSE WHO CLIMBED MT. EVEREST

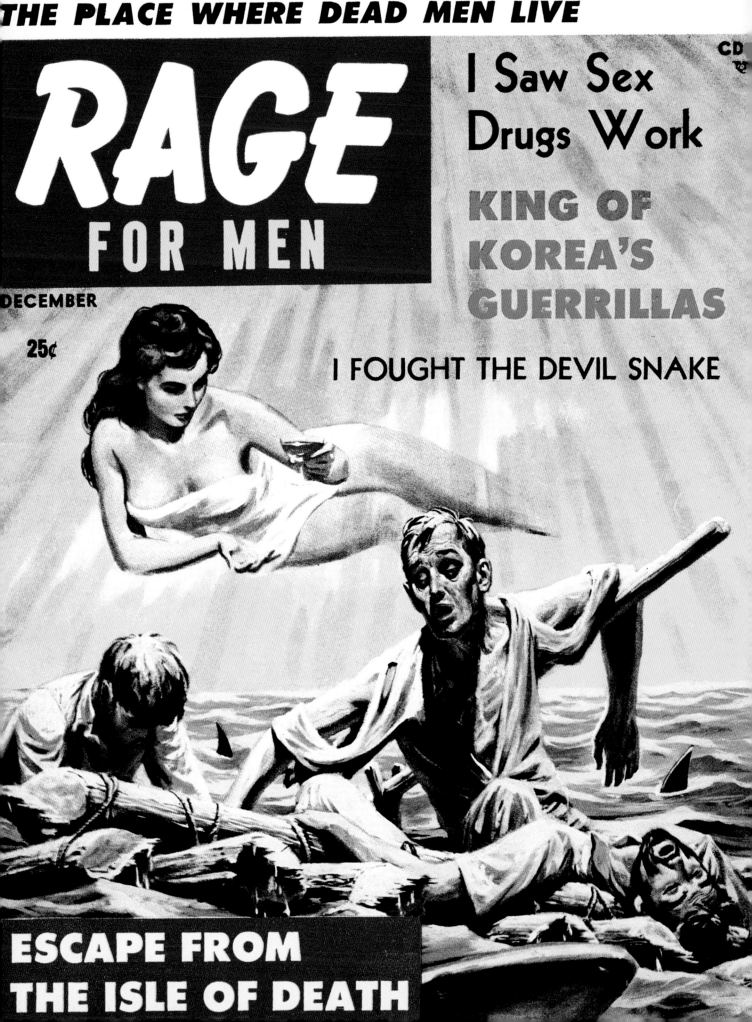

Sensational photo series:
THE PLACE WHERE DEAD MEN LIVE

RAGE
FOR MEN

DECEMBER

25¢

CD

I Saw Sex
Drugs Work

**KING OF
KOREA'S
GUERRILLAS**

I FOUGHT THE DEVIL SNAKE

**ESCAPE FROM
THE ISLE OF DEATH**

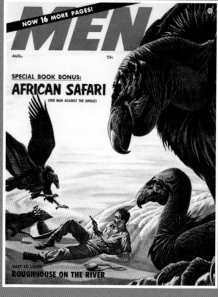

RAGE FOR MEN, December 1957. Uncredited.

TRUE MEN, October 1957. Uncredited.

MEN, August 1954. Illustration: Paul Rabut.

TRUE ADVENTURES, March 1957. Illustration: Martin Kay.

ADVENTURE, March 1957. Illustration: Emmett Kaye (Mort Künstler).

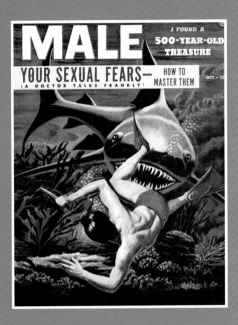

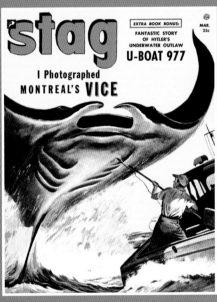

MALE, October 1953. Uncredited.

STAG, March 1954. Uncredited.

CHALLENGE FOR MEN, September 1956. Uncredited.

MEN'S PICTORIAL, February 1958. Illustration: Phil Ronfor.

MALE, April 1955. Original Illustration: Mort Künstler.

An Article Every Man Should Read—**CAN SEX ENSLAVE YOUR MIND?**

ADVENTURE

THE MAN'S MAGAZINE OF EXCITING FICTION AND FACT

Mar., 25c

AN AMAZING STORY

ARE OTHER WORLDS WATCHING US?

THE MAN WHO SWEET-TALKS MURDER

I Fought The SUEZ SEA BEAST

ADVENTURE, March 1957. Illustration: Emmett Kaye (Mort Künstler).

AMERICAN MANHOOD, June 1953. Illustration: Peter Poulton.

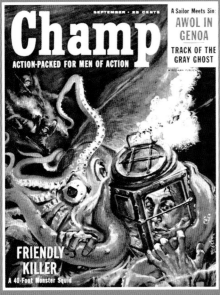

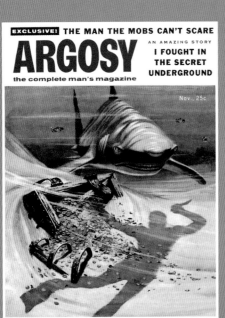

MEN'S PICTORIAL, October 1956. Illustration: Walter Popp.

CHAMP, September 1957. Uncredited.

ARGOSY, November 1955. Illustration: Ed Valigursky.

ADVENTURE, February 1956. Original Illustration: Mort Künstler.

BOLD MEN, March 1961. Uncredited.

BOLD MEN!

MARCH • 35c Ⓚ

Here's the inside on the still-at-large fiend of Buchenwald:

HOW NAZI BORMANN'S CRUEL LUST WILL BETRAY HIM!

THE DAY H'WOOD SIRENS STRIPPED IN CANNES

RIS BRISTOL
1961 Trend in
Models' Nighties

THE DEADLY LONDE WENCH OF WAIKIKI

nly Ed Conn could take
r passion and still elude
e fiendish plot she laid.

MALE

SEX LIFE OF AN UNFAITHFUL WIFE

BY DR. SHAILER UPTON LAWTON

BLOW ALL BALLAST!
(A Terrifying Submarine Adventure)

I DRIFTED TO SIBERIA
(An Episode of Pure Horror)

DEC • 2

Schulz

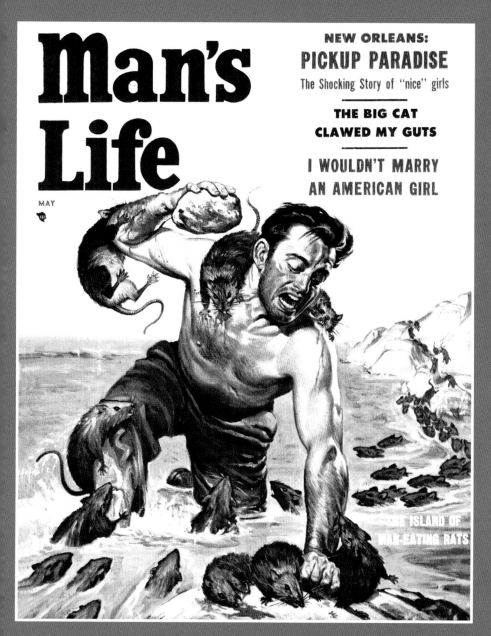

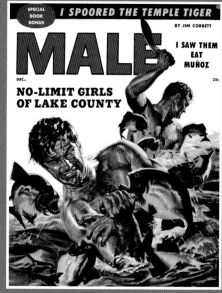

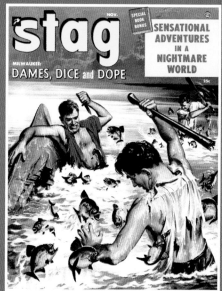

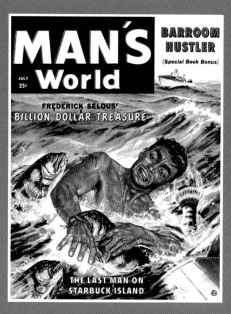

MALE, December 1953. Illustration: Schulz.

MAN'S LIFE, May 1956. Illustration: American Art Agency.

MALE, December 1955. Illustration: George Gross.

STAG, November 1954. Uncredited.

MAN'S WORLD, July 1957. Illustration: Jim Bentley.

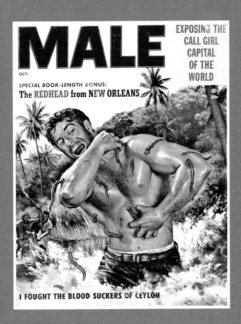

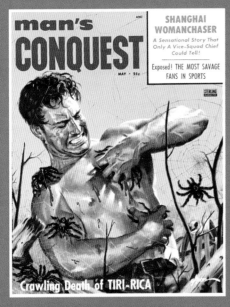

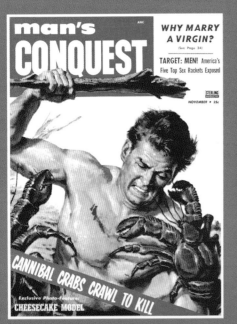

MALE, October 1955. Illustration: Mort Künstler.

MAN'S CONQUEST, May 1956. Uncredited.

MAN'S CONQUEST, November 1956. Uncredited.

MAN'S LIFE, March 1956. Illustration: "American Art Agency" (Norman Saunders).

REAL ADVENTURE, May 1958. Uncredited.

WHO TURNED THE KILLERS LOOSE?
60 Slaughtered GI's of the Malmedy Massacre cry vengeance

Confidential Guide Through The
10 WILDEST SIN TOWNS IN AMERICA

Real Adventure

MAY • 25 CENTS

A HILLMAN PUBLICATION

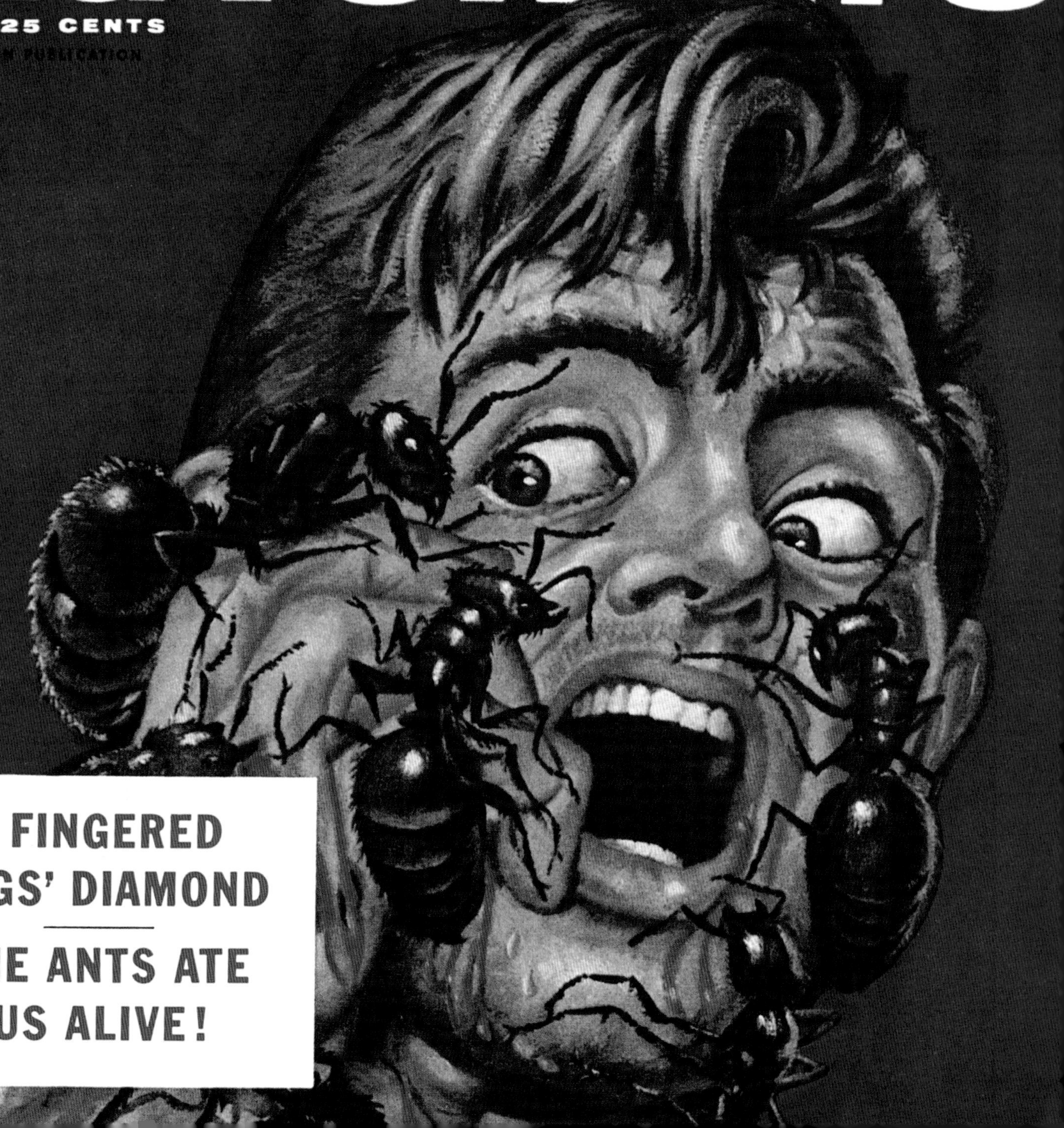

I FINGERED 'LEGS' DIAMOND
——
THE ANTS ATE US ALIVE!

TRUE ADVENTURES, May 1957. Illustration: Walter Popp.

MALE, June 1955. Original Illustration: Mort Künstler.

MEN, May 1953. Uncredited.

RAGE FOR MEN, August 1957. Uncredited.

MAN'S DARING ADVENTURES, November 1956. Uncredited.

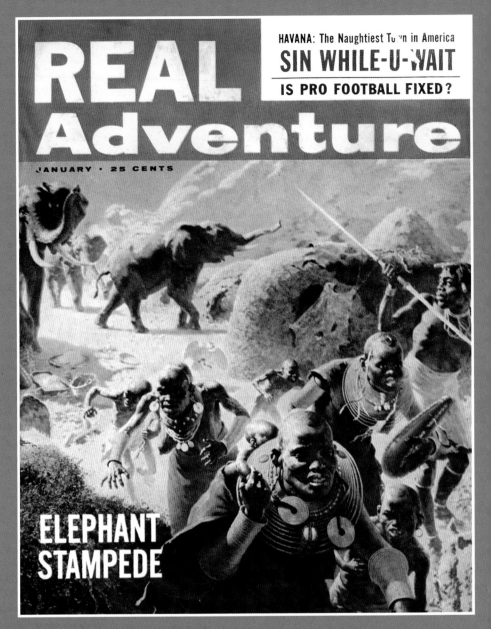

STAG, March 1955. Uncredited.

MAN TO MAN, December 1953. Illustration: Mark Schneider.

SAFARIS UNLIMITED, March 1960. Illustration: Tom Beecham.

REAL ADVENTURE, January. Uncredited.

STAG. Original Illustration: Mort Künstler.

"PEEL STREET," U. S. A.—New York's Fabulous Street of Stripper

ADVENTURE

THE MAN'S MAGAZINE OF EXCITING FICTION AND FACT • OCTOBER 25c

I ESCAPED FROM RED CHINA

by Karl Graffenried

PLUS NOVEL, STORIES, PICTURES, TRUE ADVENTURES

stag

G.

25

SPECIAL BOOK BONUS:
THE SOUTHPAW

(THE GREATEST BASEBALL STORY EVER WRITTEN)

MEN'S pictorial

MURDER ON HORSEBACK

Aug. 25¢

PLAYTIME DAMSEL

A STORY EVERY MAN SHOULD READ
ARE YOU AFRAID OF SEX?

THE SIN THEY NEVER TALK ABOUT
READ
Torture, Unlimited

They Told Me I Was Dying!

MALE 25¢
DEC.

ISLAND OF
VIOLENT LOVERS

SPORT ALL NEW!
A Adventure

JUNE

ONLY 25¢

BOOK BONUS!
The Jungle and the Damned!

"SCARE 'EM OUT OF THEIR WITS"
See p. 22

"I BATTLED A TON OF TURTLE!"

Pato: Bloody Sport For Guys With Guts

TRAPPING THE SPAWN OF HELL!

"I Was A Prisoner of the Devil Cats!"

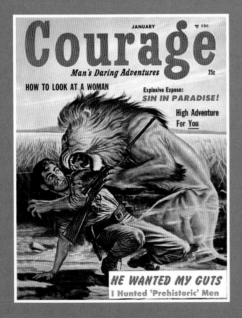

JANUARY CBC
Courage
Man's Daring Adventures 25¢

HOW TO LOOK AT A WOMAN

Explosive Exposé:
SIN IN PARADISE!

High Adventure For You

HE WANTED MY GUTS
I Hunted 'Prehistoric' Men

A SHOCKING TRUE STORY   THE MONSTER OF THE RIVER

ADVENTURE

THE MAN'S MAGAZINE OF EXCITING FICTION AND FACT

SEX TRAPS FOR BACHELORS

The Devil's Pardner
by PETER DAWSON

Sept., 25c

THE KILLER CAT of the TIETON

THE SHAME OF OUR CITIES READ THE STREET WHERE SIN WAS KING

8 MORE PAGES

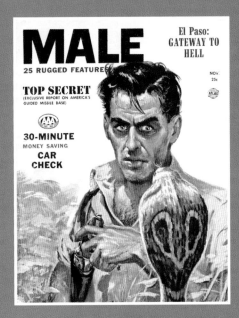

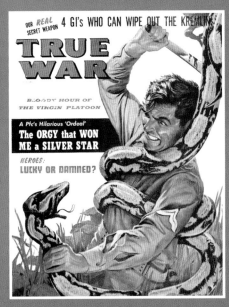

previous page: **SAFARIS UNLIMITED**, May 1960. Illustration: Tom Beecham.

previous page: Original Illustration: Mort Künstler.

MALE, November 1952. Uncredited.

TRUE WAR, January 1958. Illustration: Mal Singer.

MAN'S CONQUEST, July 1956. Uncredited.

HUNTING ADVENTURES, Summer 1956. Illustration: Rafael DeSoto.

MALE, November 1956. Illustration: Stan Borack.

SPECIAL $4.50 BOOK BONUS:
MY 15-YEAR ADVENTURE
(FROM THE ARCTIC TO THE JUNGLES)

MALE

SIX DROPS of POISON

NOV.

25

LISBON'S SECRET **SEX CIRCUIT**

(EXPOSING EUROPE'S SIN CENTER)

HOW NORMAL IS YOUR SEX LIFE
according to the letter of the law

MAN'S ADVENTURE

Revealing a shocking medical secret
YOU CAN CATCH CANCER

A report on the love-happy housewives of suburbia
NYMPHOS WITH A RANCH HOUSE

MARCH   35¢   PDC

Torture and death in New Guinea
SHOWDOWN ON CANNIBAL RIVER

The unbelievable but true story of how the Army saved the Marines
THE BLOODY BEACHES OF GUAM

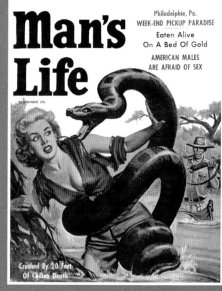

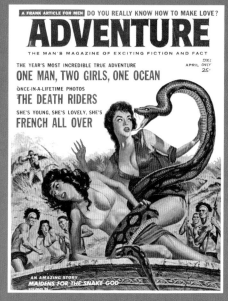

MAN'S ADVENTURE, March 1962. Uncredited.

MAN'S SMASHING STORIES, June 1959. Uncredited.

MAN'S LIFE, September 1957. Illustration: Will Hulsey.

PERIL, December 1960. Uncredited.

ADVENTURE, April 1961. Illustration: Vic Prezio.

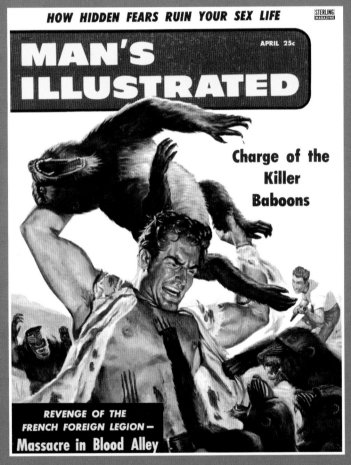

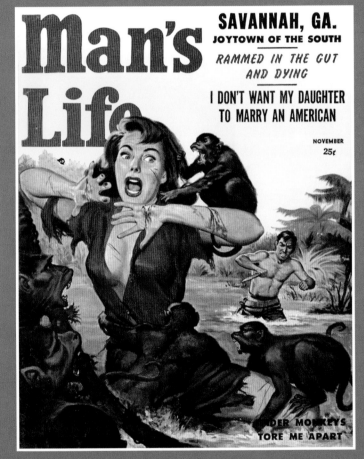

RAGE FOR MEN, April 1957. Uncredited.

MAN'S ILLUSTRATED, April 1956. Uncredited.

MAN'S LIFE, November 1957. Illustration: Will Hulsey.

MAN'S ADVENTURE, March 1961. Uncredited.

EXPOSING TABOOS THAT
GOVERN THE MOVIES   SEX ON THE SILVER SCREEN

MAN'S
ADVENTURE

MARCH   PDC   35¢

Right in the middle of a
Florida swamp, a hoard of gold
is waiting for salvage

**THE TREASURE
THAT'S YOURS
FOR THE
TAKING**

Sure it's a racket, but every
week a million guys are putting
their cash on the line for . . .

THE WOMEN
WHO RAFFLE
THEIR LOVE

Josephine loved a
practical joke but
one day she played
her tricks on
the wrong man and

**SHE LAUGHED
HER WAY
TO MURDER**

EXOTICA

BIRD CALLS. XYLOPHONES. The drone of a mosquito goes from one speaker to the other. Behind the bamboo bar are two Edgar Leeteg black velvet paintings of Tahitian lovelies. On top of the bar lay two magazines. On one cover a startled, scantily-dressed white woman looks outside the vacation hut where a brown-skinned savage holds a huge, bloody knife. Another magazine shows an Indiana Jones-style explorer, a cap perched on his head, whip by his side.

The strange Goddesses and Amazons were particularly violent toward, or beholden to, American suburbanites spying their buxom, cappuccino-skin colored rituals with beheading savages or Komodo dragons.

American exotica, circa 1957. The way to enjoy potent mixed drinks while recognizing, almost subliminally, the superiority of the white American male as victors of the Pacific War, the sort desired by beautiful South Pacific women, and needed to fight back their mates, almost always seen as being darker-skinned and far more vicious than their women.

This pulp and Hollywood apparatus was used time and again since the turn of the century as cheap set decoration, and also to promote the American moral imperative to invade the lands of backward people and save their women and children from—what?—themselves. The same imperial goal is even used today, primarily as distraction from the true reason behind interest in conquering the savage arena, namely, resources.

The exotic clarion call also bugled for the longtime Gary Cooper obsession with French Legionnaires, violent peons of the "dark continent," and Arabs, the Rimsky-Korsakov kind obsessed with white slavery, jewelry, fezzes, and white flowing robes, oil wells drilling behind them.

Before the African became the African-American, and the cannibal gag was finally rested. And before the South Seas became a fond memory of the Pacific War.

Illustration: Norm Saunders.

ESQUIRE, April 1944. Uncredited.

SOUTH SEA STORIES, December 1939. Illustration: Rod Ruth.

SAGA, September 1934. Illustration: "Hurst."

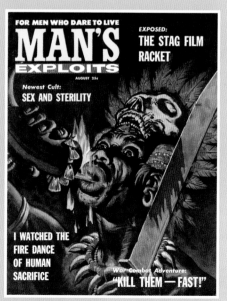

FURY, May 1956. Illustration: Tom Beecham.

STAG, "Ceremonial Dance." Original Illustration: Mort Künstler.

SAFARI, November 1956. Illustration: Robert Doares.

SIR!, December 1954. Illustration: Mark Schneider.

MAN'S EXPLOITS, August 1957. Uncredited.

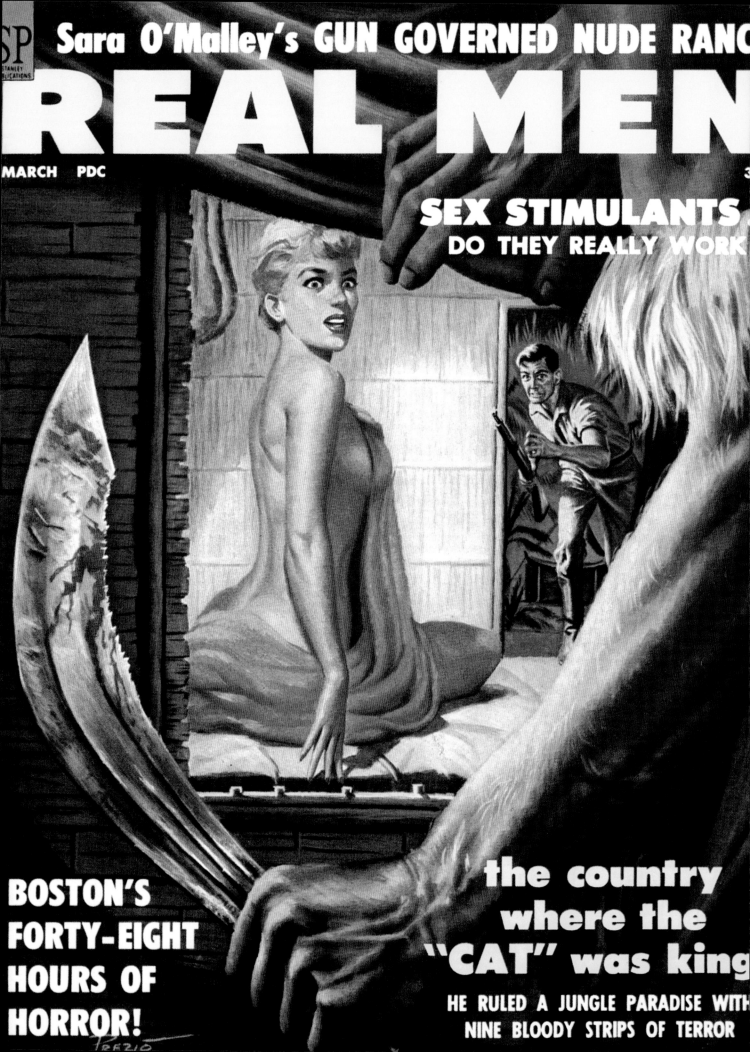

REAL MEN, March 1959. Illustration: Vic Prezio.
EXOTIC ADVENTURES, Vol. 1 No. 2. Illustration: Hirtle.

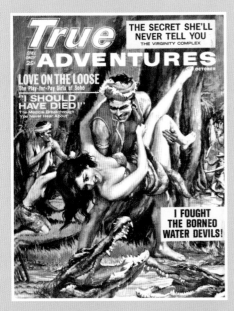

SPUR, June 1959. Uncredited.

TRUE ADVENTURES, October 1963. Illustration: Vic Olson.

MAN TO MAN, October 1958. Uncredited.

MAN'S ADVENTURE, January 1959. Illustration: Vic Prezio.

REAL ACTION, January 1958. Illustration: George Eisenberg.

REAL
ACTION
G-B GAS:
Deadlier Than the H-Bomb
THE BROTHEL THAT STOPPED A BATTLE
THE CAR DETROIT WON'T GIVE YOU
MURDER IS MY BUSINESS
BIRTH CONTROL PILLS CAN RUIN YOU
WHY FIGHTERS FIGHT DIRTY

NOW 25c

FOR MEN

WILD

DECEMBER - 1957

ACE

SANTIAGO.

PASSIO
PIT
OF THE
ANDES

SLAUGHTER at APACHE Pa

THE DAY FRISC
WENT BERSER

BLOODY PANG
STORY OF 'MAU MAU' TERF

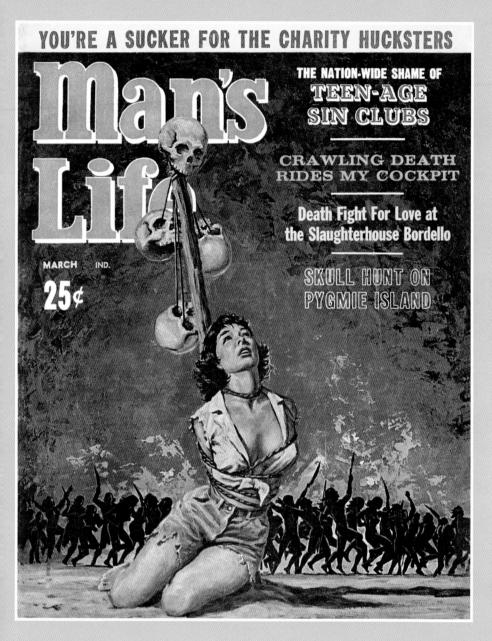

Man's Life

THE NATION-WIDE SHAME OF
TEEN-AGE SIN CLUBS

CRAWLING DEATH RIDES MY COCKPIT

Death Fight For Love at the Slaughterhouse Bordello

SKULL HUNT ON PYGMIE ISLAND

MARCH IND.

25¢

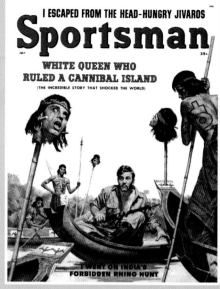

I ESCAPED FROM THE HEAD-HUNGRY JIVAROS
Sportsman
WHITE QUEEN WHO RULED A CANNIBAL ISLAND
(THE INCREDIBLE STORY THAT SHOCKED THE WORLD)
JULY 35¢
TWENT ON INDIA'S FORBIDDEN RHINO HUNT

The DANCE HALL GIRL and her TOMBSTONE KILLER — SPECIAL BOOK BONUS
FOR MEN ONLY
JULY 25¢
ISLAND OF STRANGE WOMEN
"THERE'S NO PILOT ON THIS PLANE!"
(THE MOST FANTASTIC AIR ADVENTURE EVER TOLD)

From behind the scenes in a German women's prison...
THE SEX-MAD MONSTERS OF DORTMUND
The hotrodders who stopped the U.S. Army cold
THE GUNNERS OF SAN PATRICIO
REAL MEN
The cures are there, but your doctor is afraid to use them
the lawsuits that threaten your life
PDC OCT. 25¢
The latest gimmick in the call-girl game
SWIMMING POOLS OF PASSION

WILD, December 1957. Uncredited.
MAN'S LIFE, March 1961. Uncredited.
SPORTSMAN, July 1958. Uncredited.
FOR MEN ONLY, July 1956. Uncredited.
REAL MEN, October 1960. Uncredited.

MAN TO MAN, January 1962. Illustration: Shores.

FURY, April 1954. Illustration: J.G. Woods.

MAN'S ADVENTURE, October 1958. Illustration: Clarence Doore.

MALE, May 1956. Illustration: Stan Borack.

SPECIAL BOOK BONUS   **SLAUGHTER STREET**
A STORY OF MOBSTERS, MOLLS AND MURDER

MALE

RAID OF THE
JIVARO
HEADHUNTERS

MAY

25c

E 16 WIVES
OF BEN
E HERMIT

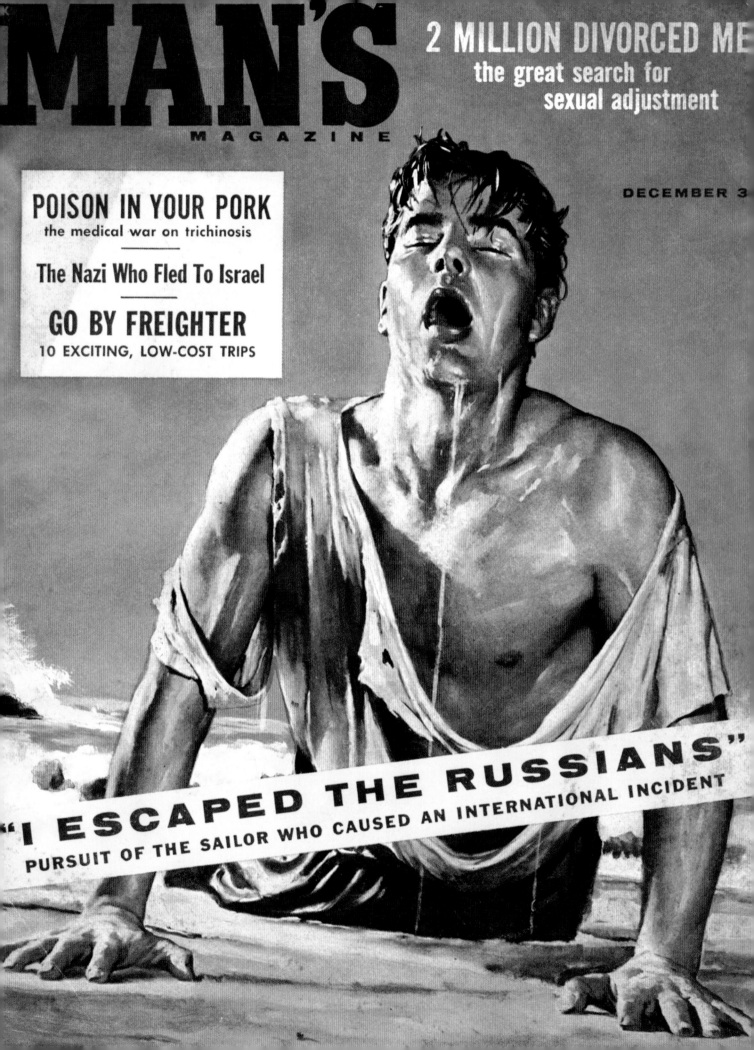

MAN'S
MAGAZINE

2 MILLION DIVORCED ME
the great search for
sexual adjustment

DECEMBER 3

POISON IN YOUR PORK
the medical war on trichinosis

The Nazi Who Fled To Israel

GO BY FREIGHTER
10 EXCITING, LOW-COST TRIPS

"I ESCAPED THE RUSSIANS"
PURSUIT OF THE SAILOR WHO CAUSED AN INTERNATIONAL INCIDENT

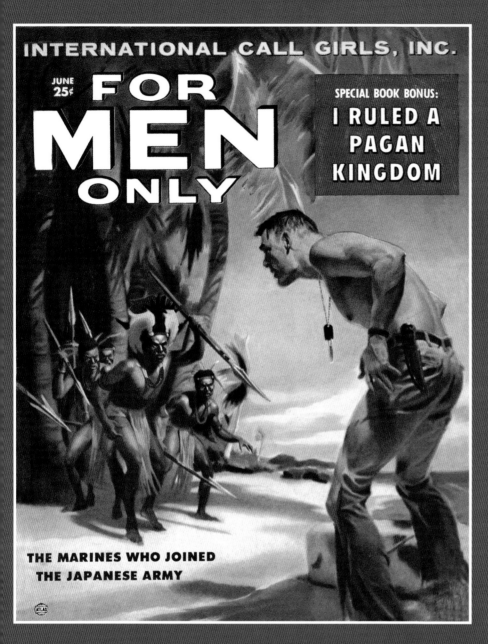

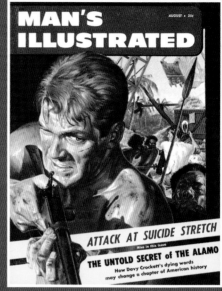

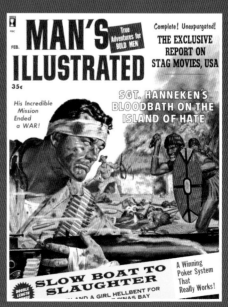

MAN'S MAGAZINE, December 1958. Illustration: Robert E. Schulz.

FOR MEN ONLY, June 1957. Uncredited.

MAN'S ILLUSTRATED, August 1956. Uncredited.

MAN'S EXPLOITS, January 1958. Uncredited.

MAN'S ILLUSTRATED, February 1960. Uncredited.

TRUE ADVENTURES, October 1960. Illustration: Vic Prezio.

STAG, September 1957. Original Illustration: Mort Künstler.

WILDCAT, April 1960. Uncredited.

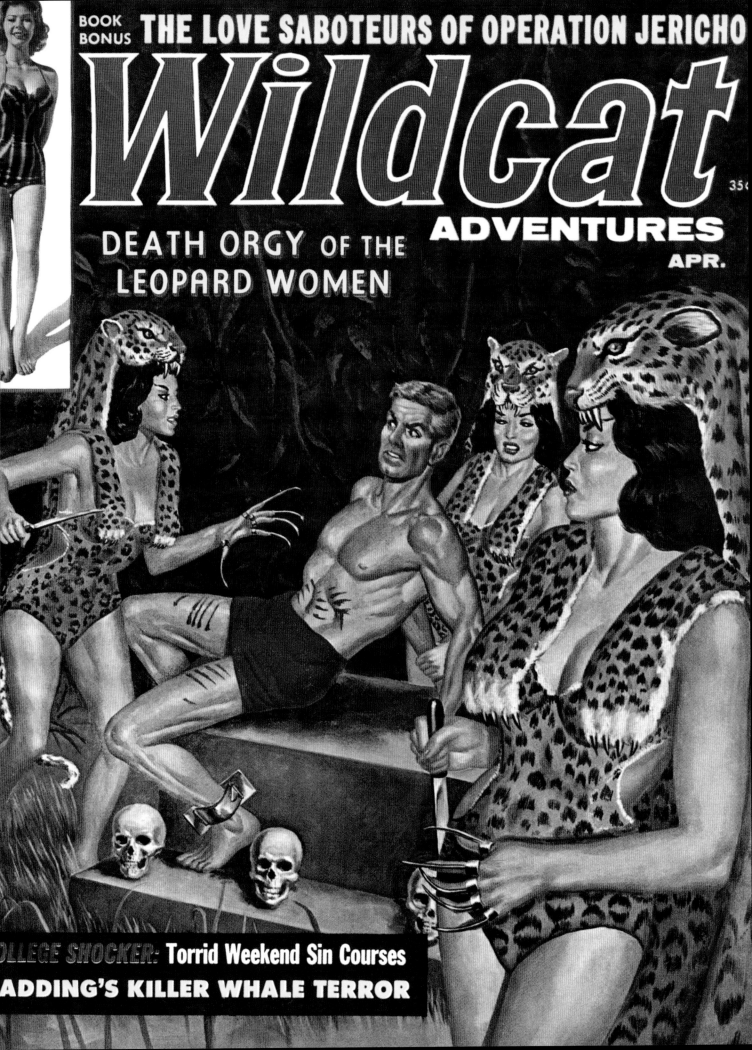

COMSTOCK'S LAST QUEEN OF VICE

JAN. 25¢

SIR!

√ SMUT On The Streets Of Paris

√ My Wife Was a White Slave

√ The Man Who Wouldn't Hang

Why Giants Won't Score in Frisco

HAS OUR LOST MISSILE BECOME A PAGAN GOD?

THE FLOATING HAREM OF BULLY HAYES

IND.

ESCAPE

SEPT. **TO ADVENTURE** 35c

JONY JOHNSON ▶

the HORROR of the VICTORIAN WHITE SLAVE RINGS

those COLLEGE CROWD CAPERS AT FT. LAUDERDALE

the STRIPPER who WHIPS MEN   DEATH to SGT. HAYATO!

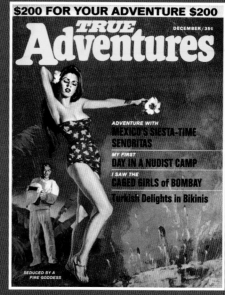

$200 FOR YOUR ADVENTURE $200

TRUE Adventures

DECEMBER / 35c

ADVENTURE WITH
MEXICO'S SIESTA-TIME SEÑORITAS

MY FIRST
DAY IN A NUDIST CAMP

I SAW THE
CAGED GIRLS of BOMBAY

Turkish Delights in Bikinis

SEDUCED BY A FIRE GODDESS

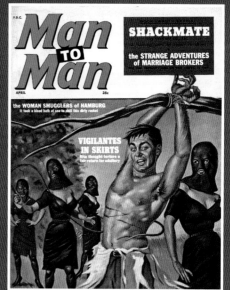

P.D.C.

Man TO Man

SHACKMATE
the STRANGE ADVENTURES of MARRIAGE BROKERS

APRIL 35c

the WOMAN SMUGGLERS of HAMBURG
It took a blood bath of sea to abill this dirty racket

VIGILANTES IN SKIRTS

SIR!, January 1958. Uncredited.

ESCAPE TO ADVENTURE, September 1961. Uncredited.

TRUE ADVENTURES, September 1965. Illustration: Basil Gogos.

MAN TO MAN, April 1961. Uncredited.

ADVENTURE, December 1966. Illustration: Vic Prezio.

DECEMBER 35c

Adventure

THE NUMBER 1 ADVENTURE MAGAZINE FOR MEN

Six Strike-It-Rich Islands

TRAVEL GUIDE FOR MEN ONLY

Cure For Lonesome Males

LET'S HAVE FARMER GIRLS

LURED BY THE MISTRESS OF THE COBRA TREASURE

TRUE ADVENTURES, October 1961. Illustration: Vic Prezio.

ADVENTURE, December 1961. Illustration: Raphael M. DeSoto.

THE TRUTH ABOUT OVERSEXED GIRLS

ADVENTURE

THE MAN'S MAGAZINE OF EXCITING FICTION AND FACT

STILL ONLY 25¢ DECEMBER

THE YANK WHO BECAME AN ISLAND GOD
Sailor Morrell and His Hundred Brides

AN EXCLUSIVE
The Murders You Never Hear About
RUB-OUT

PLAYGIRL OF THE MONTH

POISON-PEN SEX MANIACS ON THE LOOSE!

NEW **MAN'S PERIL**

OCT.
35¢
CDC

THE SIN-DOLLS WHO TRAPPED THE REDS' ACE MASTER SPY!

THE MADAM WHO BOSSED THE BIZARRE BORDELLO'S VICE & CRIME RING!

WE BATTLED THE MAN-STARVED NYMPHOS OF CORUMBA...

THE DAY THE SOUTH RAIDED VERMONT

stag

SEPT. 25¢

MY LIFE WITH NEW GUINEA'S AMAZON WOMEN

(THE STRANGE TRUE ADVENTURES OF CONRAD STRECK)

EXOTIC Adventures

50¢

THE ARABIAN SLAVE-GIRL RACKET

ISLAND OF LOVE-STARVED WOMEN

TERROR IN THE FAR EAST: THE WOLF-WOMEN OF INDIA

Plus: MISS BERLIN: FABULOUS, FANTASTIC, EXOTIC!

Man's World

25¢ FEB.

SYNDICATE MADAM
SHE RAN THE EAST'S BIGGEST VICE RING

THE GUNSLINGER WITH 200 NOTCHES

PARIMU'S MISTRESS

THE CANNIBAL HAREM OF CHARLIE SAVAGE
(INCREDIBLE SAGA OF A WHITE MAN WHO BECAME KING OF THE FIJIS)

man's world

TRUE BOOK BONUS: HELMET FOR MY PILLOW

THE FOUR-FINGERED SPY
(1000 AGENTS HUNT THIS DEADLY RED HATCHET MAN)

CHAMPION FOR MEN, November 1959. Illustration: Clarence Doore.

MAN'S PERIL, October 1965. Uncredited.

STAG, September 1957. Uncredited.

EXOTIC ADVENTURES, Vol. 1 No. 5. Uncredited.

MAN'S WORLD, February 1958. Illustration: Charles Copeland.

MAN'S WORLD, August 1958. Illustrator: Mort Künstler.

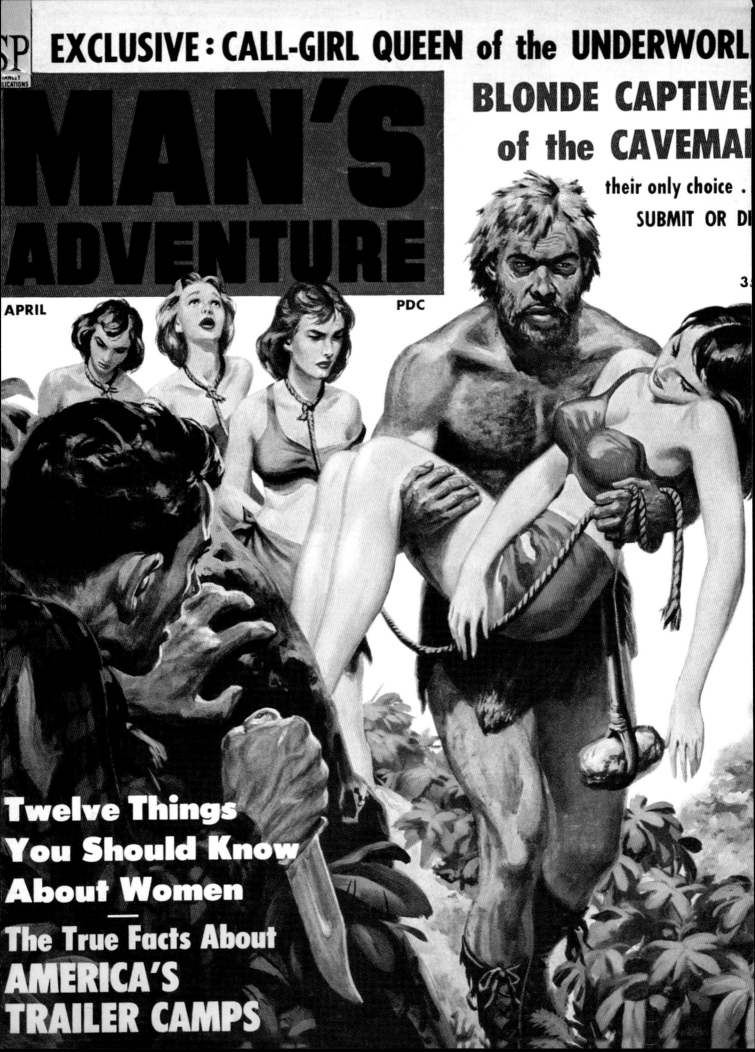

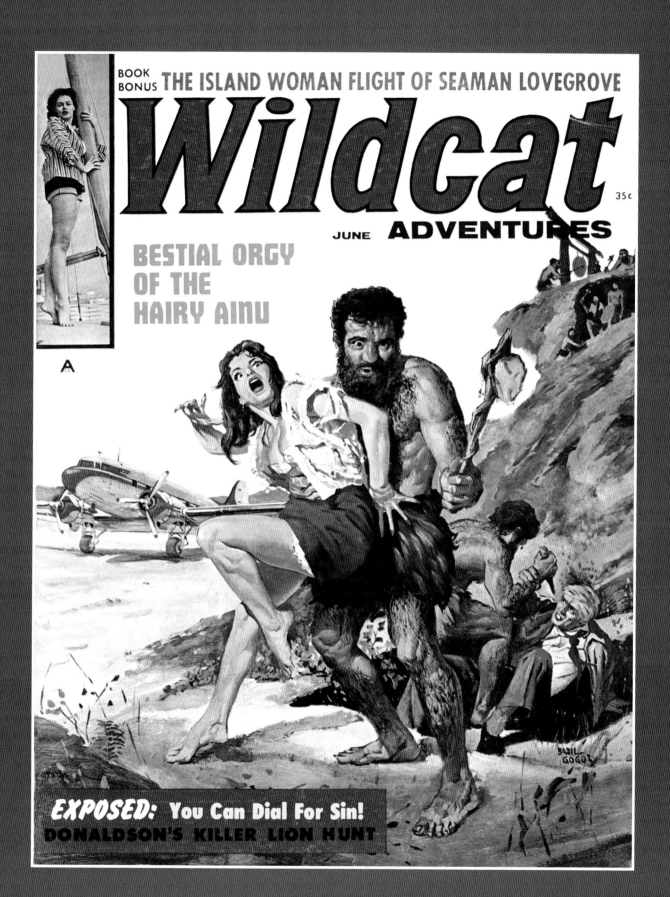

MAN'S ADVENTURE, April 1959. Uncredited.

WILDCAT, June 1960. Illustration: Basil Gogos.

SIR!, October 1953. Illustration: Mark Schneider.

SAGA, November 1954. Original Illustration: Mort Künstler.

MAN TO MAN, Spring 1963. Uncredited.

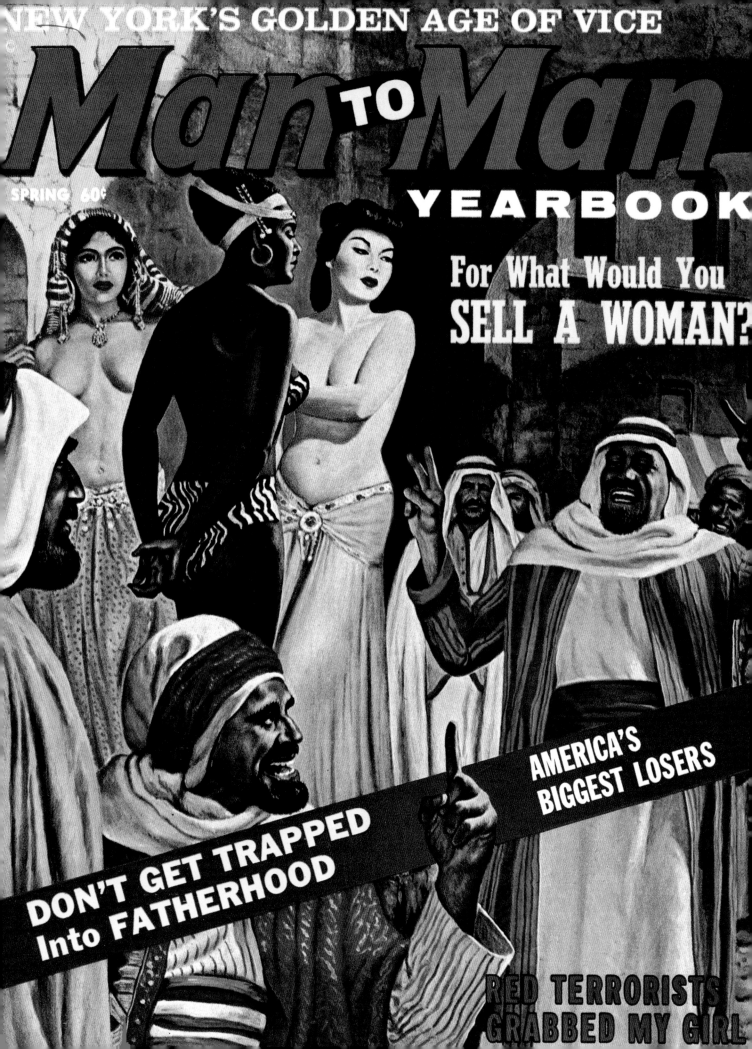

the case of Donald Hume: **HOW TO GET AWAY WITH MURDE**

DOWIE'S ELECTRIC BED: the Do-It-Yourself project no woman could resis

REAL

B·O·O·K - B·O·N·U·S:
THE MAN KILLER

the amazing confession of an assassi
who changed today's history

JUN
35

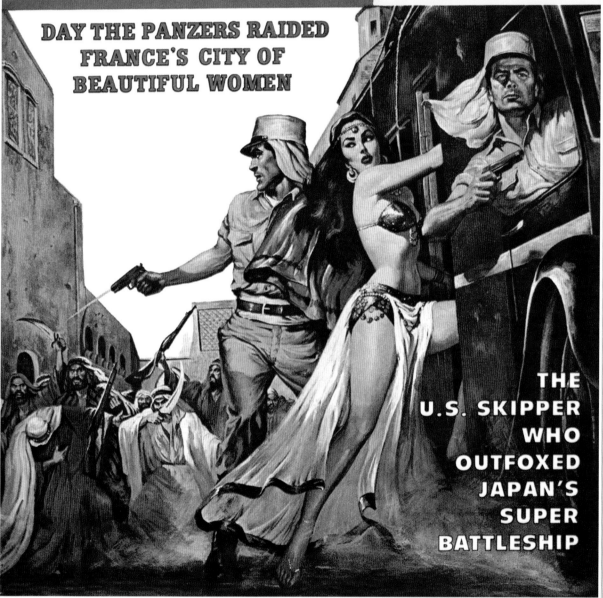

REAL, June 1960. Illustration: Michael Aviano.

TRUE ACTION, August 1961. Illustration: Charles Copeland.

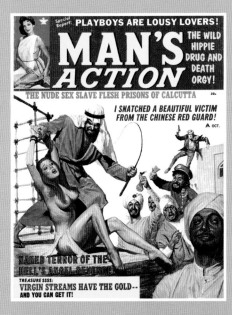

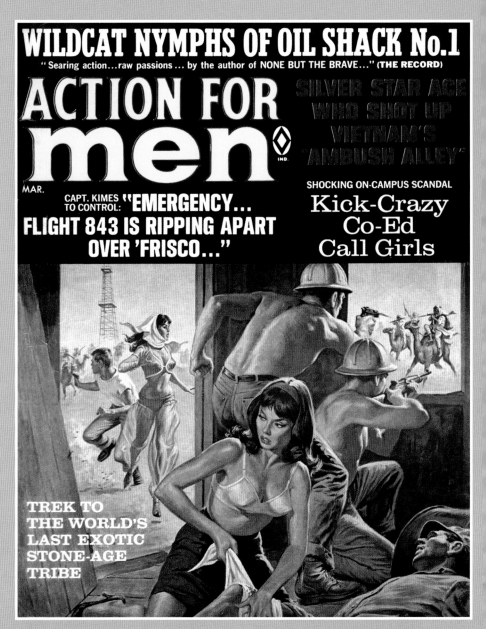

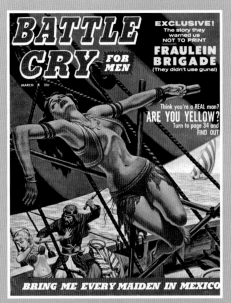

TRUE ADVENTURES, December 1960. Illustration: Vic Prezio.

MAN'S ACTION, October 1959. Uncredited.

BATTLE CRY, March 1960. Uncredited.

ACTION FOR MEN, March 1966. Illustration: Earl Norem.

UNTAMED, July 1959. Illustration: Ed Emsh.

UNTAMED

ACE

July/35¢

What You Don'
Know About
Nymphomaniac

RASHED THE
ORDELLO FOR MILLIONAIRES ONLY

he Day They Roasted
Charlie Savage

essie Darling's Thirty-Hour Ordeal

true

RICO TOMASO

THE AIRCREWMAN

SEE PAGE 37 — A TRIBUTE BY
REAR ADMIRAL ARTHUR W. RADFORD
ACTING CHIEF OF
AIR OPERATIONS, U. S. N.

NATIONAL WAR FUND

FOR OUR OWN—FOR OUR ALLIES

WORLD WAR II

IN THE WAR YEAR 1943, the long-running men's magazine *Argosy* traded in its pulp fiction emphasis to become a "slick" of true stories. In this transitional period *Argosy* replaced the illustrated cover with a photograph, and its former pulp dimension became oversized, early *Life*-style. It took *Argosy* about five years to realize that covers with posed photography looked a touch like weird put-ons. Well-executed standard-sized illustrated covers were more easily accepted by the mainstream, and in the '50s they helped *Argosy* to replicate *True*, and in so doing energize the circulation enough to become the second most purchased men's magazine.

It took until the height of the Korean War [1950–1953] for men's adventure magazines to find readers, and themselves, leading at once to amoebic self-reproduction. Called a "non-fun war" by Mario Puzo, the designation applied to the Korean War was later attached to the Vietnam War. If featured on the cover, the non-fun wars had a poisonous effect on sales.

Publishing during wartime had its own tricky obligations. Covers often featured a patriotic ribbon and a phrase (like the yellow ribbons of the Gulf War), so as not to be perceived as supporting the enemy or cultivating a lavender-like affection for art. Ironically, Korean War-period men's magazines didn't make the mistake of too often featuring the ongoing and politically confusing "non-fun war," preferring instead to remember the Great War in which good and evil were more easily understood.

As Mario Puzo also pointed out, World War II was a "gold mine"— successfully exploited for its light-and-dark/good-and-evil horrorshow of Big Emotions. Editors in search of new material expanded the evil of the Axis logarithmically year by year. Battles and atrocities were freshly discovered every issue, the new ones revealed to be even more extreme than last month's. The evil Asians seen menacing helpless American women in '30s pulps became pint-sized Nazis with Napoleonic complexes after Pearl Harbor. Writers and illustrators often confused Japanese for Korean for Vietnamese for Red Chinese. Very little effort was made to distinguish Asian nationalities, even to get the uniform right, as long as the teeth were bucked and the eyes slanted. And the evil was forever cryptic.

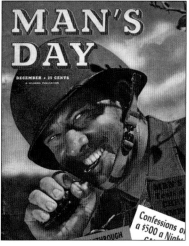

But illustrators and writers never seemed to have a problem distinguishing Nazis from other European nationals, such as incapable but good-hearted Frenchmen. General Rommel, the sole Nazi portrayed by the postwar American media with nominal regard, was depicted as scarred and grimacing when his head filled the cover of *Man's Magazine*. Goering was seen as being predictably worse—a gaggle of white slaves and a movie camera are positioned behind him on the cover of *War Criminals* magazine, presumably for the purpose of shooting snuff pornography. Men's adventure magazines reveal why Nazis lost the war: the nasty screwballs focused every living moment into inventing ways to procure and torture busty American women with futuristic swimwear and hairdos.

Most of the publishers and illustrators of the Nazi freak show avoided taking proper credit for their work, but a major celebrity—Ed Gein—publicly admitted that these magazines had given him great pleasure and inspiration.

TRUE, November 1964. Illustration: Rico Tomaso.

G.I. JOE, May 1946. Illustration: Uncredited.

MAN'S DAY, December 1952. Uncredited.

WAR ACES, 1941. Uncredited.

MAN'S
MAGAZINE

JANUARY 35¢

"MY 23 YEARS IN THE DEATH HOUSE"
BY TEXAS' DON REID, JR.

THE GI WHO GOT V.D.

RUSSIA'S "OPERATION KIDNAP"
HOW THE KREMLIN ABDUCTED DR. WALTER LINSE

FLAMING DEATH OF ADMIRAL YAMAMOTO
Tom Lanphier's Mission: Destroy the Jap Who Plotted Pearl Harbor

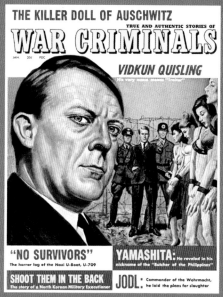

MAN'S MAGAZINE, January 1961. Illustration: Mel Crair.

CHALLENGE FOR MEN, August 1959. Illustration: Mel Crair.

MAN'S MAGAZINE, October 1958. Uncredited.

WAR CRIMINALS, January 1964. Uncredited.

WAR CRIMINALS, August 1961. Uncredited.

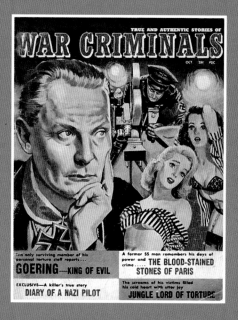

Men in Adventure

SEXUAL ADJUSTMENT IN MARRIAGE

The FRENCH MADAM and her BROTHEL of BLOOD

NOVEMBER • 35 CENT

THIS COVER PAINTING WAS DONE IN COMBAT BY LIEUT. MITCHELL JAMIESON, USNR

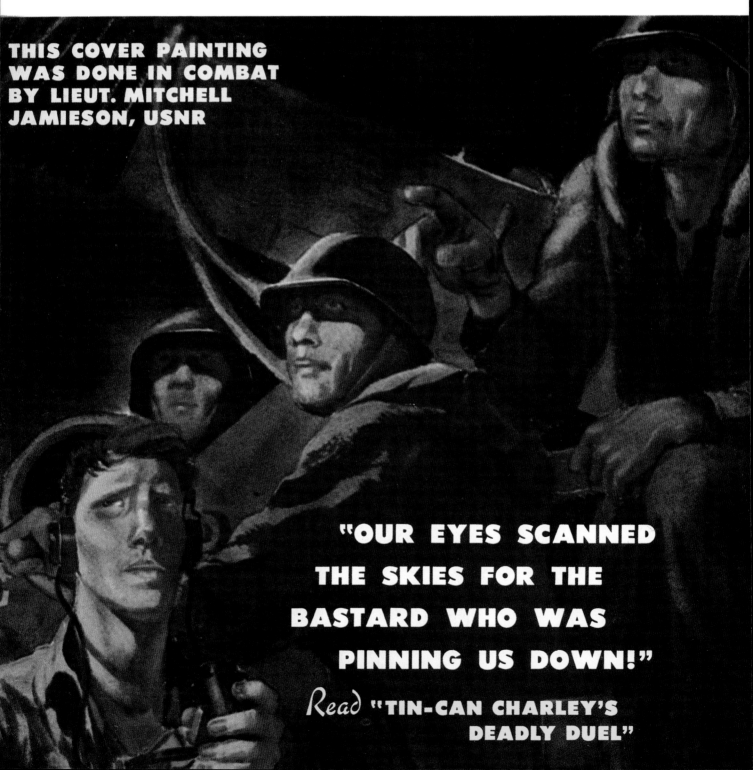

"OUR EYES SCANNED THE SKIES FOR THE BASTARD WHO WAS PINNING US DOWN!"

Read **"TIN-CAN CHARLEY'S DEADLY DUEL"**

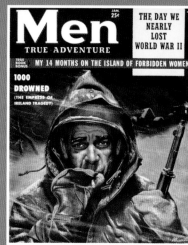

MEN IN ADVENTURE, November 1959. Illustration: Lt. Mitchell Jamieson.

MAN'S LIFE, November 1952. Illustration: Leonard Steckler.

MEN TRUE ADVENTURE, January 1958. Illustration: Mort Künstler.

MEN, June 1953. Illustration: James Bama.

MEN, October 1952. Uncredited.

MALE, May 1952. Uncredited.

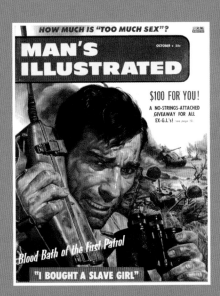

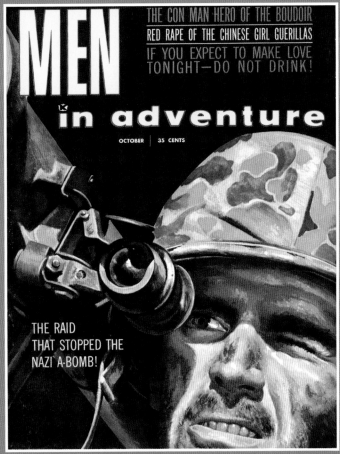

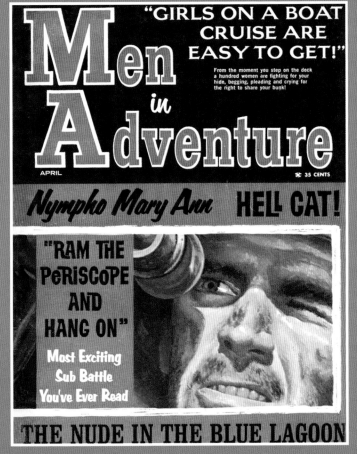

MAN'S ILLUSTRATED, October 1956. Uncredited.

MAN'S CONQUEST, June 1965. Uncredited.

MEN IN ADVENTURE, October 1960. Uncredited.

MEN IN ADVENTURE, April 1965. Uncredited.

MAN'S MAGAZINE, February 1961. Illustration: Mel Crair.

MAN'S
MAGAZINE

EBRUARY 35¢

HITLER'S HUMAN SANDBAGS
BOOK BONUS FROM THE BEST-SELLER
"THE BRIDGE"

BLOODY CHRISTMAS
THE DAY LOS ANGELES
HUNG ITS HEAD IN SHAME

"THEY CARVED KKK ON MY SKIN!"

SECRETS OF SATISFYING WOMEN
by Dr. Shailer Upton Lawton

hat the
.S. Army
n't tell...

STARTLING TRUTH ABOUT THE 77 AMERICAN VICTIMS OF
NERVE GAS

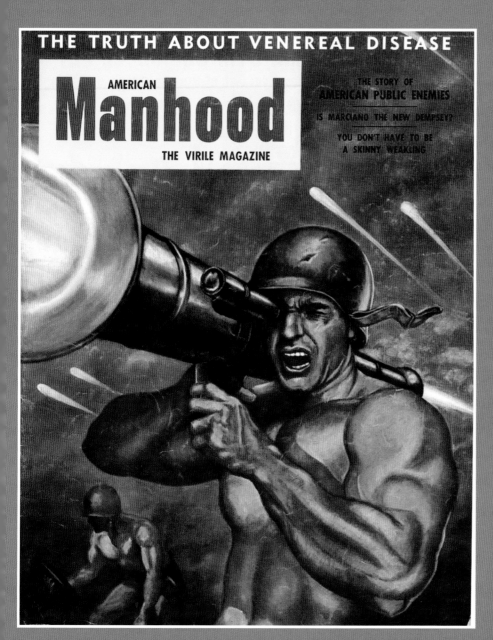

THE TRUTH ABOUT VENEREAL DISEASE

THE STORY OF
AMERICAN PUBLIC ENEMIES

IS MARCIANO THE NEW DEMPSEY?

YOU DON'T HAVE TO BE
A SKINNY WEAKLING

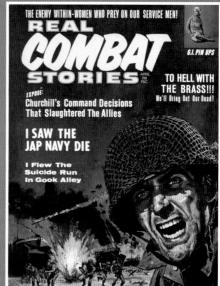

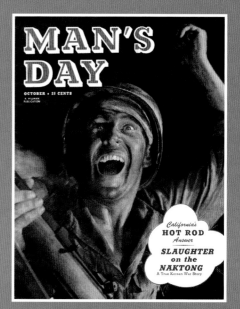

Illustration: Norman Saunders.

AMERICAN MANHOOD, February 1953. Uncredited.

MAN'S MAGAZINE, October 1952. Uncredited.

REAL COMBAT STORIES, April 1964. Uncredited.

MAN'S DAY, October 1952. Uncredited.

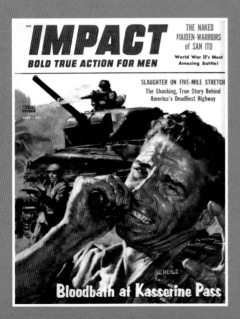

previous page: **MEN IN COMBAT**, July 1957. Illustration: Norman Saunders.

previous page: Illustration: Norman Saunders.

STAG, June 1956. Uncredited.

FOR MEN ONLY, March 1957. Illustration: Mort Künstler.

IMPACT, June 1957. Illustration: Schulz.

Illustration: Norman Saunders.

MAN'S WORLD, April 1964. Uncredited.

APR.

MAN'S WORLD

50¢

OKLENGTH EXTRA   *From the Sizzling International Best Seller*

Hell Sub Nymph

. ED ABERSOLD,
**Fighting C. O. of
et Nam's All-Ace
ystery Squadron**

SPECIAL BONUS FICTION

The **Sinful Sisters**

OW IN
ULL-ACTION
OLOR

'WILD WENDELL' PHILLIPS
**Gun-Toting U.S. Millionaire
Who Found The Sahara's
River Of Oi**

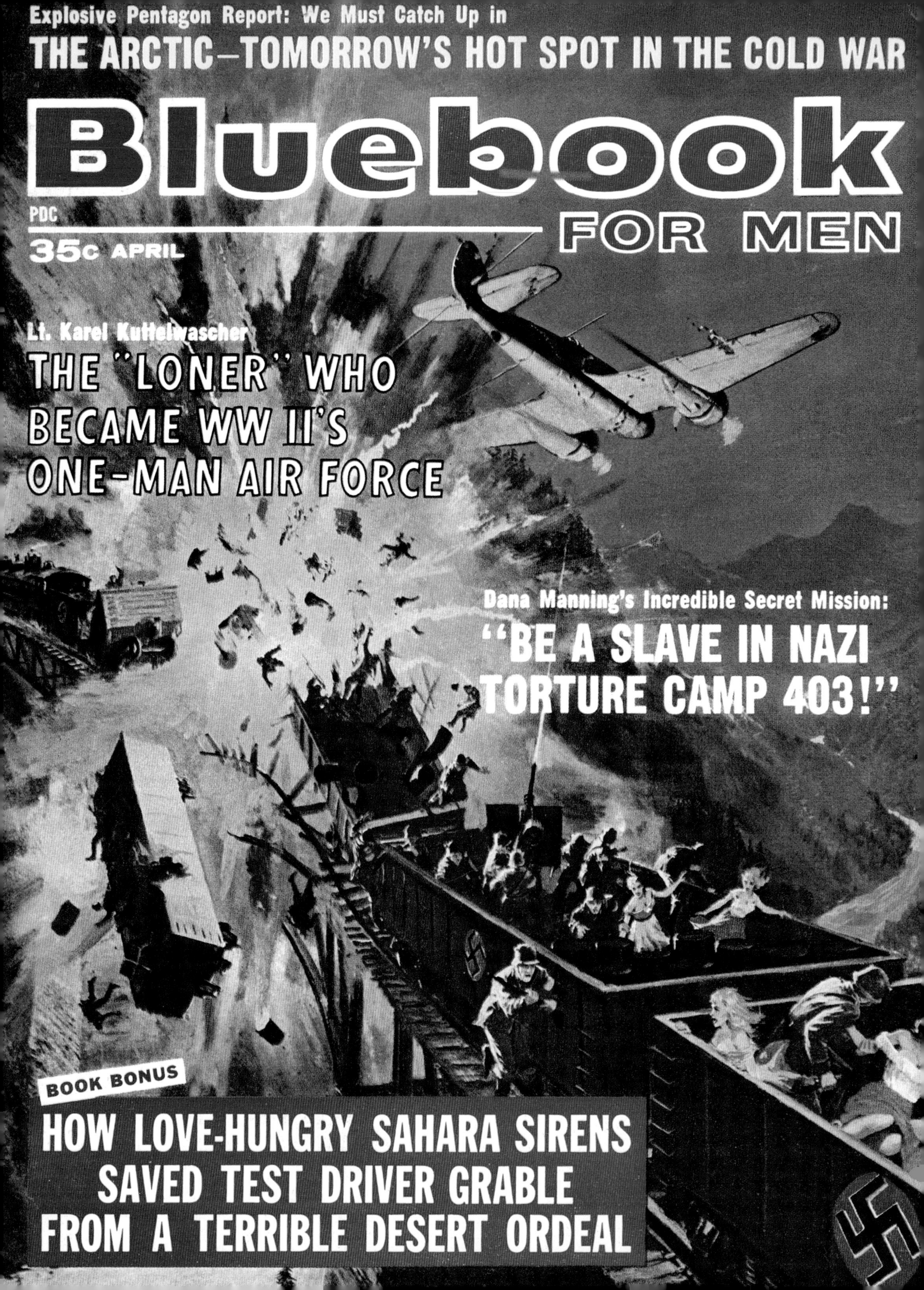

Explosive Pentagon Report: We Must Catch Up in
THE ARCTIC—TOMORROW'S HOT SPOT IN THE COLD WAR
Bluebook
PDC
FOR MEN
35c APRIL
Lt. Karel Kuttelwascher
THE "LONER" WHO BECAME WW II'S ONE-MAN AIR FORCE
Dana Manning's Incredible Secret Mission:
"BE A SLAVE IN NAZI TORTURE CAMP 403!"
BOOK BONUS
HOW LOVE-HUNGRY SAHARA SIRENS SAVED TEST DRIVER GRABLE FROM A TERRIBLE DESERT ORDEAL

BLUEBOOK FOR MEN, April 1963. Illustration: Bob Schulz.

MEN'S PICTORIAL, December 1957. Illustration: Phil Roncor.

STAG, February 1962. Original Illustration: Mort Künstler.

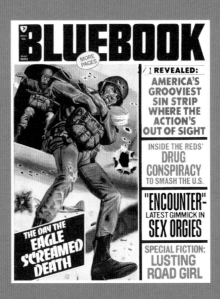

BLUEBOOK, May 1971. Uncredited.

FOR MEN ONLY, February 1964. Original Illustration: Mort Künstler.

BATTLE CRY, April 1957. Illustration: Clarence Doore.

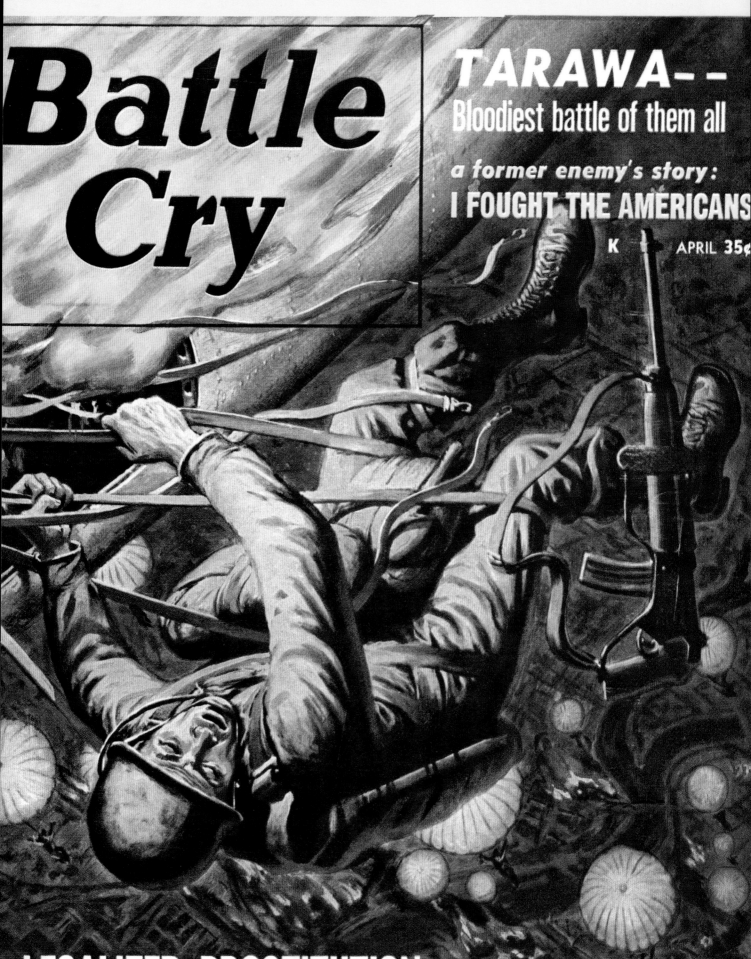

THE DIEPPE RAID: *an epic of* CANADIAN *courage*

Battle Cry

TARAWA--
Bloodiest battle of them all

a former enemy's story:
I FOUGHT THE AMERICANS

K   APRIL 35¢

LEGALIZED PROSTITUTION: *a cure for military ills?*

Real Adventure

OVEMBER · **25 CENTS**

A HILLMAN PUBLICATI●

Shocking Story of 20th Century Voodoo!

SATAN'S SEX CULT

THE MAN WHO STOLE A COUNTRY

HELL-BOAT!

Days in an Open Boat
d 40 of Us Would Die!

previous page: **STAG**, May 1963. Original Illustration: Mort Künstler.

previous page: **REAL ADVENTURES**, November 1956. Uncredited.

BATTLE STATION, November 1961. Illustration: Doug Weaver.

MALE, October 1958. Original Illustration: Mort Künstler.

MAN'S CONQUEST, January 1963. Uncredited.

MALE, February 1958. Illustration: James Bama.

STAG, July 1961. Illustration: Mort Künstler.

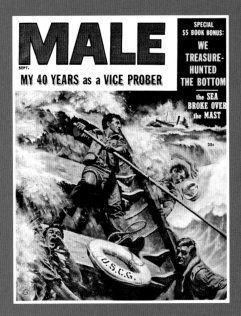

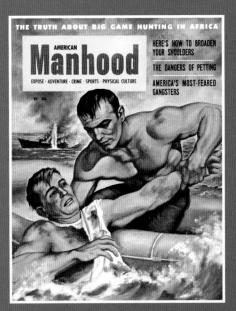

MALE, September 1955. Illustration: Mel Crair.

CHALLENGE, May 1957. Illustration: Mel Crair.

AMERICAN MANHOOD, May 1953. Uncredited.

"US Sub. Captain." Illustration: Mort Künstler.

SEE, January 1960. Uncredited.

THE PREGNANT INNOCENTS:
sterilization's secret scandal

SEE
K

JAN.
35¢

HE MAN
HO ATE HIMSELF

REFFIELD'S
CREDIBLE
EX CULT

Y LIFE BEHIND
HE GUN
unforgettable
ok-bonus by
MES D. HORAN
thor of
E D. A.'s MAN

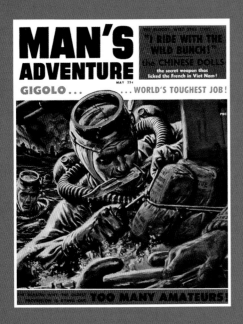

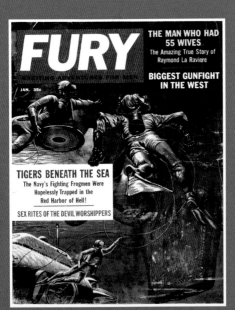

MAN'S ADVENTURE, May 1958. Illustration: Clarence Doore.

AMERICAN MANHOOD, December 1952. Illustration: Peter Poulton.

FURY, January 1959. Uncredited.

MEN IN ADVENTURE, September 1959. Uncredited.

Illustration: Mort Künstler.

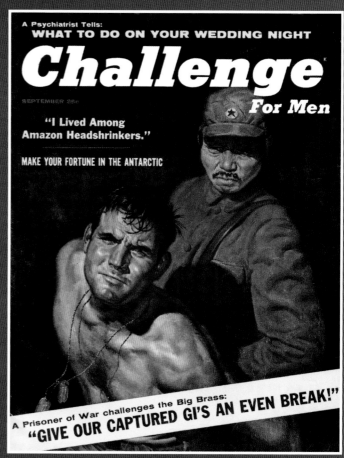

RUGGED MEN, February 1961. Illustration: Vic Prezio.

MAN'S TRUE ACTION, June 1956. Illustration: L.B. Cole.

HIGH ADVENTURE, June 1958. Illustration: John Leone.

CHALLENGE FOR MEN, September 1955. Illustration: Tom Ryan.

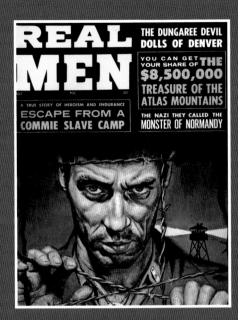

REAL MEN

THE DUNGAREE DEVIL
DOLLS OF DENVER

YOU CAN GET
YOUR SHARE OF THE
$8,500,000
TREASURE OF THE
ATLAS MOUNTAINS

A TRUE STORY OF HEROISM AND ENDURANCE
ESCAPE FROM A
COMMIE SLAVE CAMP

THE NAZI THEY CALLED THE
MONSTER OF NORMANDY

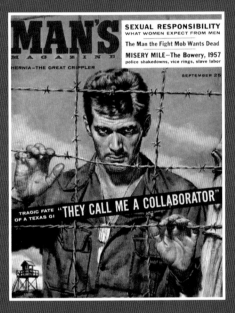

MAN'S
MAGAZINE

HERNIA—THE GREAT CRIPPLER

SEXUAL RESPONSIBILITY
WHAT WOMEN EXPECT FROM MEN

The Man the Fight Mob Wants Dead

MISERY MILE—The Bowery, 1957
police shakedowns, vice rings, slave labor

SEPTEMBER 25¢

TRAGIC FATE
OF A TEXAS GI   "THEY CALL ME A COLLABORATOR"

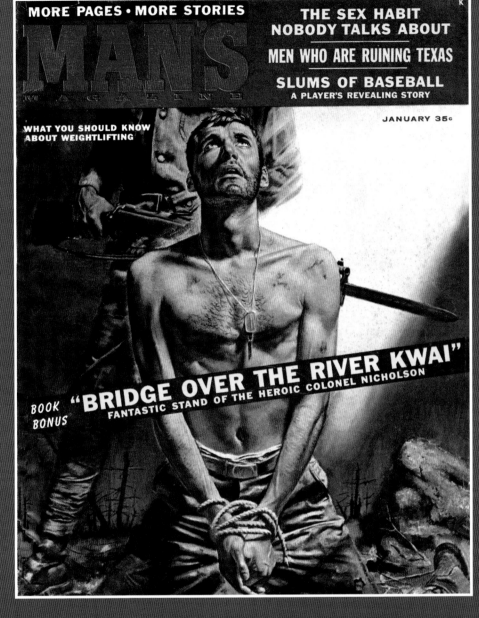

MORE PAGES • MORE STORIES

MAN'S
MAGAZINE

THE SEX HABIT
NOBODY TALKS ABOUT

MEN WHO ARE RUINING TEXAS

SLUMS OF BASEBALL
A PLAYER'S REVEALING STORY

WHAT YOU SHOULD KNOW
ABOUT WEIGHTLIFTING

JANUARY 35¢

BOOK
BONUS   "BRIDGE OVER THE RIVER KWAI"
FANTASTIC STAND OF THE HEROIC COLONEL NICHOLSON

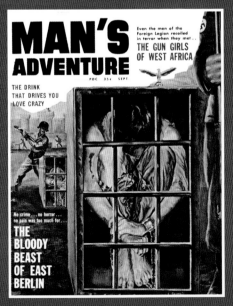

MAN'S
ADVENTURE

Even the men of the
Foreign Legion recoiled
in terror when they met...
THE GUN GIRLS
OF WEST AFRICA

PDC 35¢ SEPT

THE DRINK
THAT DRIVES YOU
LOVE CRAZY

No crime... no horror...
no pain was too much for...
THE
BLOODY
BEAST
OF EAST
BERLIN

REAL MEN, September 1964. Uncredited.

MAN'S MAGAZINE, September 1957. Illustration: Mel Crair.

MAN'S ADVENTURE, September 1960. Illustration: T. Canierio.

MAN'S MAGAZINE, January 1958. Illustration: Mel Crair.

STAG, May 1954. Illustration: Mort Künstler.

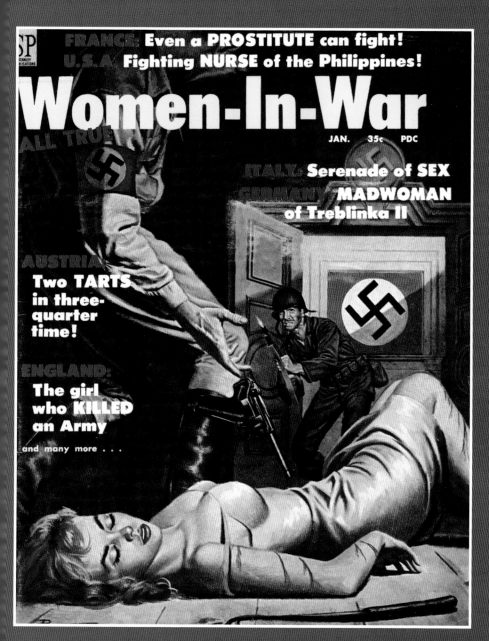

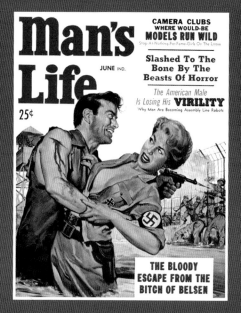

Illustration: Mort Künstler.

WOMEN-IN-WAR, November 1959. Illustration: Vic Prezio.

MAN'S LIFE, April 1960. Illustration: Will Hulsey.

MAN'S BEST, November 1961. Uncredited.

MAN'S LIFE, June 1959. Uncredited.

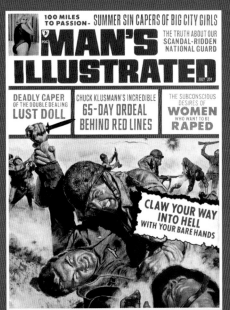

MEN'S MAGAZINE, June 1964. Illustration: Gil Cohen.

BIG ADVENTURE, November 1960. Uncredited.

MAN'S ILLUSTRATED, July 1960. Uncredited.

MAN'S WORLD, August 1961. Uncredited.

MALE, October 1959. Uncredited.

AMERICAN FLYBOY WHO BROKE OUT OF...

CAMP "TWO MILES DOWN"

MALE

IND.

25¢   OCT.

A blonde, a mickey in Lisbon, handcuffs, a quick trip into Axis Spain, and the American Major was a guest in Capt. Noriega's Black Hole of Madrid

TRUE BOOKLENGTH

—

YANKEE NEWSHOUND WHO GRABBED A CHINESE HAREM

TYPHOON THAT WIPED OUT TASK FORCE 38

"THE WAVES WERE 20 STORIES HIGH"

CLIMAX, May 1960. Illustration: Warren Bauggartner.

BATTLE CRY, October 1955. Uncredited.

Battle Cry

CALL ME TRAITOR!

G. I. SEX INSTRUCTION FILMS

SUICIDE SUB

DECEMBER 25¢

K

RST ISSUE!

"LAST TRIP"

THE SADISTIC BURLESQUE

"First Dr. Dicks offers his assessment of where these men ranked on a wartime scale of Nazi fanaticism, and then he attempts to discover what inner and external forces impelled these particular people to accept and carry out their gruesome roles. The evidence Dr. Dicks has assembled suggests that neither fanaticism nor identifiable psychiatric disorders were crucial factors among them. They were mostly weak-egoed, emotionally deprived individuals whose secret resentments, covered by conformity and unquestioning obedience to what were originally congenital social and group pressures and sanctions, essentially broke through, causing them to discard their previously 'civilized' behavior in order to act out to the fullest their roles as S.S. executioners."
—Cover flap description of the book *Licensed Mass Murder: A Socio-Psychological Study of Some S.S. Killers* by Henry V. Dicks.

"Iraqi refugees tell us how forced confessions are obtained: by torturing children while their parents are made to watch. International human rights groups have catalogued other methods used in the torture chambers of Iraq: electric shock, burning with hot irons, dripping acid on the skin, mutilation with electric drills, cutting out tongues, and rape."
—President George W. Bush State of the Union speech, 1/28/03

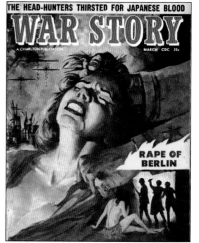

DEPENDING UPON WHOM YOU SPEAK TO, the men's adventure genre either degraded or got more interesting in the early '60s when a couple dozen magazines started offering covers showing women being bound and threatened in so many ways that DeSade's litany of perversions seems … well … limited.

Sexual perversions are suggested in these magazines through headlines ("Tormented Love," "Slaves of the Emperor of Agony," "Savage Rites of the Whip"), and only intimated by the stories themselves. But the violence in these magazines is unlimited, both in text and illustration. Women being skewered and roasted, women being stretched on a rack to be set aflame with gasoline, women being burned to death with liquefied iron, women being thrust into nail-bound coffins, women being lowered into a snake-filled canyon, women being eaten alive by piranha, women being ice-cubed to death, women being whipped and whipped and whipped. Seventy-five percent or so against women, and the remainder the torture of men by the "Bitch of Buchenwald" and the *Ilsa She Wolf* like. Strangely, the women being tortured were always centerfold material, with facial expressions that said the victims were merely being inconvenienced—or stressed, at the worst. It must have been decided to not make the tortures seem too real, possibly out of fear of instigating removal from newsstands. As Bruce Jay Friedman mentioned, the Magazine Management boys were nonplussed when some city decided to widen the censure of "leg shacklers" to their comparatively sedate magazines, *Male* and *For Men Only*. The irony here is that some of the torture slicks were actually published by Martin Goodman pseudonymously. Torture magazines of the '60s were basically a second go-round of "weird menace" pulps, such as Goodman's *Mystery Tales* of 1938. When Goodman launched a number of weird menace pulps, he signified their particular degeneracy by attaching a "red circle" emblem to their covers. Fifteen years later, Goodman used the Diamond to signify his assortment of adventure magazines. In "Unholy Jitters: Sex and Sadism in the Red Circle Weird Menace Pulps," Ed Hulse tells us that Goodman pushed pulp perversity to "an almost unimaginable degree," but he discontinued the shudder pulps soon after New York City mayor Fiorella LaGuardia started a campaign to drive unwholesome magazines off city newsstands.

Whoever owned them, three major production companies (Candar/Thunderbird, EmTee/Reese, and Stanley Publications) and a few minor ones (Escape Magazines, Periodical Publishers and Picture Magazines) issued torture to the masses. The sadistic burlesques of the '60s even shared illustrators and scenarios with the weird menace pulps seen decades earlier. The major difference in the latter torture 'zines was that the hooded or topless villain now wore a swastika.

REAL, April 1960. Illustration: Carl Hantman.

WAR STORY, March 1956. Uncredited.

THE NATIONAL POLICE GAZETTE, February 1956. Uncredited.

TRUE, June 1940. Uncredited.

Damsels have been distressed since the turn of the century in pulps, but nearly always the illustrations suggested that a hero was nearby, and his rescue pending. When adventure slicks of the early '60s came to feature a torture scene, they initially included the possibility of heroic entry by a good American to save the girl. But heroes came to play an increasingly minor role in illustrations until being completely phased out by the mid-'60s, coincidentally the time of the Vietnam War's escalation and the emergence of feminism.

"Teases Die Hard!" warned an article, intimating that good-looking women were responsible for provoking their agonizing death if they strutted their stuff and frustrated the testosterone-enhanced.

Publishers discovered that readers no longer felt that saving women from torture was on any level heroic. The new, unspoken heroes were not saviors, but the hardest and most degenerate torturers who wear Satanic hoods and are assisted by hunchbacked horror film outcasts. Even the long-despised swastika is seen as symbolizing a suppressed manhood that rids itself of women who humiliate and degrade by virtue of the superiority of their looks.

The torture magazines' illustrations may not be the best-drawn, but they are the most interesting, as they reveal a suppressed side of the American male, percolating with hate and vengeance. These fetish-strokers were published for many years and by the dozen, raising the stakes every month to stimulate and satisfy weak male egos—a disturbingly large quantity of them.

It's strange to consider that throughout the '60s, boys were allowed to purchase magazines that promoted wholesale violence against an entire gender, while *Playboy*-style girlie mags that revered women and their bodies were considered unfit material for the underage.

SCOOP, December 1942. Photo: Hal Reiff.

DETECTIVE FICTION, February 1942. Uncredited.

ARGOSY, August 1942. Uncredited.

15¢

ARGOSY

AUGUST

SEX OUTRAGES BY JAP SOLDIERS

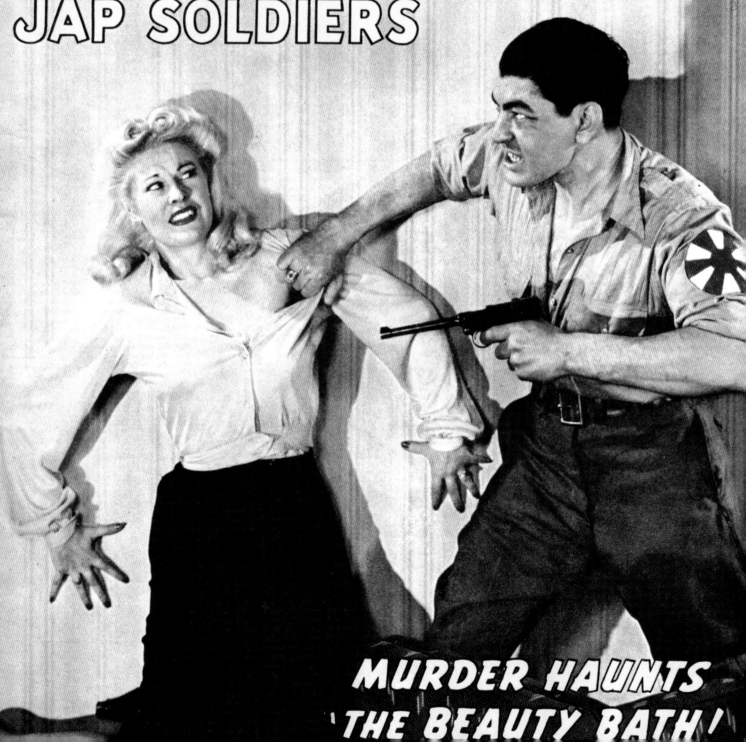

MURDER HAUNTS 'THE BEAUTY BATH!'

The story of the sex queen of the concentration camps

THEY CALLED HER "FRAULEIN TORTURE"

TRUE AND AUTHENTIC STORIES OF

WAR CRIMINALS

35¢   PDC

AUG.

The incredible saga of the world's bloodiest master
murder... **ADOLPH EICHMANN**

Martin Bormann
MAN WITHOUT MERCY

Dachau and Buchenwald
THIS IS THEIR MONUMENT

Heydrich: THE HANGMAN

An illustrated catalogue of brutality
INSIDE TORTURE CHAMBERS

WAR CRIMINALS, August. Uncredited.

MAN'S ADVENTURE, July 1961. Uncredited.

ALL MAN, May 1964. Uncredited.

MAN'S STORY, November 1963. Original Illustration: Norm Eastman.

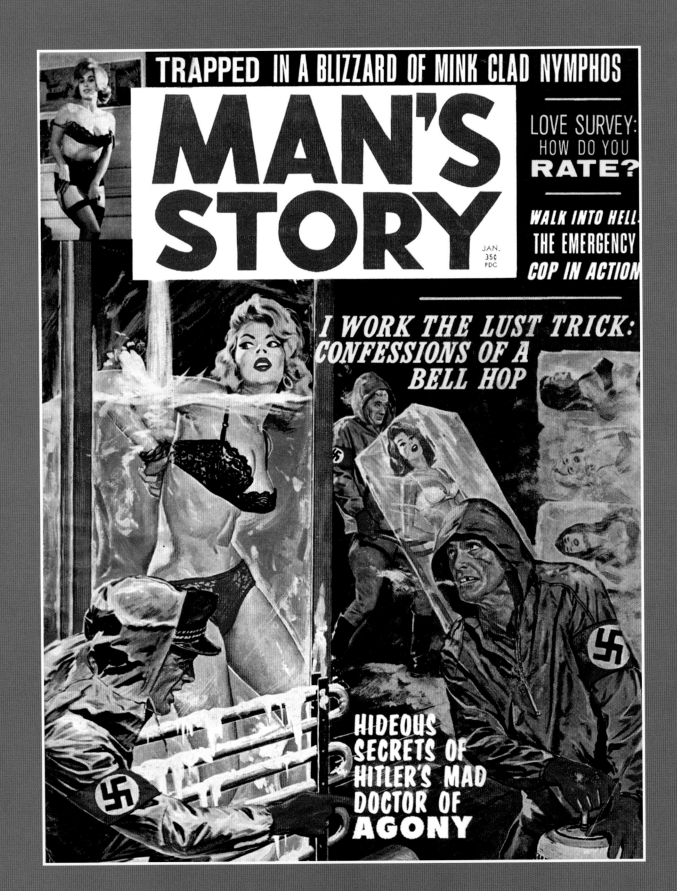

TRAPPED IN A BLIZZARD OF MINK CLAD NYMPHOS

MAN'S STORY

JAN.
35¢
PDC

LOVE SURVEY: HOW DO YOU **RATE?**

WALK INTO HELL: THE EMERGENCY COP IN ACTION

I WORK THE LUST TRICK: CONFESSIONS OF A BELL HOP

HIDEOUS SECRETS OF HITLER'S MAD DOCTOR OF **AGONY**

MAN'S STORY, January 1963. Uncredited.

MAN'S STORY, May 1965. Original Illustration: Norm Eastman.

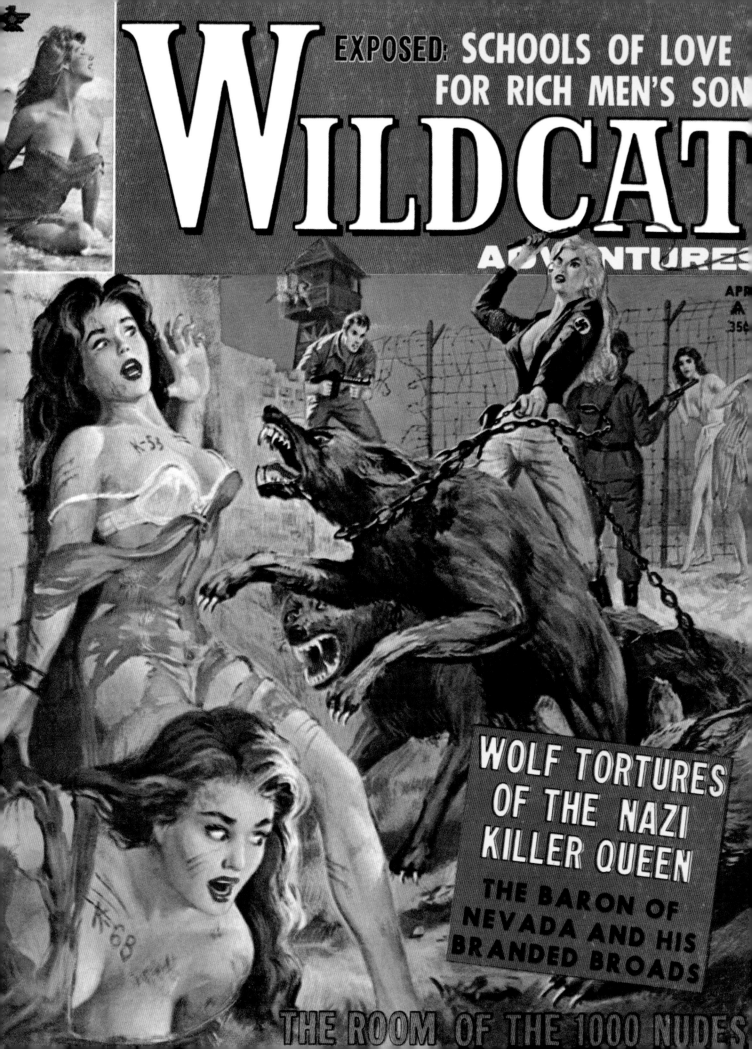

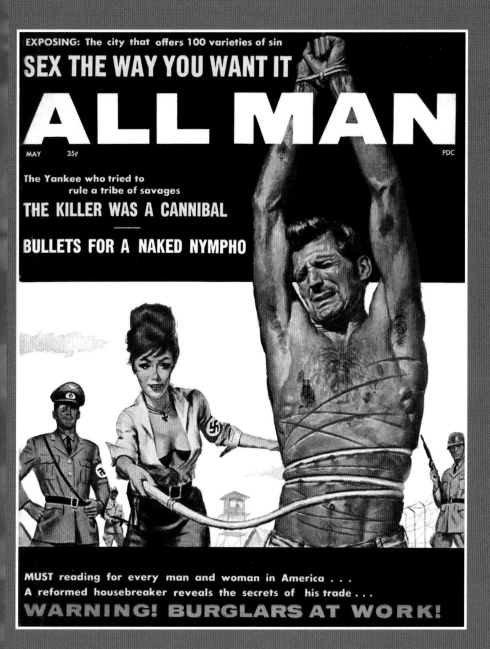

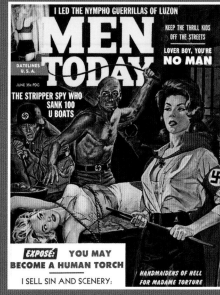

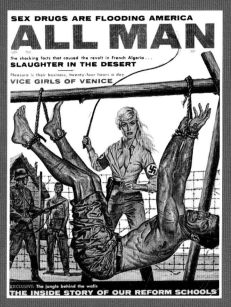

previous page: **MAN'S EPIC**, April 1965. Original Illustration: Norm Eastman.

previous page: **MAN'S STORY**, September 1964. Original Illustration: Norm Eastman.

WILDCAT ADVENTURES, April 1962. Uncredited.

ALL MAN, May 1962. Uncredited.

MEN TODAY, June 1962. Uncredited.

ALL MAN, November 1961. Illustration: Norm Eastman.

MAN'S ACTION, April 1968. Uncredited.

THE WIFE SWAP CLUB THAT COVERS THE COUNTRY

MEN
IN CONFLICT

DEC   PDC   35¢

BEHIND THE SCENES AT A STAG SHOW

SEX GIRLS WHO WORK IN PRIVATE

EVERY SECOND OF HIS ESCAPE
WAS A BATTLE WITH SUDDEN DEATH

I BROKE FREE FROM THE BERLIN WALL!

GOLD, $30,000,000 WORTH, STIL
LITTERS THE BOTTOM OF MANTA B

I FOUND THE TREASURE OF VENEZUELA

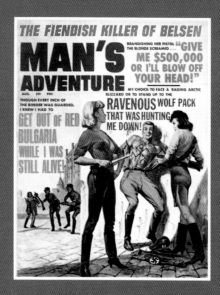

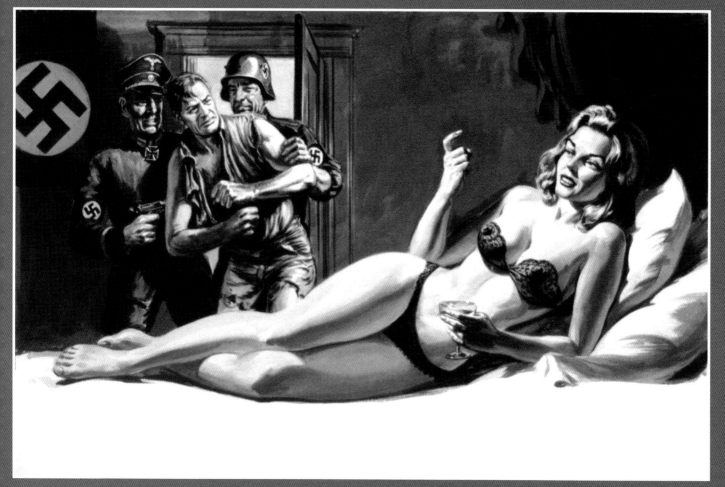

MEN IN CONFLICT, December 1965. Illustration: Anton Mandolini.

MAN'S ADVENTURE, August 1966. Uncredited.

Illustration: Norman Saunders.

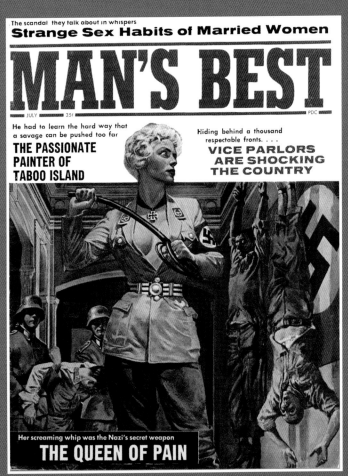

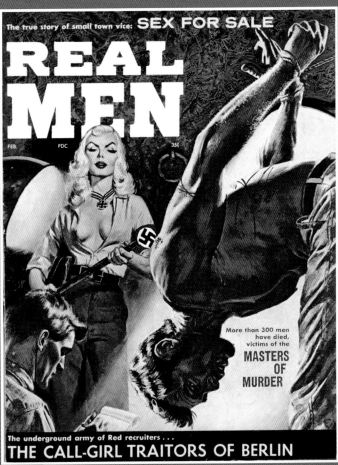

MAN TO MAN, April 1962. Uncredited.

MAN'S BEST, July 1962. Illustration: Vic Prezio.

REAL MEN, February 1961. Uncredited.

REAL MEN, June 1961. Uncredited.

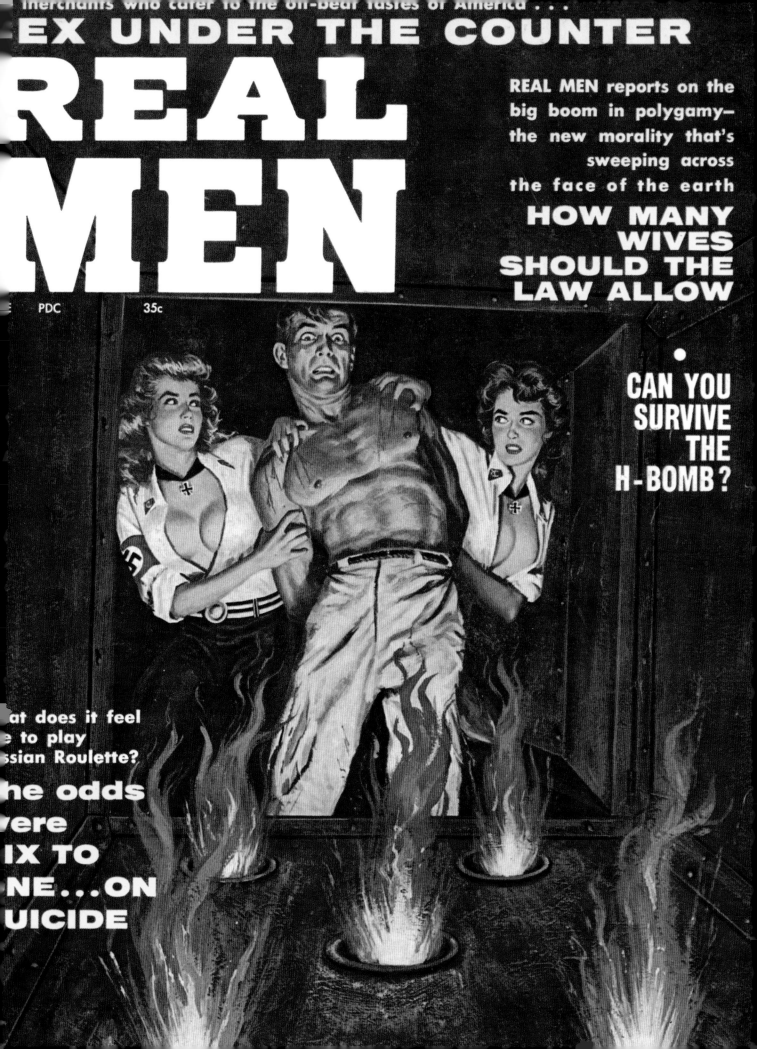

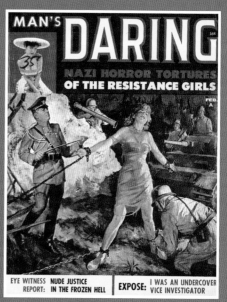

Reese, EmTee Publishing. Illustration: Norman Saunders.

MAN'S STORY, February 1964. Original Illustration: Norm Eastman.

MAN'S STORY, October 1967. Illustration: Norm Eastman.

MAN'S DARING, May 1961. Uncredited.

MEN TODAY, August 1965. Illustration: Norm Eastman.

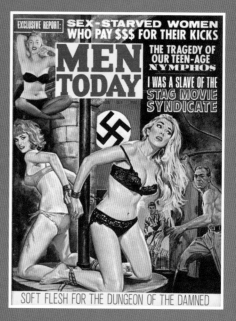

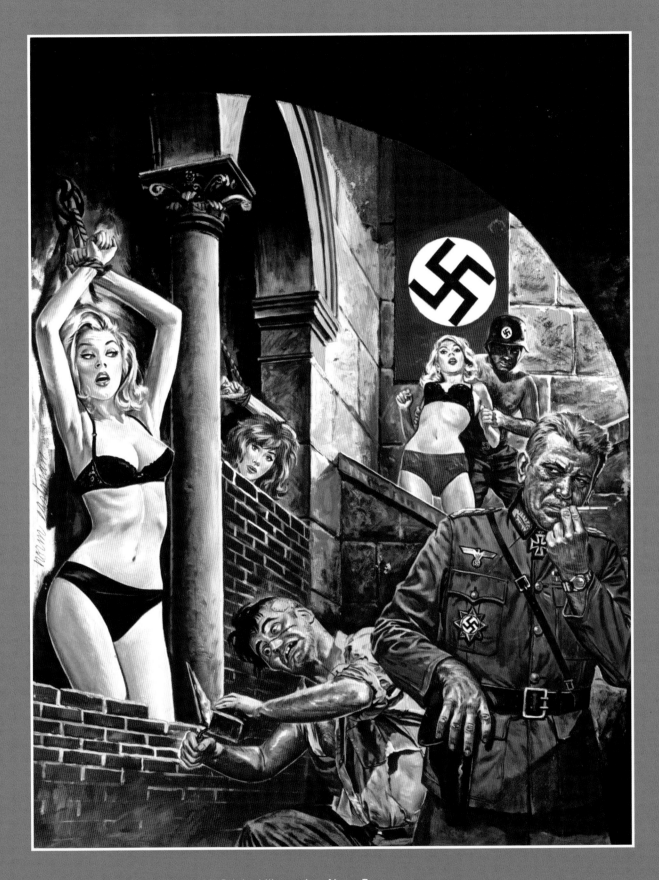

MAN'S STORY, December 1963. Original Illustration: Norm Eastman.

ALL MAN, January 1962. Uncredited.

e floating house of joy **SEX IN THE ISLANDS**

ALL MAN

JAN   PDC   35¢

-hungry
girls prowling for
sion . . . **SCHOOL**
for **NYMPHOS**

d to lie there screaming
helpless . . .

WATCHED THEM
T MY FLESH!

y female captive is
th her weight in
d . . .

WOMEN
E MY SLAVES

He sold his soul for the
power of pain . . .

TRAITOR
WITH A WHIP

Is Lesbianism A Cure For Frigid Women

REAL MEN

A fortune in war loot, lost in the jungles of Burma...

$16,000,000 I RUBIES And It STILL THERE!

APR. 35¢ PDC

I Escaped from the Red Killers of East Berlin

THE DOLL WHO TRADED A COLONEL'S LEG FOR 227 GI'S!

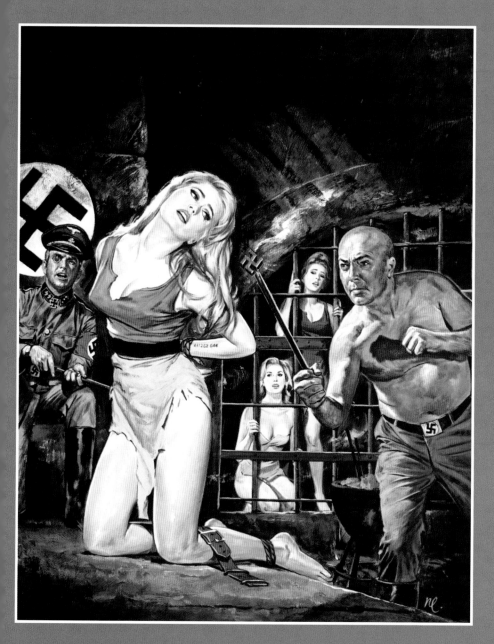

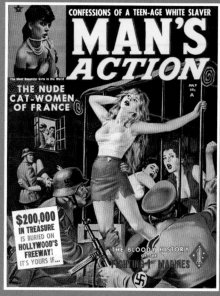

REAL MEN, April 1964. Uncredited.

MAN'S STORY, August 1967. Original Illustration: Norm Eastman.

MAN'S ACTION, July 1962. Uncredited.

WILDCAT ADVENTURES, July 1963. Uncredited.

TRUE MEN STORIES, August 1967. Uncredited.

Reese, EmTee Publishing. Illustration: Norman Saunders.

MAN'S ADVENTURE, March 1967. Uncredited.

E CROWDS ARE GETTING BIGGER EVERY MONTH

VE STAG SHOWS--FOR MIXED AUDIENCES!

MAN'S ADVENTURE

MAR.   35¢   PDC

THE SOUTH PACIFIC'S WILDEST EPISODE

THE WORLD WAR II CRUISE OF THE SHIP OF SEX!

KORZEN: THE NAZI WHO OUTWITTED THE ALLIES!

STRIPPER'S METHOD OR KEEPING HER ODY AT IT'S OUNCING BEST

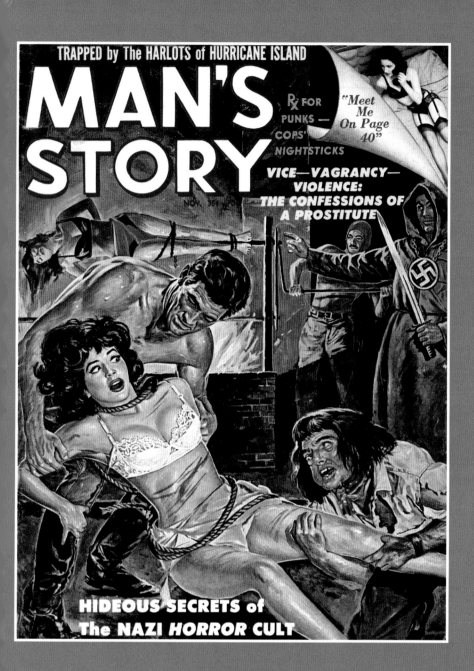

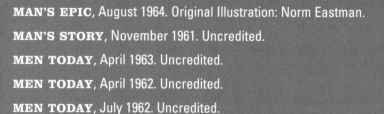

MAN'S EPIC, August 1964. Original Illustration: Norm Eastman.

MAN'S STORY, November 1961. Uncredited.

MEN TODAY, April 1963. Uncredited.

MEN TODAY, April 1962. Uncredited.

MEN TODAY, July 1962. Uncredited.

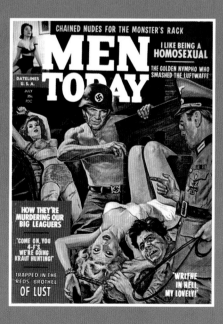

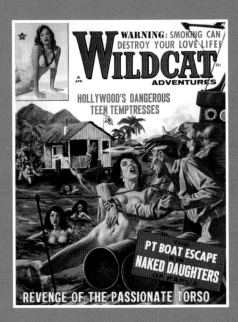

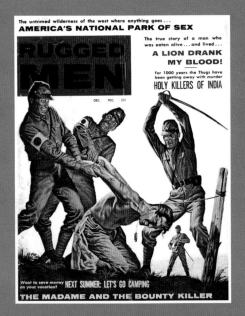

WILDCAT ADVENTURES, April 1964. Uncredited.

MEN IN CONFLICT, March 1967. Uncredited.

RUGGED MEN, December 1968. Uncredited.

MEN TODAY, December 1961. Uncredited.

MAN'S ADVENTURE, September 1961. Uncredited.

ngle sip will lead to writhing passion—
THE DRINK THAT DRIVES YOU LOVE CRAZY

MAN'S ADVENTURE

PDC   35¢

UNCENSORED
The scandal that even
shocked the French . . .
THE JAIL-BAIT NYMPHOS OF PARIS

A TRUE story of horror
NIGHTMARE ON YUCCA FLAT

wild man who fought
Nazis to defeat . . .
E-ARMED KILLER
THE SKIES

MEN TODAY

ONE TICK TO DOOM
THE BOMB SQUAD IN ACTION

LOVE CAPTIVE OF CASTRO'S EXECUTIO SQUAD HARLOTS

FEB.
35¢
PDC

ATELINES
U.S.A.

LL
EW
RIES

SOFT MAIDENS FOR THE MONSTER'S DEVIL FISH

BRIDES OF
AGONY IN THE
RAID OF HORROR

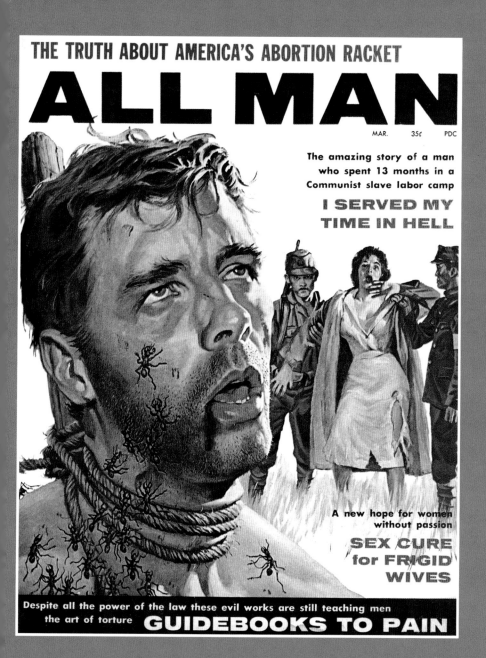

THE TRUTH ABOUT AMERICA'S ABORTION RACKET

ALL MAN

MAR. 35¢ PDC

The amazing story of a man who spent 13 months in a Communist slave labor camp

I SERVED MY TIME IN HELL

A new hope for women without passion

SEX CURE for FRIGID WIVES

Despite all the power of the law these evil works are still teaching men the art of torture **GUIDEBOOKS TO PAIN**

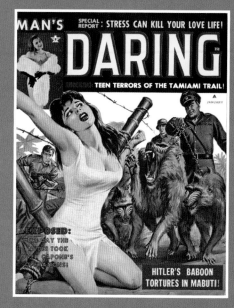

SPECIAL REPORT : STRESS CAN KILL YOUR LOVE LIFE!

MAN'S **DARING** 35¢

TEEN TERRORS OF THE TAMIAMI TRAIL!

A JANUARY

EXPOSED: THE DAY THE FEDS TOOK AL CAPONE'S PLEASURES!

HITLER'S BABOON TORTURES IN MABUTI!

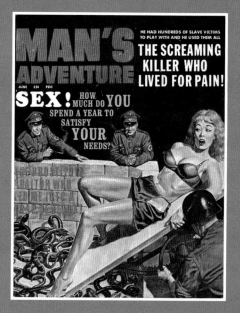

HE HAD HUNDREDS OF SLAVE VICTIMS TO PLAY WITH AND HE USED THEM ALL

MAN'S ADVENTURE

THE SCREAMING KILLER WHO LIVED FOR PAIN!

JUNE 35¢ PDC

SEX! HOW MUCH DO YOU SPEND A YEAR TO SATISFY YOUR NEEDS?

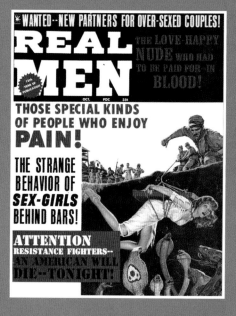

WANTED--NEW PARTNERS FOR OVER-SEXED COUPLES!

REAL MEN

THE LOVE-HAPPY NUDE WHO HAD TO BE PAID FOR--IN BLOOD!

OCT. PDC 25¢

THOSE SPECIAL KINDS OF PEOPLE WHO ENJOY **PAIN!**

THE STRANGE BEHAVIOR OF **SEX-GIRLS** BEHIND BARS!

ATTENTION RESISTANCE FIGHTERS-- AN AMERICAN WILL DIE--TONIGHT!

MEN TODAY, February 1963. Uncredited.

ALL MAN, March 1961. Uncredited.

DARING, January 1962. Uncredited.

MAN'S ADVENTURE, June 1967. Uncredited.

REAL MEN, October 1967. Uncredited.

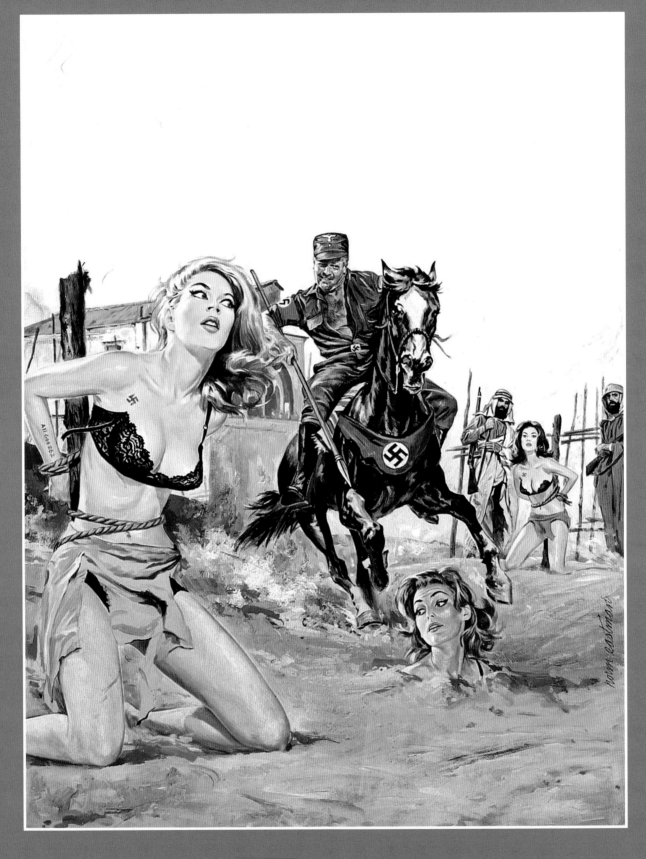

MEN TODAY, November 1963. Original Illustration: Norm Eastman.

MEN TODAY, January 1963. Uncredited.

MEN TODAY

"WRITHE MY LOVELY, IN
THE TENT OF TORTURE!"

DATELINES
U.S.A.
N.

FETTERED NUDES For The MONSTER'S COLLAR Of AGONY

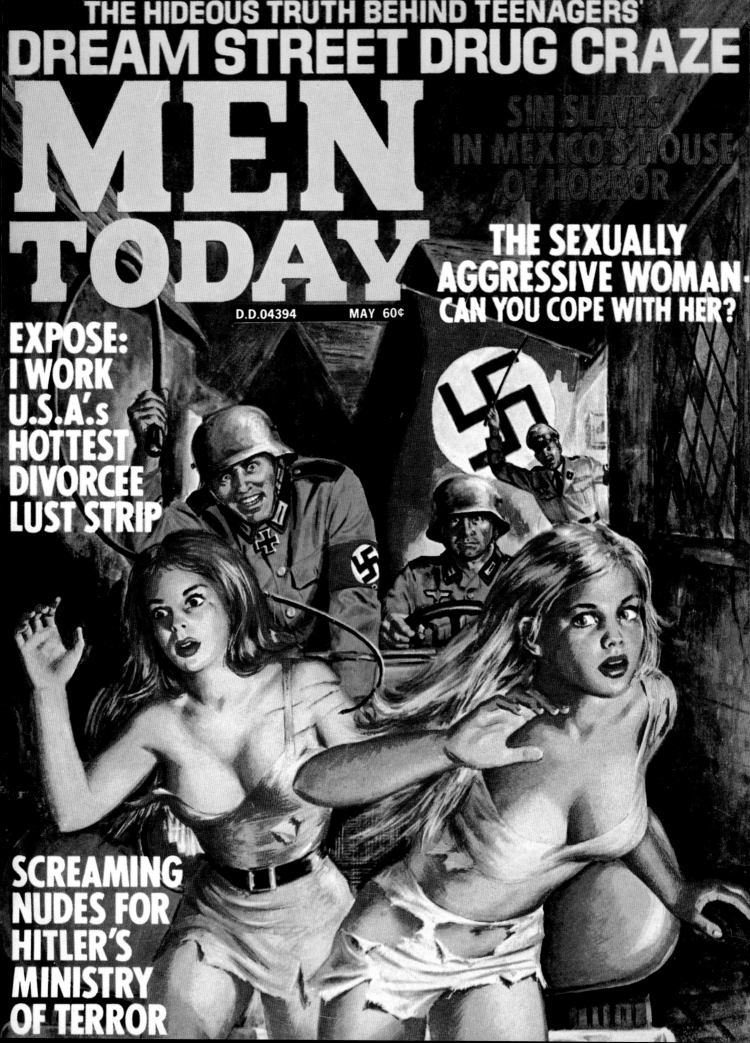

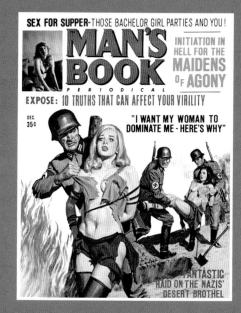

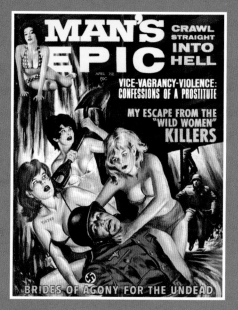

MEN TODAY, May 1975. Uncredited.

WORLD OF MEN, November 1965. Uncredited.

MAN'S BOOK, December 1967. Uncredited.

MAN'S EPIC, April 1964. Uncredited.

NEW MAN, January 1965. Uncredited.

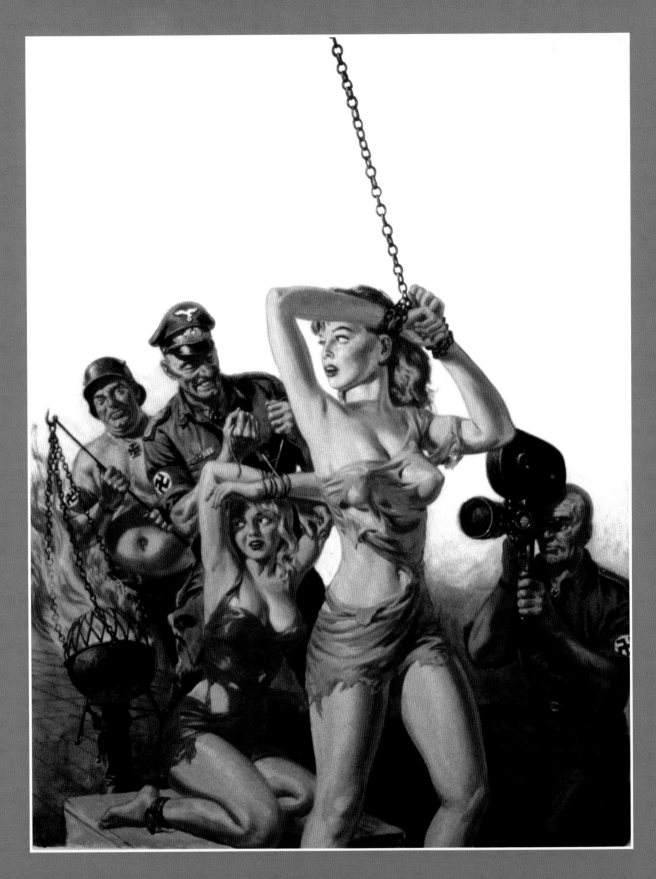

Reese, EmTee Publishing. Illustration: Norman Saunders.

MEN, December 1967. Illustration: Gil Cohen.

hy Young Girls urn Into Unbridled Sex Kittens

THE BEDROOM REBELS

DEC.

MEN

40¢

IND

ensational Book Bonus

he Thrill-Kill Pack

ptures the in-the-raw emotions of
lifornia's Sin Surf World..." THE RECORD

p Priority Mission
r a G. I. Rescue Ace

REE THE WOMEN OF
OVE CAPTIVE STALAG

'ROTTEN MEAT'
BOOTLEGGERS
30 Million Americans Are
Unaware Suckers

PDC

MAN'S
MAGAZINE

JUNE 35c

THE DESERTER
Strange Fate of an Infantry Hero

SEX and YOUR CHILDREN
how to tell them the facts of life

THE HOBO WHO RAN AWAY FROM $5,000,000

FROM THE BEST-SELLING BOOK
BAND OF BROTHERS
MISERY MISSION
ABLE COMPANY'S BLOODY STAND

to Ex- Champion Ezzard Charles:
"GET OUT OF BOXING"
by his own manager

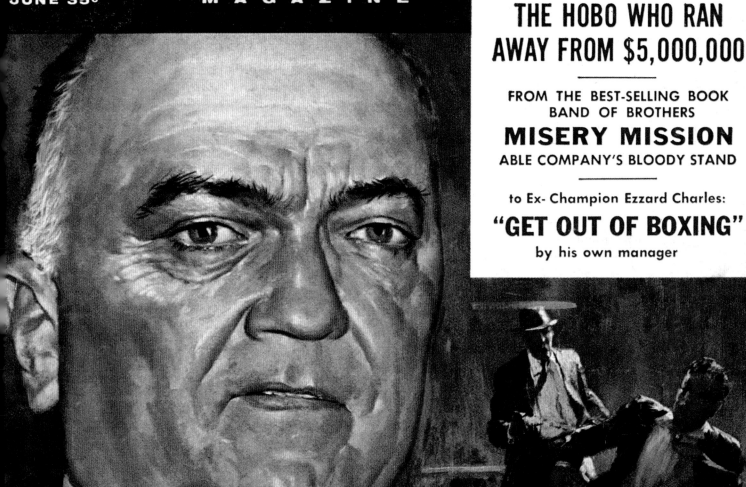

CRIME BUSTER HOOVER

FBI

Violent Story of America's Toughest Cop J. Edgar Hoover, and his Fighting G-Men

THE COLD WAR

WITH A NEARLY RABID PATRIOTISM pitched to a war vet readership, men's adventure magazines increased their circulation during the height of those uneasy days known as the Cold War. The magazines themselves helped disseminate Cold War code words, issuing anxiety, paranoia, Red Threat, and Yellow Peril every month, though it did so in many issues with a Terry Southern sort of satirical exaggeration.

The Cold War started after the powers divided postwar spoils at Yalta, and the Soviet Union cloaked itself in an Iron Curtain, and the United States expanded its economic control by Marshall Plan pocketbook and the support of dictator appointees in the Third World.

In a time with unimaginable military buildup and state secrecy sponsored by KGB and CIA, the Cold War was a time of Joseph McCarthy, atomic bomb tests, domino theory paranoia, state assassination and cover-up. Super wars between superpowers were avoided but fought nonetheless in "proxy" wars like Korea and Vietnam for the United States, and Afghanistan and Hungary for the Soviets.

In men's magazines, the Cuban issue always seemed a hot topic. Fidel Castro replaced Nazi and Jap with his own variety of sadistic torture of very white American women, peppered with suggestive Spanish commentary. Cover illustrations sometimes portrayed the missiles that had brought readers through a recent stomach-churning crisis. If anything, the men's adventure magazines made the apocalyptic reality seem a little less drastic, almost a *Mad* magazine style of acknowledgement for the sake of humor.

Even then, the Americans ducking and covering were also looking to Tomorrowland, and the extravagant scientific conquests of outer space, a colonialist lure when Yuri Gagarin successfully took off into orbit and touched down later that same day.

Unlike World War II, which produced the good soldier who reflected the group mind, the Cold War produced James Bond, the superspy whose forte was to detect an enemy far more obscure than the Nazis of decades past. The Cold War, when wars were fought by minds and not by bullets, blacks and whites merged into grays, and the individual was elevated into superstar celebrity status.

MAN'S MAGAZINE, June '59. Illustration: Bob Schulz.

NEW WORLDS: FICTION OF THE FUTURE, 1946. Apocalyptic sci-fi magazine from England.

MAN TO MAN, April 1958. Uncredited.

WHISPER, November 1959. Gossip mag goes to Cuba.

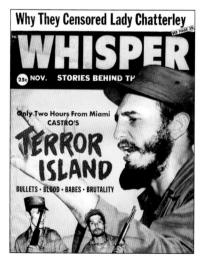

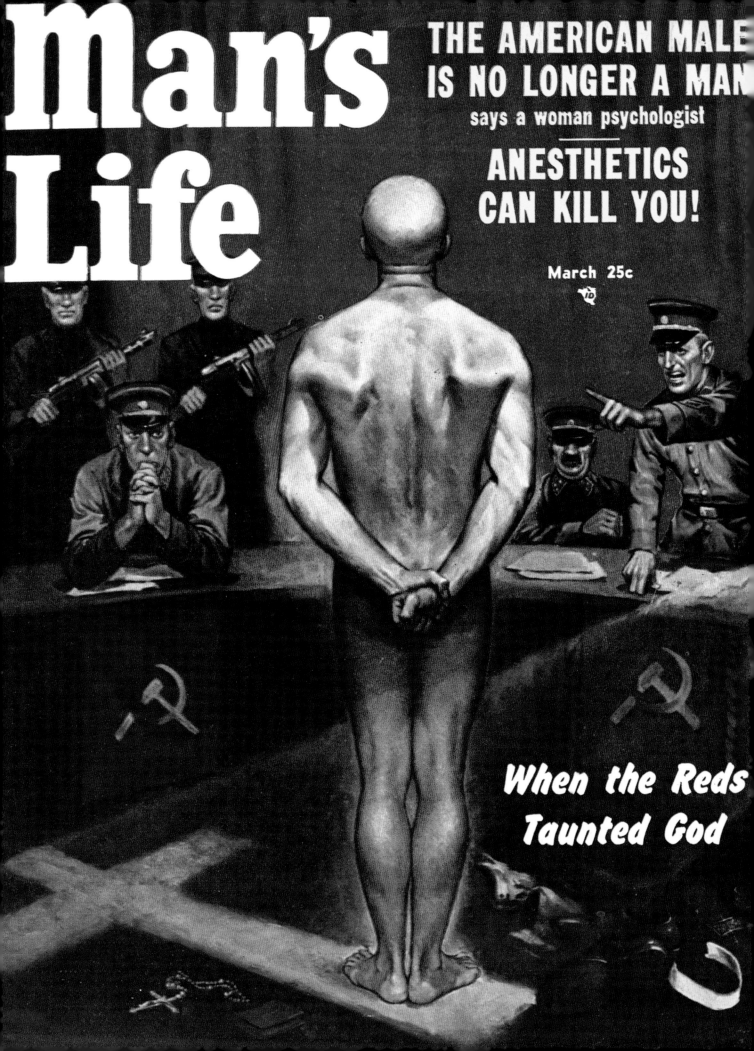

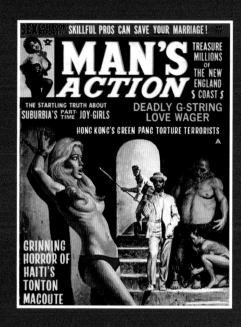

MAN'S LIFE, March 1955. Illustration: Milton Luros.

MEN IN CONFLICT, December 1962. Uncredited.

MAN'S ACTION, February 1969. Uncredited.

BATTLE CRY, August 1961. Uncredited.

MAN TO MAN, November 1961. Illustration: Pike.

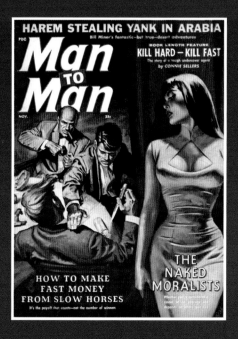

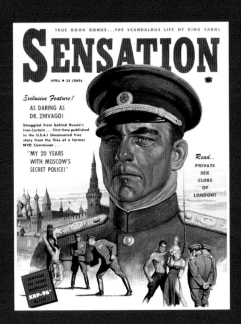

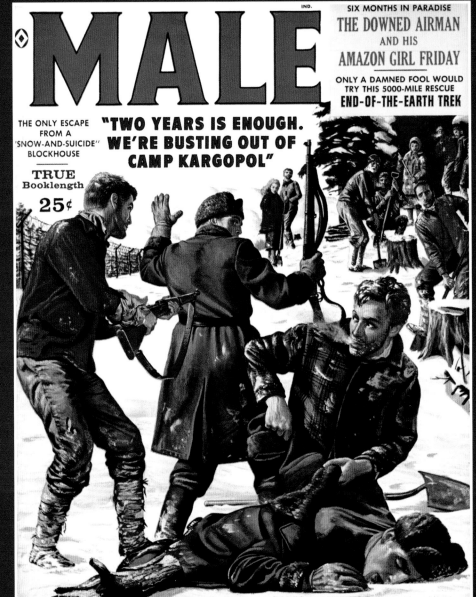

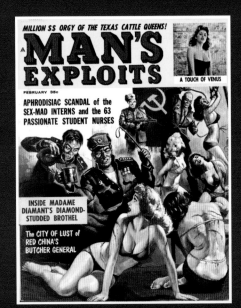

SENSATION, March 1959. Illustration: Rafael DeSoto.

SIR!, January 1961. Uncredited.

MAN'S EXPLOITS, March 1963. First issue. Uncredited.

MALE, November 1959. Illustration: Mort Künstler.

EXPOSÉ, October 1959. Illustration: Stan Borack.

HE BOOKS THEY COULDN'T BAN!

• LADY CHATTERLEY'S LOVER • The Homosexual BLACK DIARIES of ROGER CASEMENT

EXPOSÉ

FOR MEN!

OCTOBER • 35 CENTS

HOURS AFTER THIS WAS WRITTEN THE AUTHOR WAS DEAD!

y Commie Assignment Was: **KILL THE GERMAN V.I.P.!"**

BERLIN 60 km.

Acclaimed!
Book Bonus
China Bomb!
"Red-raw adventure" —FT. WORTH PRESS

MALE

DEC.

40¢

I Was An Offic
'PASSION
LOTTERY
GIRL

A FINANCIAL WIZARD'S
SURE-FIRE PLAN TO BEAT THE
Credit Gougers

Incredible Saga of Anna Hoegerova,
MOB GODDESS 2000 MAFI
GUNMEN COULDN'T KILL

Great Extra-Length Adventure
Yank Agent Who Penetrate
The Nazi High Command's
Love Swap Circus

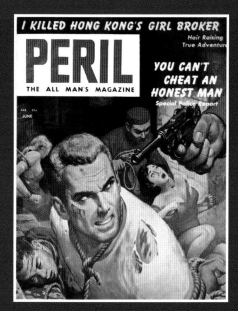

MALE, December 1967. Illustration: Mort Künstler.

FOR MEN ONLY, March 1967. Illustration: Mort Künstler.

WILDCAT ADVENTURES, August 1961. Illustration: Basil Gogos.

ALL MAN, February 1960. Uncredited.

PERIL, March 1960. Uncredited.

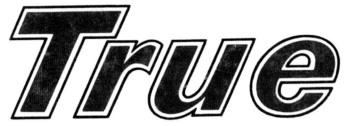

True ADVENTURES

FOR MEN—EXCLUSIVE

Don't be a "Love Coward"

STILL ONLY 25¢

OCTOBER

FIRE SETTER:

AT LAST—THE REAL STORY OF THE MORRO CASTLE

A NIGHT IN HONG KONG'S OPIUM DENS

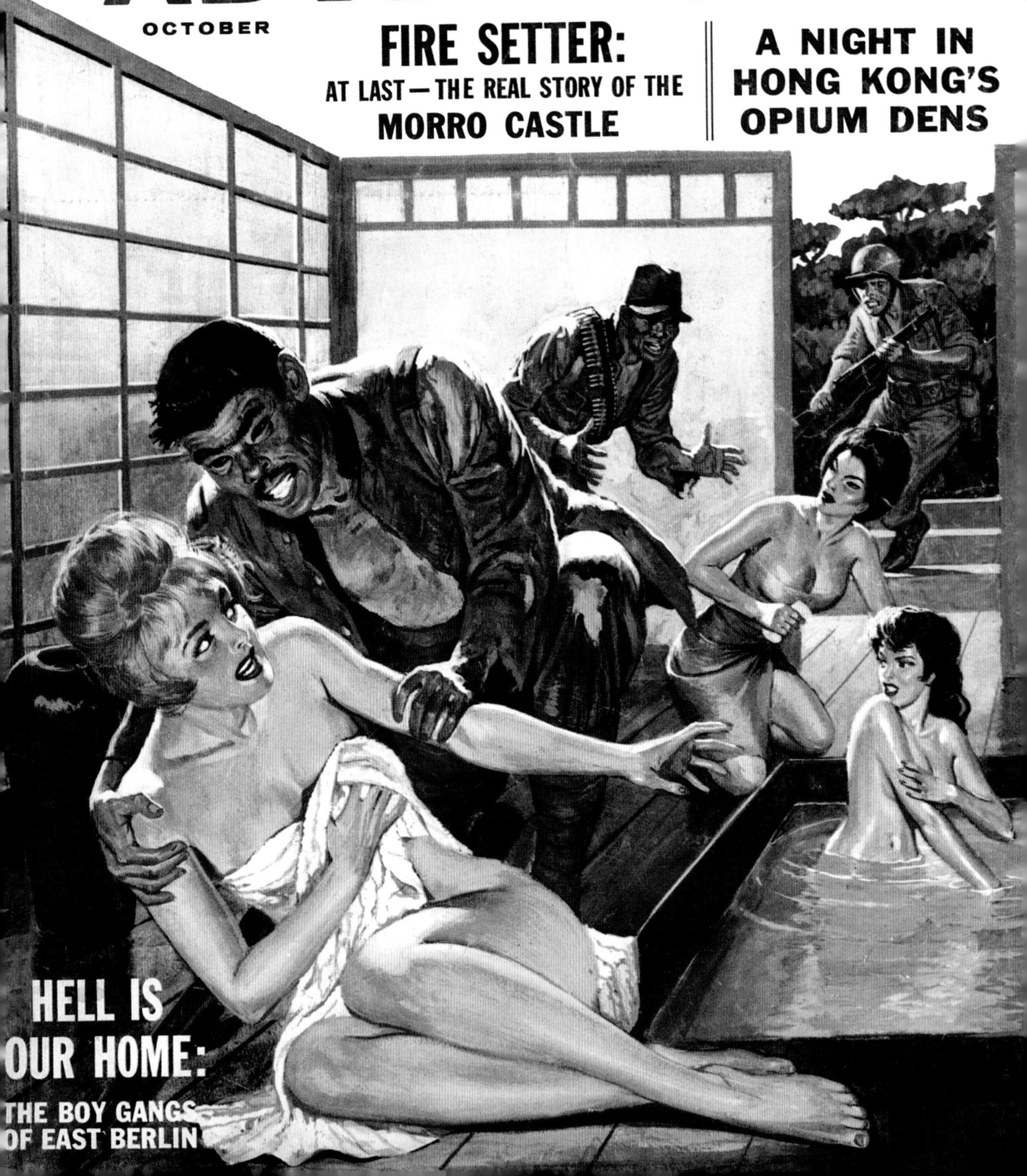

HELL IS OUR HOME:

THE BOY GANGS OF EAST BERLIN

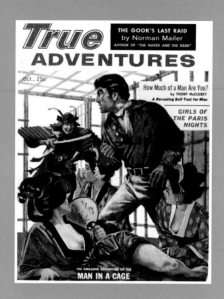

TRUE ADVENTURES, October 1962. Illustration: Rafael De Soto.

TRUE ADVENTURES, October 1958. Illustration: John Styga.

Magazine Management Illustration: Mort Künstler.

MALE, December 1966. Original Illustration: Mort Künstler.
MAN'S STORY, December 1970. Uncredited.

EXPLODED—10 MYTHS ABOUT POTENCY & PASSION

MAN'S STORY

DEC. 50c MAC

THE
DAMNED VIRGINS
AND THE HORROR
THAT WOULDN'T DIE

AMERICA'S
HOMOSEXUAL REVOLT
FUN AND GAMES
OR DEADLY PERIL?

PSYCHOLOGICAL REPORT
CHAINED
WOMEN:
SEX SLAVES WHO
BEG TO BE TORTURED

THE DEAL
S DAMES, DRUGS
AND DEATH,
McGRADY!"

FOR MEN ONLY, August 1964. Original Illustration: Mort Künstler.
Magazine Management Illustration: Mort Künstler.

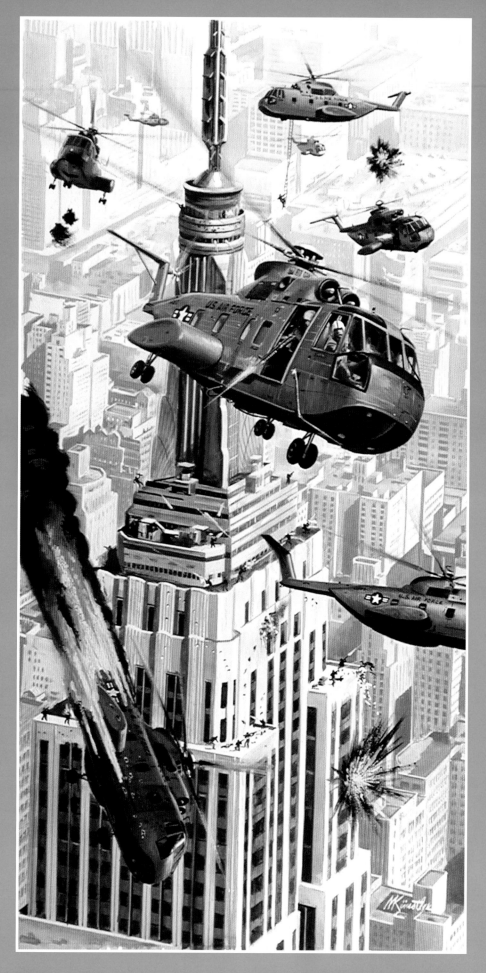

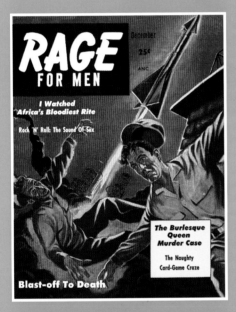

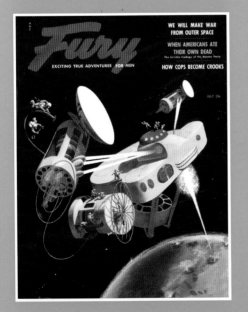

MR. AMERICA, January 1953. First issue. Uncredited.

RAGE FOR MEN, December 1956. Uncredited.

REAL, June 1967. Illustration: Jon Dahlstrom.

FURY, July 1956. Illustration: Tom Beecham.

PERIL, March 1962. Uncredited.

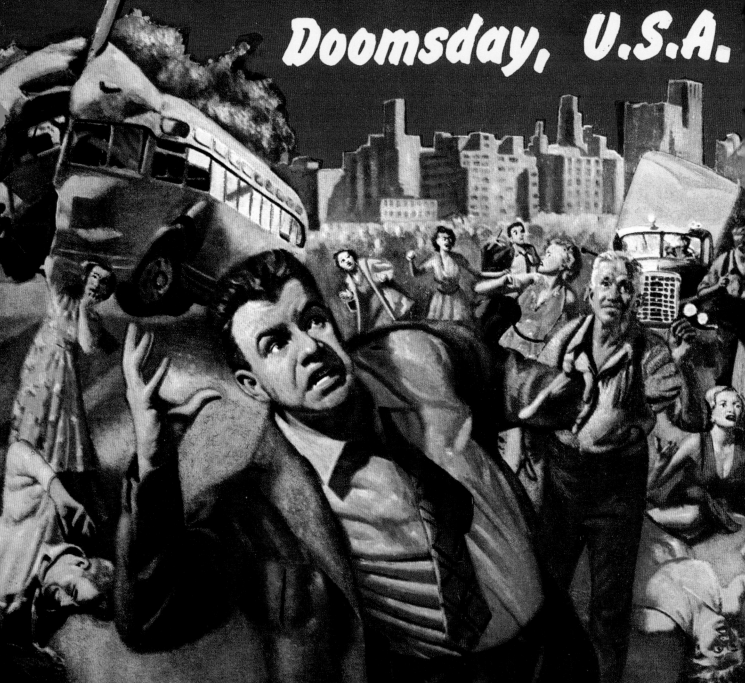

Man's Life

SEX FILMS
A New Low in Filth
—
They Drowned Screaming
—
FOOTBALL FORECAS

November 25¢

Doomsday, U.S.A.

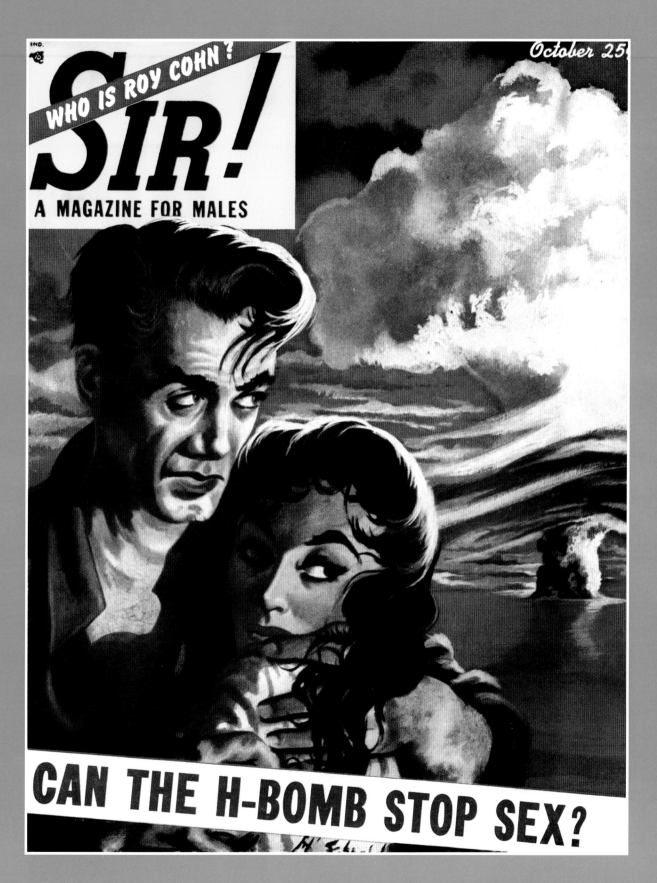

MAN'S LIFE, November 1954. Illustration: John Fay.

SIR!, October 1954. Uncredited.

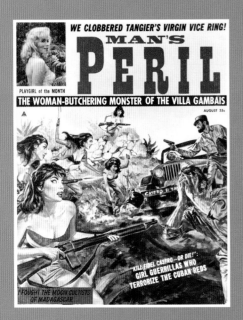

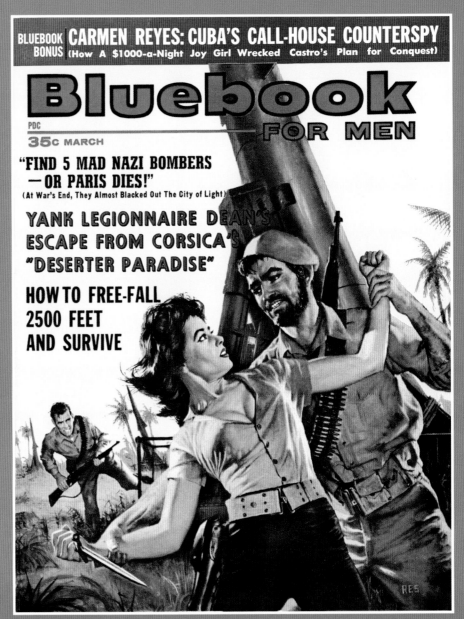

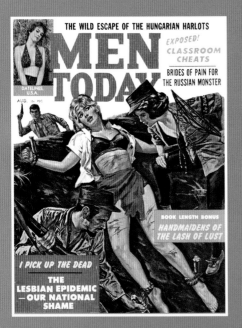

MAN'S PERIL, August 1963. Uncredited.

ADVENTURE, December 1963. Illustration: George Gross.

MEN TODAY, August 1961. Uncredited.

BLUEBOOK FOR MEN, March 1963. Illustration: Bob Schulz.

SEE FOR MEN, May 1963. Illustration: George Gross.

NEW MAN, November 1967. Original Illustration: Norman Saunders.

TRUE ADVENTURES, April 1961. Illustration: Basil Gogos.

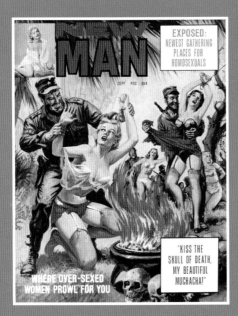

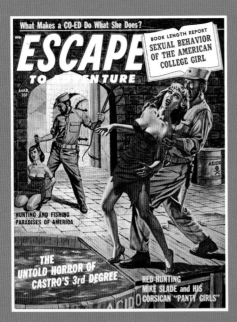

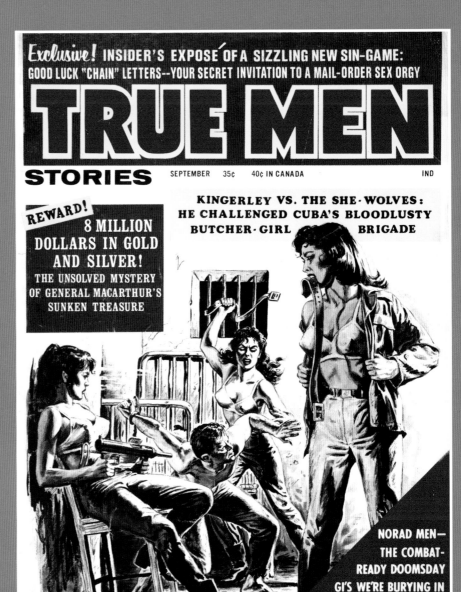

NEW MAN, September 1965. Illustration: Norman Saunders.

MEN TODAY, April 1961. Uncredited.

ESCAPE TO ADVENTURE, March 1964. Illustration: Sid Shores.

TRUE MEN, September 1965. Uncredited.

MAN'S STORY, September 1965. Original Illustration: Norm Eastman.

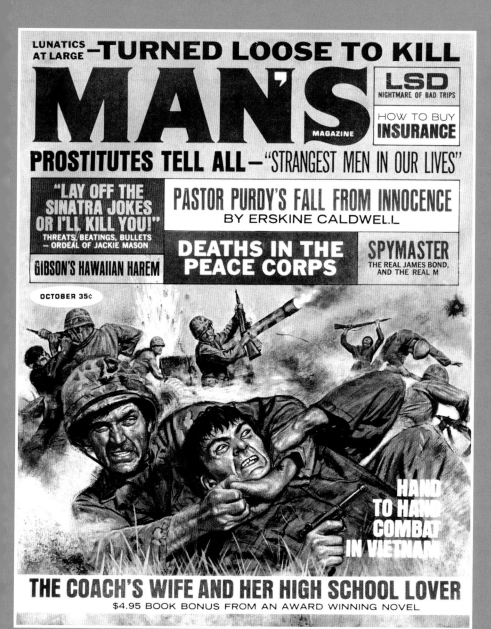

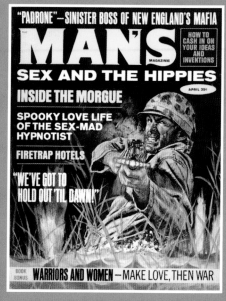

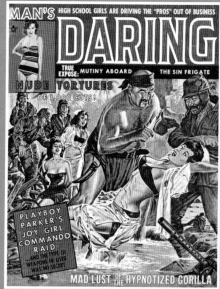

BLUEBOOK, June 1967. Original Illustration: Norm Eastman.

MAN'S MAGAZINE, October 1967. Illustration: Mel Crair.

MAN'S MAGAZINE, April 1968. Illustration: Mel Crair.

DARING, January 1962. Uncredited.

MAN TO MAN, May 1964. Uncredited.

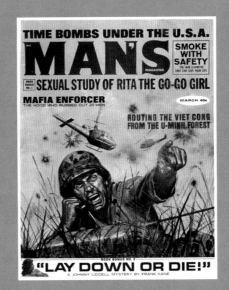

MAN'S MAGAZINE, March 1967. Illustration: Mel Crair.

WORLD OF MEN, March 1967. Original Illustration: Norm Eastman.

MAN'S STORY, March 1967. Original Illustration: Norm Eastman.

MAN'S WORLD, February 1967. Uncredited.

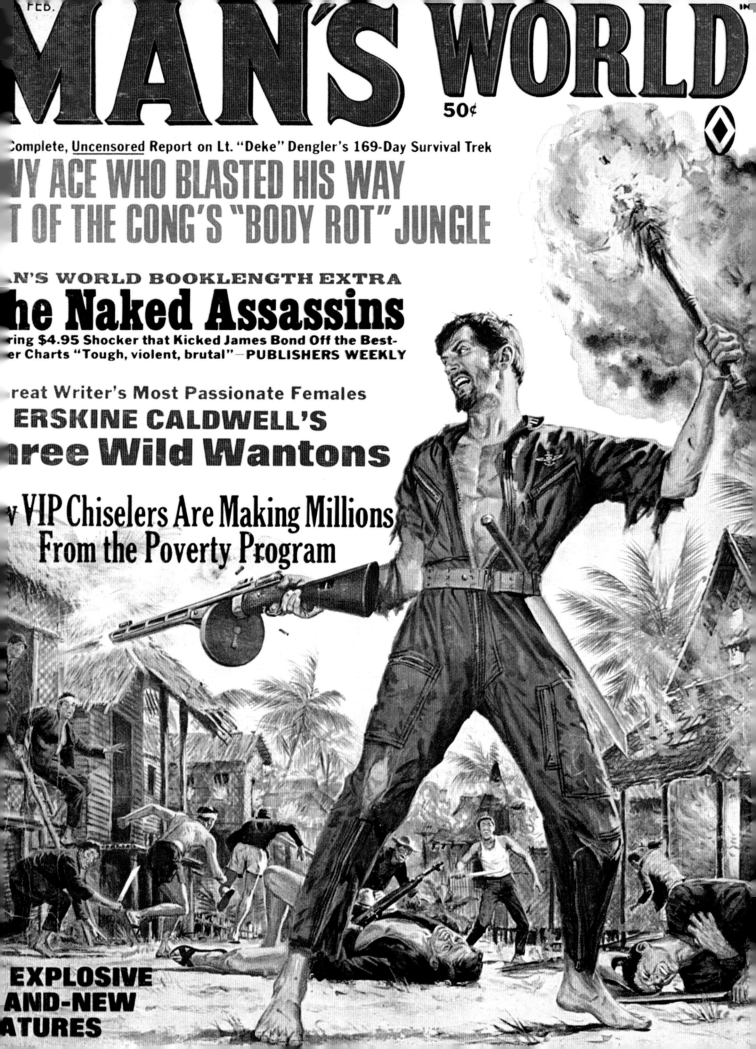

FEB.

MAN'S WORLD

50¢

Complete, Uncensored Report on Lt. "Deke" Dengler's 169-Day Survival Trek

VY ACE WHO BLASTED HIS WAY
T OF THE CONG'S "BODY ROT" JUNGLE

AN'S WORLD BOOKLENGTH EXTRA

he Naked Assassins

ring $4.95 Shocker that Kicked James Bond Off the Best-
er Charts "Tough, violent, brutal"—PUBLISHERS WEEKLY

reat Writer's Most Passionate Females

ERSKINE CALDWELL'S
hree Wild Wantons

v VIP Chiselers Are Making Millions
From the Poverty Program

EXPLOSIVE
AND-NEW
ATURES

NEW MAN, October 1967. Original Illustration: Norm Eastman.

STAG, February 1968. Illustration: Mort Künstler.

CTION-CHARGED
OOK BONUS
"REDHEAD" SWINGER
"...outrageous girls...amazing adventures...to be a smash movie..." POST-PRESS

stag IND

FEB.   50c

FROM AN ASTOUNDING
JUNGLE TREK DIARY
EXPEDITION TO THE
'STRANGE WOMEN
TRIBE
OF NEW GUINEA

UR FOREIGN FRIENDS"
THEY GRAB
OUR AID
BUT HATE
OUR GUTS

MARRIED
COUPLES
WHO ADD
A THIRD
SEX PARTNER

THE LOOTERS

MEN

50¢

DEC.

THE MAFIA STORY OF THE YEAR!

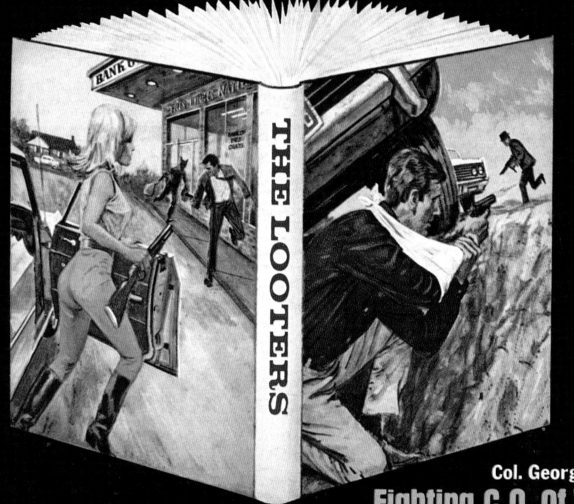

FROM THE $4.50 BEST SELLER

THE LOOTERS

Col. George S. Patton, 3rd
Fighting C.O. Of Viet Nam's Cong-Blasting "Tankers"

BOOKLENGTH SPECIAL
Latest Diversion For Bored Couples

"I Joined A Go-Naked Swap Cult"

Fiction Extra

"PILLOW GIRL"

Bill Lear Bets His $40 Million That—
You Will Drive A Super-Speed Steam Car In 3 Years

THE WAR COMES HOME

AS THE COLD WAR MOVED INTO THE '60s, fear increasingly moved out of the bedroom and into the streets. Escalating crime and wars — race war, gender war, generational war — brought hostilities home to American soil.

Circulation of adventure magazines started to fall precipitously when, as Mario Puzo put it, the "non-fun" Vietnam War was seen every evening on television, complete with dull jungle footage and droning fatality counts. Art directors tried a number of ways to regain interest, and sales. Illustrations were reduced and headlines multiplied on covers, suggesting the early pulp tactic of cheap quantity. When this didn't work, illustrations veered into territory more fitting for the true crime and detective genre. Satanic bikers, longhaired hippy killers, and juvenile delinquents of a murderous stripe populated adventure magazines in the late '60s and early '70s. All were hateful, sure, but buyers less and less felt a need to purchase an exaggerated portrayal of the morning headline.

Adventure magazines finally gave up the ghost when the last few became cheap third-rate *Playboy* wannabes at a time when *Hustler* arrived and made girly magazines rather gynecological.

Today, a new feast of magazines, led by *Maxim*, attempts to appeal to heterosexual male readers with unapologetic gender exclusivity. When flags started waving and exotic villains started appearing, after 9/11, men's adventure magazines of decades past seemed, somehow, weirdly pertinent once again.

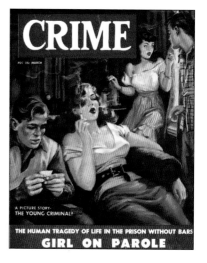

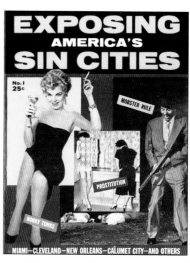

MEN, December 1968. Illustration: Bruce Minney.

CRIME, March 1953. Uncredited.

PERIL, February 1959. Cover: Vinnie Grosso and John Lowell.

EXPOSING AMERICA'S SIN CITIES, Winter 1956.

previous page: Magazine Management Illustration: Mort Künstler.

previous page: **FOR MEN ONLY**, August 1961. Illustration: Mort Künstler.

previous page: Magazine Management Illustration: Mort Künstler.

Illustration: Norm Eastman.

SAGA, June 1952. Illustration: Rico Tomaso.

SAGA

True Adventures for Men

JUNE

Korea Veterans Tell:
HOW TO SURVIVE COMBAT

NYFD

25¢

A Bellyful of Smoke • GOLD Where You Can Find It

The man who built the only legal harem in America . . .

HOUSE OF A HUNDRED LOVERS

MAN'S ADVENTURE

JAN   PDC   35¢

The truth about the Sex Drug that's sweeping the country . . .

LITTLE PILLS OF PASSION

Stanley Ketchel:
KILLER IN THE RING

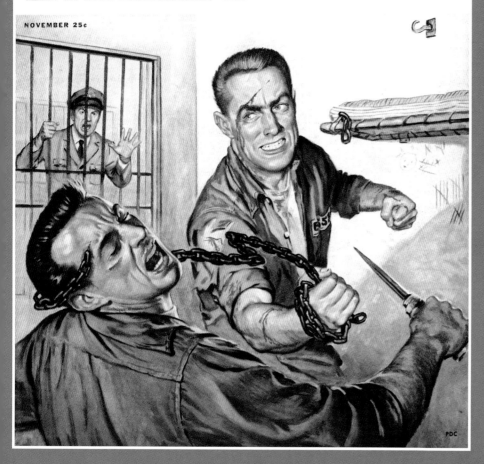

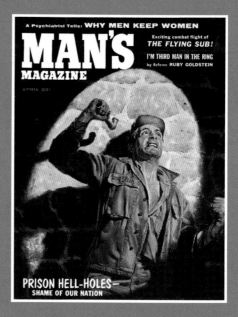

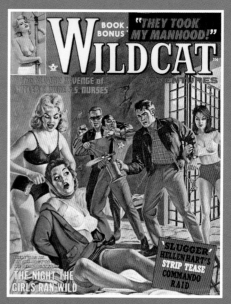

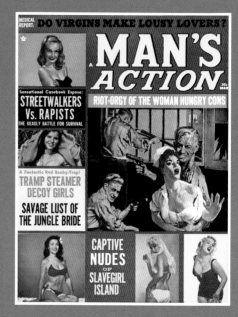

MAN'S ADVENTURE, January 1961. Uncredited.

REAL MEN, November 1956. Illustration: Milton Luros.

MAN'S MAGAZINE, April 1956. Illustration: Frank Cozzarelli.

WILDCAT ADVENTURES, October 1962. Uncredited.

MAN'S ACTION, March 1966. Uncredited.

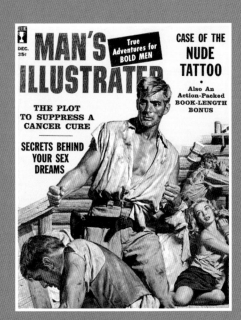

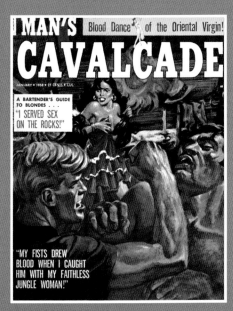

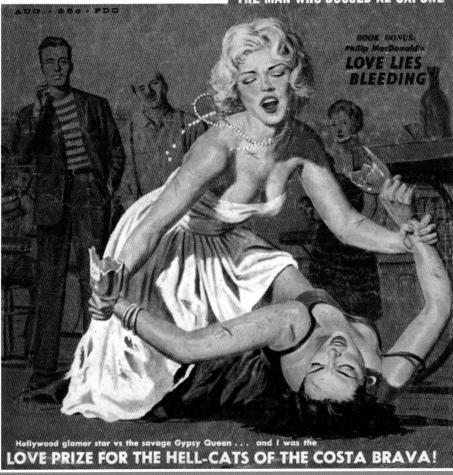

Hollywood glamor star vs the savage Gypsy Queen . . . and I was the

LOVE PRIZE FOR THE HELL-CATS OF THE COSTA BRAVA!

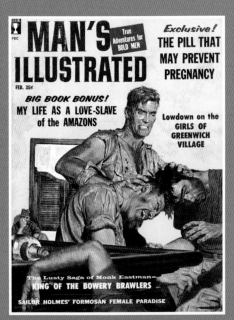

MAN'S ILLUSTRATED, December 1959. Illustration: George Gross.

MAN'S CAVALCADE, January 1958. Uncredited.

MAN'S ILLUSTRATED, February 1959. Illustration: George Gross.

REAL MEN, August 1959. Illustration: John Leone.

MAN'S MAGAZINE, December 1955. Illustration: John Leone.

MAN'S
MAGAZINE

HOW TO JILT A WOMAN

THE LOWDOWN ON PUNCH-DRUNK FIGHTERS
by RAY ARCEL, famous trainer

DECEMBER 25¢

et the Man Who Outguesses Our Intelligence Service:
AMERICA'S NUMBER ONE PRIVATE SPY

REAL, December 1962. Illustration: George Gross.

"The Fantastic Escape of Conrad Grimes and Singapore Kate," 1963. Magazine Management Illustration: Mort Künstler.

MAN'S ADVENTURE, July 1965. Uncredited.

Magazine Management Illustration: Mort Künstler.

SEE FOR MEN, May 1962. Illustration: George Gross.

NEW YORK'S

LESBIAN SEX PARTIES

SEE

MAY
35¢

FOR MEN

THE PLANE
THEY
COULDN'T
KILL

ALMOST
NEVER
ON SUNDAY

Life of a Stripper—
the Backstage Story

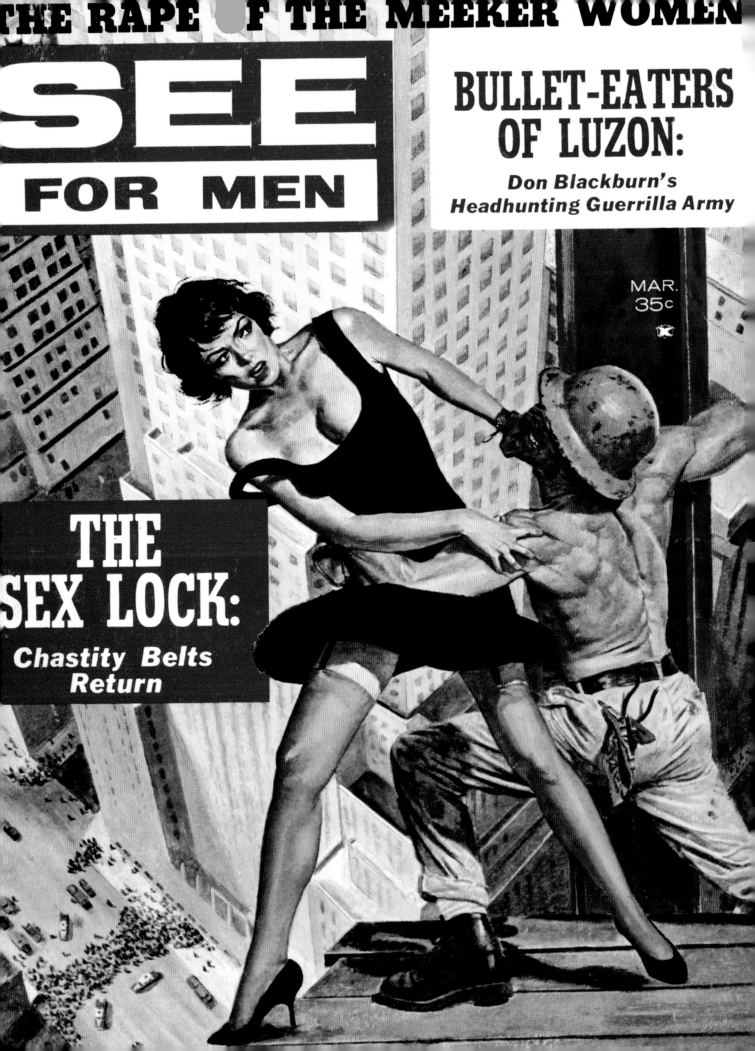

THE RAPE OF THE MEEKER WOMEN

SEE
FOR MEN

BULLET-EATERS OF LUZON:
Don Blackburn's Headhunting Guerrilla Army

MAR.
35c

THE SEX LOCK:
Chastity Belts Return

SEE FOR MEN, March 1962. Illustration: George Gross.

REAL, April 1960. Original Illustration: Norman Saunders.

Magazine Management Illustration: Mort Künstler.

FOR MEN ONLY, July 1964. Uncredited.

CITING BOOK BONUS

35¢
OF IN
NADA

IND. ◆

ULY

KILL and RUN NUDE

...fast-paced...graphic...
action-crammed...THE DIGEST

FOR MEN ONLY

"Lend-Lease" Vice Girls

OUR LATEST IMPORTED SEX RACKET

lay Pigeons
f St. Lô.

00 Trapped GI's Heroic Stand
at Saved the
rmandy Beachhead.)

OW YOUR BOSS
PIES ON YOU

Illustration: Norm Eastman.

Magazine Management Illustration: Mort Künstler.

INDIA'S ALL-TIME SEX MANUAL

IND.

ESCAPE

MAY **TO ADVENTURE** 35¢

JEANMARIE LUSSIER

MY SOJOURN WITH THE CHIN MAIDENS

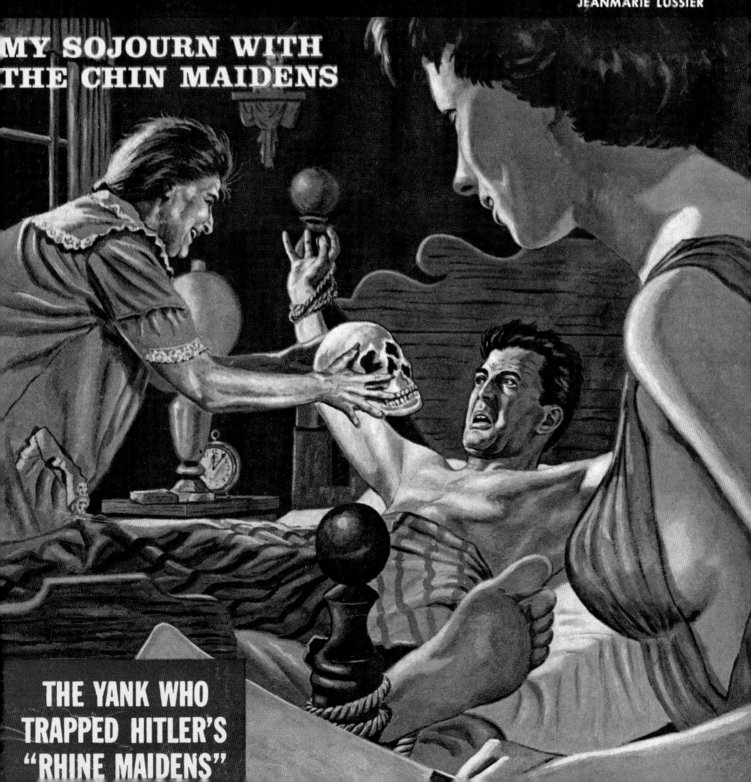

THE YANK WHO TRAPPED HITLER'S "RHINE MAIDENS"

ESCAPE TO ADVENTURE, May 1962. Uncredited.

MAN'S BEST, September 1962. Uncredited.

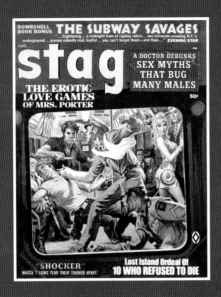

STAG, August 1968. Illustration: Emmett Kaye (Mort Künstler).

Magazine Management Illustration: Mort Künstler.

DARING, March 1963. Uncredited.

REAL

THE MAN WHO TERRORIZED TITO

BEWARE THE HORSEPOWER HUCKSTERS

MOST DARING COMMANDO RAID

AP
35

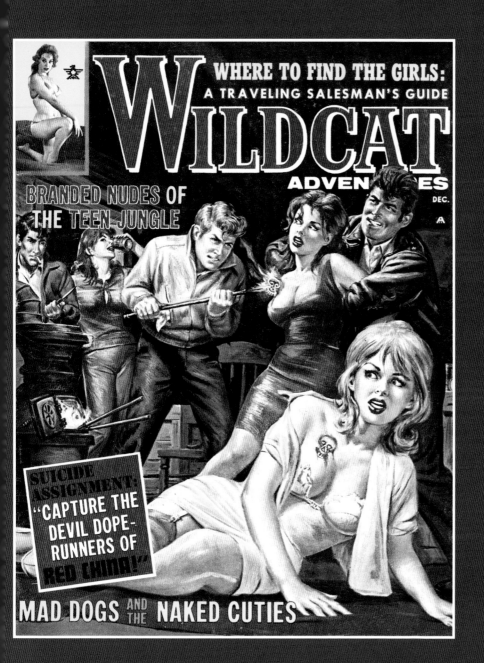

REAL, April 1963. Illustration: George Gross.

WILDCAT ADVENTURES, December 1962. Uncredited.

SEE, September 1959. Uncredited.

DARING, May 1963. Uncredited.

PERIL, January 1963. Uncredited.

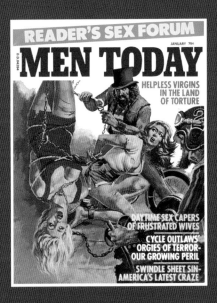

MEN TODAY, January 1976. Uncredited.

STAG, February 1971. Original Illustration: Gil Cohen.

MEN TODAY, March 1967. Original Illustration: Norm Eastman.

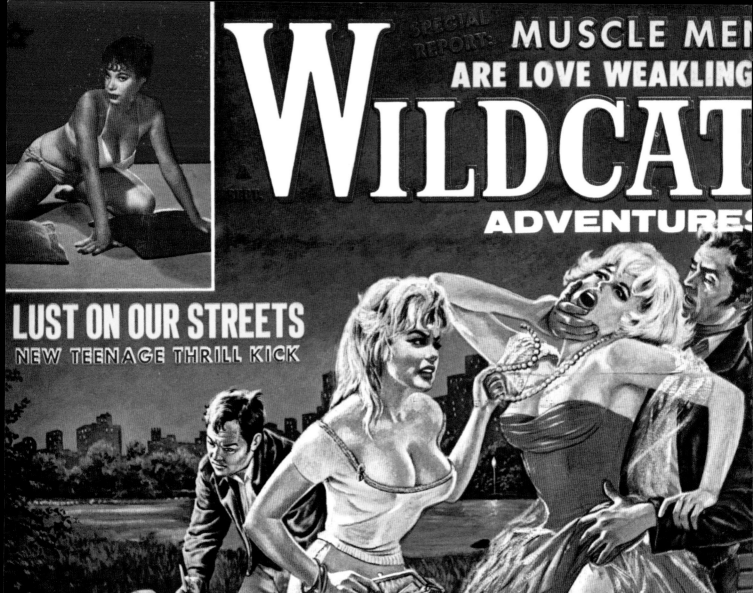

SPECIAL REPORT:

MUSCLE MEN
ARE LOVE WEAKLING

Wildcat
ADVENTURES

LUST ON OUR STREETS
NEW TEENAGE THRILL KICK

WHY BRIGITTE BARDOT
CAN'T HOLD HER MAN

THE SADISTIC FUEHRER
OF THE NEW NAZI BEAST

WILDCAT ADVENTURES, September 1963. Uncredited.

DARING, July 1961. Uncredited.

Illustration: Norman Saunders.

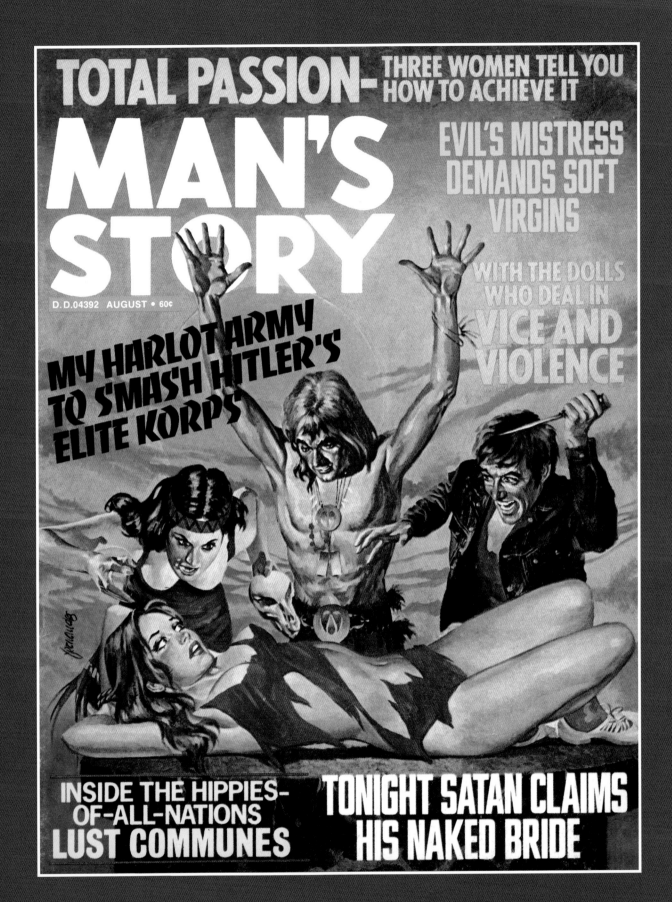

MAN'S STORY, August 1974. Illustration: Fernandez.

NEW MAN, February 1970. Illustration: Norman Saunders.

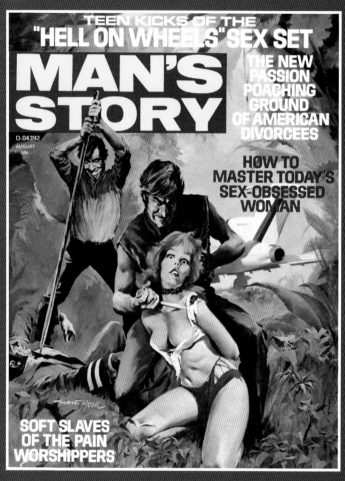

MAN'S BOOK, August 1972. Uncredited.

MEN TODAY, March 1972. Uncredited.

MAN'S STORY, August 1973. Illustration: "Martin Poll."

next page: FOR MEN ONLY, January 1968. Original Illustration: Mort Künstler.

Bill Devine

DEVINE'S GUIDE to MEN'S ADVENTURE MAGAZINES

In 1997, men's adventure magazine collector Bill Devine put together what was, and still remains, the most complete checklist of the genre: the titles, the length of their existence, their illustrators and whenever possible, circulation data. Further material has been added to Devine's guide from a list provided by the collector Andrew Barbanti, as well as the book's author's own discoveries. Devine believes the guide is still incomplete, and wishes further updates from interested parties, who can pass along information to Mr. Devine at 702 Middle St., Bath, ME 04530. (And send Feral House your corrections for any future printing.)

This abbreviated guide does not include Devine's introductory text on how he accumulated his collection, as well as a brief history of the magazines, covered elsewhere in this book. This indefatigable collector estimates that well over 130 men's adventure magazine titles were released, a collection of over 6,000 individual issues. Devine acknowledges certain publishers, particularly Fawcett Publications for *True*; Ned Pines for Nedar/Standard comics and magazines that had a run from the late '40s to late '50s; Everett Arnold for his brief men's adventure career after selling Quality Comics to DC Comics in 1956; Stanley Morse (Stanmor), famous for pre-code horror comics, who converted the *Battle Cry* comic into a magazine in issue #21 after the comics code became a problem. Other publishers acknowledged by Devine for both comic books and adventure mags include Prize/Feature/Crestwood/Hillman and Star (L.B. Cole). Martin Goodman, famous for his "Diamond" imprint on his various magazines, is acknowledged for his prolific nature. Elsewhere in this book, David Saunders, son of illustrator Norm Saunders, suggests that Martin Goodman was pseudonymously involved in the publication of torture magazines, an idea verified by Goodman's involvement with "Red Circle" band Weird Menace pulps of the late '30s, many of which feature covers that were later modified to become Nazi and Jap torture with the sadistic burlesque variety of men's adventure mags. (It should be noted here that in his guide, Devine does not put forward the controversial idea that Goodman might have been involved in torture slicks.)

Mr. Devine wishes to thank the following individuals for assisting with his guide: David Alexander and Terry Stroud of The American Comicbook Co., Michael Blessing, George Haenauer, John Matricardi, Gerald Tilley, The Antiquarian Bookstore of Portsmouth, NH, and Now and Then Comics of Lexington, KY.

HOW TO SCORE MASCULINITY TEST ON PAGE 47

1. Score 3 for (a), 4 for (b), 2 for (c), 1 for (d), 5 for (e), 0 for (f)
2. Score 5 for (a), 3 for (b), 1 for (c), 0 for (d)
3. Score 5 for (a), 2 for (b), 3 for (c), 0 for (d)
4. Score 5 for (a), 3 for (b), 0 for (c)
5. Score 1 for (a), 3 for (b), 5 for (c)
6. Score 0 for (a), 3 for (b), 5 for (c)
7. Score 0 for (a), 4 for (b), 5 for (c)
8. Score 5 for (a), 3 for (b), 4 for (c), 2 for (d), 1 for (e)
9. Score 5 for Yes, 0 for No
10. Score 5 for (a), 4 for (b), 3 for (c), 2 for (d), 0 for (e)
11. Score 5 for (a) and 0 for (b)
12. Score 5 for No, 0 for Yes
13. Score 4 for (a), 5 for (b), 1 for (c)
14. Score 5 for (a), 2 for (b), 0 for (c) (married)
    Score 5 for (a), 2 for (b), 0 for (c) (single)
15. Score 5 for Yes, 0 for No
16. Score 0 for (a), 5 for (b), 2 for (c)
17. Score 5 for No, 0 for Yes.
18. Score 5 for No, 0 for Yes.
19. Score 5 for (a), 2 for (b), 0 for (c)
20. Score 1 point for each capital letter response

YOUR RATING

90 to 100	Brute
80 to 89	Real he-man
70 to 79	Good man
60 to 69	Man, all right
50 to 59	A man, but not by much
40 to 49	Weak sister
Less than 40	Scratched

TITLE/PUBLISHER	FIRST ISSUE/DATE	LAST ISSUE/DATE	ISSUES

1. TITLE is listed as it appears on the indicia.

2. PUBLISHER is listed as it appears on the indicia or by the publishing group that it belongs to. For example, "Atlas/Diamond" is a group of magazines, "Vista" is one of the corporate names.

3. FIRST ISSUE/DATE is the earliest known issue. Not every title began with #1, some resulted from renaming titles; others, such as Jalart House, didn't use issue numbers. There may be earlier issues, not yet known to me.

4. LAST ISSUE/DATE is the last known issue. Later issues are bound to exist, I just don't know them as yet.

5. ISSUES is an estimate of how many issues were published for that title. Based on frequency, first and last known dates, I've made these estimates.

6. COMMENTS AND NOTES for each title. I've compiled information on cover subjects, stories and illustrations. More info will be disclosed as it becomes available.

7. COVER ART lists artists whose work has been credited or signed by the artist. I've done no guesswork, many covers are not identified as they are neither signed or credited.

8. INTERIOR ILLUSTRATIONS lists all the artists that have been credited or have signed their work for a title. Again, only signed or credited illos have been listed. Many illos were not credited or signed. Spellings vary in some cases.

9. PAID CIRCULATION has been obtained from the annual publisher statements printed in each title. After 1960, these numbers (subscriptions plus newsstand sales) were required to be divulged. I've used the 12-month average, not the latest issue.

TITLE/PUBLISHER	FIRST ISSUE/DATE	LAST ISSUE/DATE	ISSUES

ACE   #3 '57 OCT   #5 '58 FEB   5?
Four Star. Formerly *Sport Adventure*, "The Complete Man's Magazine." The #4 '57 DEC and #5 '58 FEB are both in the adventure style with painted covers. This title took over from *Sport Adventure* at some unknown number. Format changed to a "pin-up" style mag as early as the '58 JUN issue. Cover art: G.S. Eisenberg; Inside art: Fay, Kirkbride, Waterhouse.

ACTION   v1#1 '53 MAR   v1#6 '53 DEC   6+
Picture Magazines, Inc. Action and adventure painted covers. Cover art: Schneider, Szakoli; Inside art: Gaboda, V.S.

ACTION FOR MEN   v2#2 '58 MAR   v21#5 '77 JUN   132+
Published by Hillman, after '59 JUN by Vista (Atlas/Diamond) Publications. Many excellent painted covers through at least 1970, later issues had photos of girls on covers. Cover art: Bama, Copeland, Künstler, Norem. Inside art: Bama, Copeland, DeSoto, Ray Johnson, Kuller, Künstler, Little, Minney, Norem, Osterling, Paul, Pollen, Powell, Prezio, Roberts, Al Rossi, Stanley, Stirnweis, E. Wilson. Paid circulation, 1962: 136,308; 1966: 142,758.

ACTION LIFE   v3#3 '63 AUG   v4#3 '64 AUG   16
Published by Atlas, part of the Atlas/Diamond group. Cover art: James Bama. Inside art: James Bama, Ted Lewin, Earl Norem, Walter Popp, Bob Powell, Al Rossi, Harry Schaare, Bob Stanley.

ADVENTURE   v126#6 '53 APR   v147#2 '70 OCT   100+
Popular and New Publications. This title began in the early part of the century in the "pulp" format. 8 1/2 by 11 large format issues began in the early '50s and painted action covers lasted 1965. 1967 covers featured girls in a "pin-up" style and then bikini photos took over. Cover art: F. Bolivar, Herb Mott, Vic Prezio, Philip Ronfor. Inside art: Bama, Bolivar, Dumas, Feck, Gogos, P. Howe, Kastel, Kuller, Lewin, Lynch, Means, Mott, Obie, Olson, Powell, Prezio, Rahilly, Stanley, Sternweis, Stevens. Paid circulation, 1966: 112,484.

ADVENTURE FOR MEN   v5#1 '59 JUL   V5#4 '59 OCT   4
Sterling Group. Indicia says, "formerly *Man's Illustrated*." Seemingly a temporary name change... becomes *Man's Illustrated* again after four issues. Cover art: Stan Borack. Interior art: Doug Allen, Phil Berry.

ADVENTURE FOR MEN   '65 OCT   '74 MAR   45–52
ADVENTURE FOR MEN YEARBOOK #2 '68 SEP, others are likely Jalart House, Rostam and G.C. London. Many covers and stories were reprinted from earlier titles. Many good action-type covers, '74 MAR has a bondage, lingerie, hypodermic torture cover, reprinted from *Man's True Danger* 7/64. Inside art: Stan Borack, Mel Crair, Howell Dodd, Luis Dominguez, H.W. Johnson, Robert Lopshire, Newquist.

ADVENTURE LIFE   #2 '57 APR   v2#5 '58 NOV   10+
Published by Vista Publications, part of Atlas/Diamond group. Interior art: Doore, C. Frace, Ray Johnson, Waldman.

ADVENTURE LIFE   #2 '61 AUG   v3#2 '63 MAY   10+
Published by Atlas. Second series, nice action covers. Reprints of stories from first series, from Vista. Cover art: Stan Borack; Interior art: Kuller, Little, Norem, Pollen, Soltesz, Stanley, Stirnweis.

ADVENTURE TRUE STORY   '71 MAR   1?
Jalart. Photo cover, three illustrations inside. Indicia says portions reprinted from *Thrilling Adventures*; however, these reprints did appear previously in *Adventure For Men* 7/68. Photo cover; Interior art: H.W. Johnson, Newquist.

ALL MAN   #1 '59 MAR   v7#12 '67 MAY   62–64
Stanley Publications. Great title published 6 to 9 times per year. Many Nazi torture and bondage covers from '63 through '67. 4/66 cover reprinted from *Battle Cry* 10/61. Title changed over to a "pin-up" mag beginning '67 JUN or '67 JUL, and as a girlie mag the magazine lasted at least until 1975. Cover art: Vic Prezio. Interior art: Arnesen, Budelis, Correa, Donnermacher, Doore, Franklin, Gorenson, Hirtle, Lewin, Liljegren, Litman, Mark, McDonald, Waldman, Bill Ward (cartoons), Zachs, Zussman. Paid circulation, 1962: 103,945.

AMERICAN MANHOOD '53 JUN onwards   12 +
Weider Publications. Illustrated covers feature non-hairy gay bodybuilder type males.

ANIMAL LIFE   v1#2 '54 MAY
Weider Publications. Outdoor adventures, animals attacking people.

A-OK FOR MEN   #2 '62 OCT   '63 JUN   4–5
Jalart House. (There are two #3's.) Interior art: Howell Dodd.

ARGOSY   '44 APR   v386#4 '77 NOV   400+
Popular Publications. Began in 1882, was in the pulp format and switched to magazine size around '41. Painted covers, primarily, through 1960 and then photographs. Combined fact and fiction for men, many illustrations in full color, but more tame than other titles. Cover art: Dumas, Geissmann, McDermott, Rabut, Valigursky. Inside art: Asaro, Barnett, Bates, Calle, Chiriaka, Coconnis, M. Davis, Dumas, Feck, Fisher, Galli, Glanzman, Golden, Gross, Handville, Hearne, Hook, B. Johnson, Keane, Kossin, Kuhn, Künstler, Mayan, McCall, McDermott, McDorman, Meltzoff, Meyers, Otnes, Passalaqua, Peak, Richards, Stirnweis, Styga, Valigursky.

BATTLE ATTACK   v1#2 '57 MAY   v1#3 '57 JUL   2+

BATTLE CRY   v1#21(#1) '55   v12#9 '70 SEP   110+
Published by Stanley Publications. Early issues had painted covers showing combat soldiers in realistic situations. Women and bondage covers started around '59. One *Battle Cry* special issue: "Women in War," with the same cover illustration as a Normandy Associate's *Women in War* magazine. 10/61 issue has a Nazi woman whipping POW's. Later issues have pin-up style painted covers. Cover art: Clarence Doore, Vic Prezio. Interior art: Arnesen, Biggs, Budelis, Correa, Cramer, Doore, Duncanson, E. Frace, Franklin, Hirtle, Lewin, Morton, Poppe, Prezio, Schoenherr, W. Smith, Waldman.

BATTLEFIELD   v1#1 '57   v3#5 '59 NOV   7–12
Published by Newsstand Publications, part of the Atlas/Diamond group. The first issue features Marilyn Monroe inside. Cover art: Borack; Inside art: J. Bentley, Nappi, Rosenbaum, Shores.

BIG ADVENTURE   v1#1 '60 SEP
One issue, only?

BLUEBOOK   v100#3 '61 FEB   v112#1 '73 JAN   101–103+
BLUEBOOK ANNUAL   '69   '71   3+
H.S. Publications (6/64), Hanro (Sterling) (8/64–3/66), Q.M.G. Magazine Corp. (4/67-) Mostly painted military action-style covers. Most of the art is quarter-page, and some photos were used on covers. Converted to a "gay" men's mag sometime in the '70s. Cover art: Crair, J. Davis, Gross, Minney, Bob Schulz; interior art: Crair, Gogos, Gross, Infantino, Lewin, Minney, Mott, Norem, Prezio, Zusman. Paid circulation, 1966: 143,707.

BOLD MEN!   v5#3 '61 JUN   '61 SEP   2?
Cape Magazine Management Corp.

BRAVE   v1#2 '57 FEB
Smaller than standard size, larger than a digest, has a painted cover.

BRIGADE   #2 '62 DEC was on a dealer's listing

CAVALCADE   v1#5 '58 MAR   v4#3 '61 OCT   24–28
Skye Publishing. Painted military action covers. Changes to a *Playboy*-style mag with v4#4, '61 DEC. Cover art: Stan Borack, Mel Crair, George Gross. Interior art: Borack, Gross, Dodd, H.W. Johnson, Pike, Pinkava.

CAVALIER   v1#6 '53 AUG   v12#103 '62 JAN   103+
Fawcett. Action covers, many military and air battles. Changes over to a pin-up type mag by '63 JAN or earlier. Cover art: H. Greene, McCarthy, Ronfor, Truesdale. Interior art: Baer, Bates, J. Davis, Geisen, George, H. Greene, Bill Johnson, Kalin, Keane, Kidder, Kossin, Kuhn, Lynch, McCarthy, McDermott, G. Miller, Ronfor, Scott, Schaare, Tinsley, G. Wilson.

CHALLENGE FOR MEN   #1 '55 MAR v5#6 '59 SEP   30+
Almat, part of the Pyramid group. Painted covers include ones of Nazi military. Writing by Otto Binder. Cover art: Mel Crair, John Kuller. Interior art: Doug Allen, Rudy DeRenna, John Kuller, John Leone, Lou Marchetti, Prezio, Schaare, Shores, Mal Thompson.

CHAMP   #1 '57 MAY   #5 '58 JAN   6+
Hillman Periodicals. "Action-packed for men of action." Painted action covers. Interior art: Eisenberg, Hoban, Holmann, Omar Liebman, Sorrentino.

CHAMPION FOR MEN   '59 APR   '60 JAN   4+
Stanley Publications. 11/59: "Beatnik reefer parties."

CLIMAX   #1 '53 MAR   v13#4 '64 JAN   76+
Macfadden Publications. Military action painted covers. Some photo covers in '60s. '64 JAN cover says combined with *Impact*. Possible gap between 1953 and 1959 issues, or were there two series? Becomes a "pin-up" mag by '72 FEB or earlier, lasting until '74 OCT, at least. Cover art: Borack, Cellini, Mawicke, Pucci, Saunders. Interior art: Apt, Beck, Borack, Calle, Cellini, Eichinger, R. Engle, Ferris, Fredericks, Friedman, Greenberg, Groth, Hearn, Houlihan, Harvey Johnson, Jones, Kincaid, Lemoult, Lewin, Oscar Liebman, Lowenbein, Luberoff, Lynch, McKeown, S. Mitchell, Mott, O'Sullivan, Pike, Relis, Rosenbaum, Saunders, Shaw, Stone, Summers, Todhunter, Valdez, Valigursky, Violante, C. Walker, Waterhouse, Woolhiser, Ziel, Zusman. Paid circulation, 1962: 154,536; 1963: 139,731.

CLOAK 'N' DAGGER   #2 '64 OCT   #3 '64 DEC
James Bond, etc.

COMPLETE MAN   v5#2 '65 JUN   v7#2 '67 APR   10–12
Atlas/Diamond. Has reprints from earlier and other mags. Cover art: Gil Cohen, Charles Copeland, Earl Norem. Interior art: Cohen, Copeland, DeSoto, Minney, Norem, Pollen, Al Rossi, Denzil Smith, Bob Stanley.

COMPLETE MAN'S MAGAZINE   v2#3 '57 AUG
Atlas/Diamond. Formerly titled *Ken for Men*. v2#3 is first? Interior art: John Kuller, Don Miller.

CONQUEST   v1#1 '55 APR   1(?)

COURAGE   #1 '57 NOV   #3 '58 APR   3

DARING   v7#4 '67 FEB   v7#6 '67 JUN   3
Candar Publishing. Formerly *Man's Daring* becomes a slick mag; less adventure, more pin-up style.

EPIC   #3 '57 OCT   '59 JUN   22+

EPIC   #1 '61 FEB   #2 '61 APR   2+
Published by Skye. Both have painted covers in naval settings. Cover art: "J.K." Interior art: "J.K." Newquist.

ESCAPE TO ADVENTURE   #1 '57 JUL   v7#5 '64 NOV   41+
Published by Escape Magazines. Many wild action covers and inside illos by Mark Schneider, including a great girl underground commandos vs. Nazi tank on 5/64 cover and a Sid Shores Nazi desert-torture cover on 9/64. #2 dated '57 NOV. Cover art: Mark Schneider, Sid Shores. Interior art: Leo Carty, Luis Dominguez, Jon Laurell, Kurt Lockyer, Roy McCarey, Powell, Schneider, Shores, Szokoli, Frank Tauriello.

EXOTIC ADVENTURES   #1 '58   #6   6
By Gladiator Publications. Painted action covers, girls and military. Cover of #1 was also used on *For Men Only* '57 APR. Cover art: Rafael DeSoto. Interior art: Bill Border, S. Giglio.

EXPOSE FOR MEN   v3#1 '59 JUN   '60 OCT   10+
Published by Skye. Formerly titled *Sensation*. 8/59 has painted cover of Hitler and "true account of the Fuehrer's exotic call-girl temple." Cover art: Raphael DeSoto, Howell Dodd. Interior art: Dodd, H.W. Johnson, George Kraynak, R. Lopshire.

FOR MEN ONLY   #1 '54 MAY v24#8 '77 AUG   275–279+
FOR MEN ONLY ANNUAL   #12 '74   #16 '77   4–16
Published by Canam, Newsstand, Magazine Management, all parts of the Atlas/Diamond group. One of the leading titles in the genre. Painted action covers, early numbers had western, native and safari as well as military. Bettie Page pictorial in 5/55. Starting in '63 cover art began to shrink to only one-third to at most one-half of the cover. By the '70 paintings were replaced by girlie pix. Gradually became a girlie mag although most issues still had an action story or two. Cover art: Aviano, Bama, J. Bentley, Borack, Copeland, DeSoto, Doore, Kaye, Kuller, Künstler, Little, Schaare. Interior art: Allison, Bama, Belarski, J. Bentley, Berger, Cavaliere, Chan, Cohen, Copeland, DeSoto, Eisenberg, Gross, Ray Johnson, Kinstler, Künstler, Larkin, Lavin, John Leone, Little, Lou Marchetti, McVickers, Meese, Don Miller, Minney, Nappi, Norem, Paul, G. Phillips, Pollen, Popp, Prezio, Rader, Rickard, Riger, Rose, Al Rossi, Saunders, Schaare, R. Schultz, Schulz, Soltesz, Stanley, Stone, Ben Thomas, Vebell. Paid circulation: 1963: 386,807; 1976: 111,503

FRONTIER TIMES '57 WINTER   '85 NOV
First published as a monthly historical pulp in 1923 by J. Marvin Hunter, and then taken over by *True West's* Joe Small in 1957, its publications culminating in late '85 by Oklahoma-based publishers who raised circulation to over 100,000 copies.

FURY   '54 OCT   '61 MAY   22+
Weider Publications. Cover art: Tom Beecham. Interior art: Terence Brown, Rene DeVere, Clarence Doyle (Doore?), Dwight Howe, Diana Ross.

GUSTO   #1 '57 OCT   '57 DEC   2+
"He-Man Adventures." Published by Arnold Magazines, Inc. Interior art: Matt Baker, Bill Ward (cartoons).

GUY   #1 '59 JAN   v8#2 '70 FEB   44+
GUY ANNUAL   1967   1+
Published by Banner Magazines (3/59), Pyramid Pubs (4-12/66), and Hewfred Publications (6/67-). Painted covers, smaller on later issues. Interior art: Thomas Beecham, Jim Bentley, Mel Crair, Rudy DeReyna, Basil Gogos, Larry Newquist, Dick Shelton, Bill Sherlock, Bob Stanley, Richard Van Dongan.

HE   v1#1 '53 APR
"The Magazine for Men." Digest-sized.

HIGH ADVENTURE v1#3, '59 OCT

HIS   v1#1 '53 FEB   3+

HIS WORLD   #3 '53 AUG
Westridge Publishing.

HUNTING ADVENTURES v1#1 '54 WTR   5+
Newsstand Publications, Atlas group. One cover has turtles attacking hunters, blood everywhere! Cover art: Tom Ryan. Interior art: Jim Meese.

IMPACT   #3 '53 SEP   v14#3 '64 JUN
Macfadden. Two series? *Climax* from '64 JAN says "combined with *Impact*," yet there is a '64 APR *Impact*. *Impact* from '64 MAR says "combined with *Climax*." '53 *Impact* has a painted cover, '64 photo. Inside art: Charles Beck, Raymond Houlihan, Alan Kelly, Dom Lupo, Tom O'Sullivan, Del Rossi, Leo Summers, T. Dari Walker.

IMPACT   #1 '57 JUN   #4 '57 DEC   4+
Hanro Corp., a Sterling Magazine. "Bold True Action for Men." Painted military and jungle covers on the three I've seen. Not to be confused with Macfadden's *Impact*. Cover art: Gross, Schulz. Interior art: Gross, Popp.

JUMBO MAN'S MAGAZINE #1 early '60s   1?
Inside front cover says: "rebound from the best of previous issues published by Counterpoint, Inc., 1133 Broadway, N.Y., N.Y. and affiliated corporations." This is three magazines bound under one cover. The inside mags are

missing their covers and contents pages which makes it difficult to tell what magazines are included. There may be several different combinations of magazines inside. Cover has an action painting.

KEN FOR MEN v1#1 '56 JUN 6+
Atlas/Diamond, first series, title changes to *Complete Man's*.

KEN FOR MEN V3#2, '58 NOV
Diamond group. 59 APR appears in a dealer listing. A collector reports having v4#6, '59 NOV.

KEN FOR MEN v4#1 '61 MAR
Male Publishing, Atlas/Diamond, Numbering on this title is really out of whack. Inside art: R. Houlihan, Bob Schulz, Whitney.

MALE #1 '50 JUN v27#6 '77 JUN 302+
MALE ANNUAL (YEARBOOKS) #2 64 #21 '75 21(?)
Published by Official Comics (6/51), Official Mag. (11/51), Male (1/52–9/68), Perfect Film (10–12/68) and Magazine Management (1/69–77), part of the Atlas/Diamond group. One of the leading, longtime titles in the field. Painted action covers, many jungle, wild animal in the '50s; western in late '50s; military throughout the '60s. Paintings were phased out by '70 with girl pix taking over. Became more of a girlie mag at the end, although action stories and art still used. Continued by Pantheon as a sex/girlie mag to v30#4 '80 JUL or later. Bettie Page in 10/54 issue. "Pussycat" comic strip runs in many '68 and '69 issues; by Bill Ward in 4/68 and 5/68 issues. Cover art: Bama, J. Bentley, Bolden, Borack, Clark, Doares, Englert, Greco, Gross, Künstler, John Leone, McDermott, Mott, Schaare, Soltesz. Interior art: Bama, Benney, J. Bentley, Berger, Bolle, Borack, Carden, Cavaliere, Cohen, Copeland, Crair, Cummings, David, DeSoto, Doore, Englert, Fallat, Ferguson, Gross, Holloway, Hulings, Harper Johnson, Kaye, Kidder, Kirburger, Künstler, Larkin, John Leone, Little, Lou Marchetti, McDermott, Means, Meese, Don Miller, Minney, Mott, Nappi, Norem, Olsen, O'Sullivan, Pollen, Popp, Prezio, Reldan, Runfor, Al Rossi, Ryan, Schaare, Schulz, Singer, Soltesz, Stanley, Al Sussman, Art Sussman, P. Thomas, Bill Ward (Pussycat), G. Wilson, Fred Wolff. Paid circulation, 1963: 354,018; 1966: 298,060; 1967: 315,702; 1970: 265,581; 1971: 287,392; 1974: 221,864.

MAN ABOUT TOWN v1#1 '39 MAY
Digest-sized.

MAN TO MAN '50 DEC '73 OCT 120+
MAN TO MAN YEARBOOK '63 SPR 1?
Published by Picture Magazines, Inc. Painted action covers, including many Nazi and torture covers from '61 to '64. Changes to pin-up format by '65 MAY or earlier. Cover art: Ed Moritz, Mark Schneider, Sid Shores. Interior art: Carty, Duillo, Moritz, Schneider, Shores, Szokoli. Paid circulation, 1963: 148,029.

MAN'S ACTION v1#2 '57 SEP v11#12 '76 AUG 103–105+
Published by Candar, part of the Thunderbird group. Has painted covers, but they start getting pretty tiny from '66 on. Cover art: Duillo, Rosa. Interior art: Duillo, Frace, Pablo, Powell, Rosa, Shores, Bill Ward (cartoons). Paid circulation, 1963: 114,206; 1964: 187,857 (incorrect; my estimate: 100,000); 1974: 55,263; 1975: 40,942.

MAN'S ADVENTURE #1 '57 MAY v9#2 '67 OCT 79+
Stanley Publications. Title had many wild bondage and Nazi torture covers. Title continues as a pin-up mag, v9#2 '68 JAN. Yes, there are two v9#2's, the dates are different. Is there a '67 NOV issue? Is it action-adventure type? Cover art: Clarence Doore, A. Gruerio. Interior art: Beaman, Doore, Eisenberg, Everheart, Franklin, Hirtle, Lewin, C. Lewis, McCarey, Micarelli, Parenti, Piesanto, Shores, W. Smith, Waldman.

MAN'S BEST #1 '61 SEP '67 MAR 17–35+
Normandy Associates. Nazi torture painted cover. Interior art: Bud Cramer.

MAN'S BOOK #1 '62 MAR v10#5 '71 SEP 60+
Reese (-6/63) and EmTee Publications (1/64-). Many bondage and torture covers. Interior art: Duillo.

MAN'S CAVALCADE #1 '57 APR #3 '57 OCT 3 3+

MAN'S COMBAT v1#3 '69 OCT '69 DEC 3+

MAN'S CONQUEST #1(?) '55 JUN v6#2 '72 FEB 110+
Hanro Corp., part of the Sterling Group (6/61–10/65); and Q.M.G. Magazine (10/66-). Many realistic military battle covers. Hitler painted cover on 6/61 issue. QMG cover paintings focused on babes with bikers, spies, etc. Cover art: Gross, Schulz. Interior art: Belarski, Gogos.

MAN'S COURAGE '63 OCT 3+(?)

MAN'S DARING #1 '59 JUN v7#3 '66 DEC 42–43
Published by Candar (Thunderbird group) with great torture cover paintings, but they start to get tiny on later covers. Title changes to just *Daring* with v7#4. Cover art: Duillo. Interior art: Duillo, Osterling, Powell, Rosa, Wagner.

MAN'S DARING ADVENTURES #1 '55 NOV #3 '56 JUL 3+
Published by Star Editions. Comics great L.B. Cole was publisher and cover artist. Cover art: Cole; Interior art: Hollingsworth.

MAN'S DAY #1 '60 DEC #3 '61 APR 3+
Hillman. Small cover paintings. Interior art: John Duillo, Norm Eastman, Basil Gogos, Martin Ward.

MAN'S EPIC #1 '63 SEP v10#6 '73 OCT 66+
EmTee Publishing. Great bondage and battle covers. Later covers have small art. Cover art: Mel Crair; Interior art: no credits.

MAN'S ESCAPE v2#1 '64 FEB
Pontiac Publishing.

MAN'S EXPLOITS #1 '57 JUN AUG '63 FEB 36?

MAN'S ILLUSTRATED #1 '55 JUL v17#3 '74 AUG 118+
Published by Hanro (Sterling) then Q.M.G. Painted action covers include western, jungle and military themes, including some highly detailed battle covers by Basil Gogos on 11/61 and 1/64. Cover art: Stan Borack, Basil Gogos, George Gross, Interior art: Rudy Belarski, Stan Borack, Ray DeSoto, Basil Gogos, George Gross, Ted Lewin, Walter Popp, Santo Sorrentino. Paid circulation, 1963: 114,460.

MAN'S LIFE #1 '52 NOV '74 NOV 158–160+
Published by Crestwood (-12/65) and Stanley Pubs (5/66-). Painted action covers that got quite small in '64, later returning to bigger covers mostly focusing on the scantily-clad girls. Cover art: John Fay, Milton Luros, Vic Prezio. Interior art: John Fay, Milton Luros, Vic Prezio, Marvin Stein. Paid circulation, 1962: 206,176; 1963: 202,547; 1968: 100,579.

MAN'S LOOK #1 '61 AUG #4 '62 FEB 4+
Published by Normandy Associates. #4 has a Nazi bondage cover. Interior art: Arne Arnesen, Orly Eaines, Ulbrecht Donner, Clarence Doore, Ed Frace, Ed Franklin, Hugh Hirtle, Ted Lewin, Vic Prezio, Jack Schoenherr, Sid Shores, Barry Waldman.

MAN'S MAGAZINE v2#1 '54 JUN v23#7 '75 JUL 243–260+
MAN'S MAGAZINE ANNUAL '63–'72 10+
Madison Press (-8/54), Almat Publ. Corp. 9/56–6/61); Pyramid Pubs. (7/62-6766), all part of Pyramid Group; and Hewfred (3/67-). Another steady title in the field, early numbers were larger tabloid size. Had great military and men-in-danger cover paintings. Cover art got very small in '63 as text took up to three-quarters of the space on some covers. Switched to photo covers of girls in '69. Ian Fleming's *From Russia with Love*, is 5/64 book bonus. Cover art: Borack, Crair, Schaare, Schulz, Valigursky. Interior art: Allen, Appel, Beecham, Correa, Crair, A. Davis, Jack Davis (humor), deReyna, Drucker (humor), Eastman, Eisenberg, Franklin, Gogos, Gregory, Huehnergarth, Kuller, Lewin, McConnell, Bill Micarelli, Minter, Orehek, Orlando (humor), Powell, Prezio, Rader, Rosa, Schaare, Shores, Sternbergh, Thompson, Waterhouse.

MAN'S ODYSSEY #2 '58 MAR

MAN'S PERIL v6#7 '63 MAY v8#23 '67 JAN 18+
Published by Periodical Packagers (-1/64), Natlus (5/64–6/66), and Starbright (9/66-). Took over the numbering from *Peril* magazine. The cover of 1/64 uses same art from *For Men Only* 4/57's cover by Ray DeSoto. Interior art: Bob Powell, Bill Ward (cartoons).

MAN'S PRIME #1 '63 JUL v3#23 '67 MAR 23+
Published by Normandy Associates, part of Stanley group. #1's cover painting has Nazi soldiers dragging an undressed blonde to the guillotine. Inside art: Arnesen, Donnermacher, Hirtle, Lewin, Mandolini, Warwick.

MAN'S SMASHING STORIES #1 '59 JUN #3 '59 SEP 3

MAN'S STORY v1#1 '60 FEB '75 DEC 92+
Reese Publishing (-8/63) and EmTee Pub (12/63-) Terrific Nazi bondage torture covers from '62 to '65. Great inside art also. Cover art: Norm Eastman; Interior art: Duillo, Norm Eastman. Paid circulation, 1968: 76,385.

MAN'S THRILLS '61 JAN '61 OCT 3+
6/61: Hitler's last days.

MAN'S TIME v1#4 '62 MAY
AAA Magazines, Inc.

MAN'S TRUE ACTION #1 '55 OCT #4 '56 SEP 4+
Star Editions. L.B. Cole painted the covers of #1, #3 and #4, and was listed as publisher of #3. Inside art: Nodel, George Peltz.

MAN'S TRUE DANGER #1 '62 JUN v6#19 '70 OCT 52–54+
Candar (6-10/62) and Major Magazines (6/63-12/67), and Candar, again, (1/69-), part of the Thunderbird group. Girls in bondage or in danger are the focus of this title's cover paintings. The word "MAN'S" does not appear on every cover but is listed as the proper title on the inside indicia. Cover art: Duillo; Inside art: Duillo, Osterling.

MAN'S WORLD #1 '51 JAN
Lock Publishing Corp; part of Atlas? More info needed.

MAN'S WORLD #4 '55 NOV '77 NOV 124+
Published by Medalion (11/55–5/57), Official Mag. (9/57–2/58), Olympia (10/58–4/64), Vista (4/66–12/67), Magazine Management (2/70-) part of the Atlas/Diamond group. Great cover paintings of men in danger, wild animals, military scenes. Art got very small starting in '63. Photo covers took over in '70. Turned into a girlie/sex mag but still had frequent art and action stories. Cover art: Jim Bentley, Stan Borack, Charles Copeland, Rafael DeSoto, George Gross, Mort Künstler, Harry Schaare, Bob Schulz. Interior art: Attie, Bama, Belarski, J. Bentley, P. Berry, Chan, Cohen, Copeland, Crook, DeKuh, DeSoto, Eastman, Emsh, Mort Engle, Fay, Floherty, Garber, Gross, Hulings, Künstler, John Leone, Little, Lou Marchetti, Minney, Mott, Nappi, Norem, Nostrand, Paul, Pollen, Popp, Powell, Prezio, Richards, Rickard, Riger, Al Rossi, Ryan, Schaare, Schulz, Skemp, Soltesz, Stanley, Valigursky, Waterhouse, Kirk Wilson. Paid circulation, 1960: 179,953; 1963: 165,790; 1965: 184,120; 1969: 175,309.

MEN v1#5 '52 AUG v26#9 '77 SEP 306+
MEN ANNUAL #2 '68 #19 '76 19+
Zenith Pubs. (-10/68), Perfect Film (11, 12/68), Magazine Management (1/69-) part of the Atlas/Diamond group. Another long-running title. '50s issues ran covers of military, western, jungle and some great navy scenes. Early issues were tabloid size at least through #5. Cover paintings got small in the '60s but this title did continue many full cover paintings up until '69. At that time girl photo covers came along for most issues. Pussycat comic strip runs in many '69 to '71 issues. Title continues as a girlie/sex mag through '82 FEB or later. Cover art: J. Bentley, Cohen, DeSoto, Doares, Greco, Kaye, Künstler, Mott, Norem, Oughton, Schulz, Tauss. Inside art: Baer, Bama, J. Bentley, Cavaliere, Cohen, Copeland, Crair, Cummings, Darden, David, Floherty, Garden, Holloway, Jordan, Keane, Künstler, Lance, Little, McCann, Meese, Minney, Mooney (Pussycat), Norem, Nostrand, O'Toole, Paul, Pollen, Popp, Prezio, Al Rossi, Rubeck, Saunders, Schaare, Schulz, Soltesz, Stanley, Styga, Taus, Weber (humor), B. Ward (Pussycat), Whitney. Paid circulation, 1963: 244,375; 1966: 232,227; 1968: 221,655.

MEN IN ACTION #3 '55 SEP
Medalion, part of the Atlas/Diamond group. Cover art: Clarence Doore; Interior art: Mort Künstler, Bob Schulz.

MEN IN ADVENTURE #1 '59 JUL '73 APR 44–53+
Published by Skye (-12/60), Jalart House (1/63–66) and later by Rostam (12/68-). Probable gap of three years between Skye and Jalart. V2#2 has been reported with cover dates of '60 DEC and '62 OCT. Jalart covers seem to be patched together from reprints. Cover art: Robert Lopshire. Interior art: Budd, Howell Dodd, Hal DuBose, Willard Goodman, H.W. Johnson, Newquist.

MEN IN COMBAT #1 '57 JAN '57 JUL 3+
Hanro Pubs.

MEN IN CONFLICT #1 '61 AUG v2#17 '67 MAR 27–33+
Normandy Associates (-11/66) and Stanley Publications (3/67). #1 has a great Nazi torture cover. Bondage, lingerie and torture covers common. Interior art: Arnesen, Correa, Donner, Eastman, Ed Frace, Gogos, Lewin, Minney, Preston, Schoenherr, W. Smith, Zacks, Zusman.

MEN IN DANGER #2 '55 DEC '65 APR 8+
Published quarterly by Jalart House (64–65). Small cover paintings. Much of publisher's art and stories were recycled from earlier mags. '55 listing is from

a dealer ad, most likely an unrelated series, more info needed. #5 '56 JUN, '64 OCT also known. Interior art: DuBose, H.W. Johnson, R. Lopshire.

MEN TODAY #1 '61 APR v15#1 '75 JAN 90+
Published by Reese (1/63) and EmTee (4/64-) Publications. Early issues have great Nazi torture covers. Many bondage and torture covers throughout the run. Cover art: Norm Eastman. Inside art: Duillo, Norm Eastman, Edward Moritz. Paid circulation: 1963: 98,177, 1964: 85,525; 1965: 82,308; 1968: 74,682.

MEN'S DIGEST no. 63 '66 FEB
Digest-sized.

MEN'S PICTORIAL v31#4 '56 JUN v33#3 '57 AUG 8+
New Publications. A v32#1 dated '65 AUG was on a dealer listing. Cover art: Bob Stanley. Interior illustrations: Herb Mott, H. Rosenbaum.

MR. AMERICA #1 '53 JAN '53 AUG 6+
Weider Publications. "For the man with a future." Bullfight and western painted covers on these two. Cover art: Henry Lu. Interior art: Charles Dore, J. King, Michael McCann, Tom O'Reilly, Don Ray, Fred Wolff, Andre Zaro.

NEW MAN #1 '63 APR v9#5 '71 DEC 52+
Published by Reese (8/63) and EmTee Publications. (11/65-) Has Nazi torture covers, bondage and lingerie art. 1/63 cover has Nazis, girls in torn clothes and flaming train wrecks.

NEW MAN'S LIFE v1#3 '88 APR

O.K. FOR MEN #1 '58 DEC #3 '59 APR
3 Banner Magazines. Native cover art.

OUTDOOR ADVENTURES #1 '55 AUG '58 NOV 16+
Outdoor Adventures Publications, a Joe Weider mag, "The magazine of rousing wide-open action." First issue also sports a painted back cover, unusual, as most mags ran advertising. Cover art: Clarence Doore. Interior art: Doug Allen, Orville Bell, Clarence Doore, Stanley Duff, Rocco Lo Dolce, Karl Schultz, Selby Sims, Cy Williams.

PERIL v1#1 '56 OCT v6#6 '63 MAR 33–37
Jeflin Pub., and Periodical Packagers. Posed photos on '59 covers, paintings on the rest. Became *Man's Peril* with v6#7. Interior art: Howell Dodd, DuBose, H.W. Johnson, Mort Künstler, Doug Rosa, Charles Sultan.

PIC v25#6 '54 SEP v30#1 '61 MAR 30–90
Published by Wagner Publications. '54 issue has photos on cover and is a borderline title in the adventure genre. 3/61 issue has painted action spy cover and adventure stories. Earlier incarnations of this title were similar to *Life* in size and format. There is also another PIC, a digest mag in the '60s with girlie pix and expose articles. Interior art: Ray Houlihan.

PRIVATE EYE ILLUSTRATED #1 '59 NOV
Cal York Features.

PRIZE SEA STORIES '64 SPR 1?
Macfadden-Bartell Corp. Seems to be a one-shot put out by *Saga* magazine about shipwrecks, navy and ocean adventures. Many stories are reprints from *Saga*. Cover painting has Andrea Doria at the bottom of the ocean by Ed Valigursky. Inside art: Houlihan.

RACKETS v1#1 '56 JUN 1?
Publishing Corporation. Probable one-time-only exposé mag.

RAGE FOR MEN #1 '56 '57 AUG 5+
Arnold Magazines, first series. Elvis Presley writes an article defending rock & roll in #2; issue also has stripper Blaze Starr. Inside art: "M.B." (Matt Baker), Bill Ward (cartoon).

RAGE v2#1 '61 DEC '64 JUL 12+
Natlus, Inc. Second series. Interior art: H.W. Johnson, "S.R.P." (Bob Powell), Bill Ward (cartoons).

REAL #1 '52 OCT v18#2 '67 JUN 107+
Literary Enterprises (-4/58), Excellent Publications (8/60-8/63), PAR Publications (2/64), and Arizill Realty and Publishing (4/67). Cover paintings of men in danger. 4/67 has photo cover and pictorial on Sunset Strip teen riots. Bernard Baily was editor and art director in '63. Cover art: Floherty, Gross, Ray Johnson, Lualdi, Mayers, Meese, Ronfor, A. Leslie Ross, Savitt, Sternweiss, Tomaso. Interior art: Aviano, Baumgartner, Bolle, Boltinoff,

Brusstar, Darden, Dekuh, DeSoto, Doore, Eisenberger, Ferris, Floherty, Freeman, Glanzman, Gregori, Groth, Hearne, Hilbert, Ray Johnson, Kiel, Loomis, Lupo, Maxwell, Mayers, McCann, Meese, Mott, Nappi, Popp, Prezio, Rehberger, Ritter, Ronfor, A. Leslie Ross, Saunders, Savitt, Schaare, Stanley, Stone, Summers, M. Thomas, Wing, Wolff, Zusman.

REAL ACTION FOR MEN   #1 '57 APR   #4 '57 NOV
Four Star Publications.

REAL ACTION   #1 '63 JUN   #7 '64 JUN   7+
Published by Normandy Associates. Painted action covers.

REAL ADVENTURES   #1 '55 MAR   vC#5 '58 SEP   18+
Hillman Publications. Cover art: John Leone. Interior art: Victor Olsen, Santo Sorrentino.

REAL ADVENTURES   '61 FEB   '61 MAR
"New re-issue."

REAL ADVENTURES   '70 FEB   '70 NOV   4+
Jalart House. Montage cover, photos, some art. Interior art: Budd, Hal DuBose; H.W. Johnson; R. Lopshire.

REAL COMBAT STORIES   #1 '63 OCT   V10#1 '72 JAN   44–50+
Reese Publications. Scantily dressed girls in military battles on covers and inside.

REAL FOR MEN   '53 FEB   '57 MAY

REAL LIFE ADVENTURES   v1#4 '57 OCT   '58 FEB   5+
Vista Publications (Atlas/Diamond group). Civil War battle, painted cover. Interior art: Jim Bentley, Nappi, Prezio, Al Rossi.

REAL MEN   #1 '56 MAR   v17#1 '74 APR   148–153+
Stanley Publications. Long-running title, all by the same publisher. Early cover paintings are non-military, many westerns. 4/61 has Nazi bondage and many '61-'65 also feature Nazi bondage, torture cover paintings. Covers from '69 on focus on sexy women with action in the background. 4/74 is a photo cover. Cover art: Doore, Eastman, John Leone, Luros, Prezio. Interior art: Arnesen, Biggs, Budelis, Correa, Donner, Duncanson, Eisenstein, Ed Frace, Franklin, Gorenson, Hirtle, Hughes, Kweskin, Lewin, C. Lewis, Luros, Bob Micarelli, Olson, Parenti, Popp, Schoenherr, Shores, W. Smith, Waldman, Zacks, Zusman. Paid circulation, 1962: 119,078.

REAL WAR   v1#1 '57 OCT   v2#3 '58 NOV   6+
Stanley Publications. Military cover painting. 10/58 is all "space war!" Cover art: Prezio. Interior art: Ted Lewin, Lowenbein.

RUGGED   v1#1 '57 FEB   v1#3 '57 JUN   3+

RUGGED MEN   v1#1 '56 APR   '61 FEB   14+
Stanley Publications. Western and shipwreck painted covers. #2 is dated both '56 JUN and '58 JAN, could be a gap in publiication. Title also was changed to *Spur* during 1959, then back to *Rugged Men*. See *Spur* for issue numbers. V2#3 and v2#9 are Rugged Men. Cover art: Clarence Doore. Interior art: Budelis, Correa, Doore, Franklin, Hirtle, Kaves, C. Lewis, Saunders, Schoenherr.

SAFARI   '56 JAN   '61 JAN   30+
Safari Publications. Says combined with *Animal Life* inside. Lots of gorilla covers. Cover art: Douglas Allen, Maurice Bower. Interior art: Allen, Bell, C. Bentley, Biggs, Billings, Bode, Bower, Catto, Cozzarelli, Doares, Hart, Huffman, Laraia, McBride, Pease, Pitt, Stuart, Bob Wagner.

SAGA   v1#1 '50 SEP   v55#1 '77 NOV   326+
SAGA ANNUAL   v2#5 '79
Macfadden Publications, Gambi Publications ('66–on). Unusual action cover paintings in the '50s such as deep sea divers, carnivals. Fiction by Mickey Spillane and other top writers. Photo covers take over starting in '66. Long-running men's title kept the emphasis on action and adventure writing well into the '80s as a *Hustler* clone. Cover art: Borack, Gross, Hearne, Inman, Künstler, Lynch, G. Miller, B. Phillips, Ronfor, M. Thomas, Tomaso, Ed Valigursky. Interior art: Anderson, Ashman, Sarnett, Beck, Beecham, M. Berry, P. Berry, Binger, Boyle, Brennhan, O. Brown, Calle, Cardiff, Cellini, Coggins, Cohen, Connor, Contrerras (Contreros), Copic, D'Alessio, J. Davis, M. Davis, Dye, Ernest, Feck, Freeman, Friedman, Fritz, Garrido, Geer, Glanzman, D. Greene, Groth, Hearne, Heyer, Hill, Hinds, Houlihan, Kidd, Künstler, Joe Leone, Lewin, Linscott, Lupo, Lynch, Maguire,

D. Martin, F. Martin, Mawicke, Mays, McDermott, McGinnis, McKeown, Meltzoff, Mott, Nicholas, Polseno, Popp, Prezio, Privitello, Quigley, Richards, Ronfor, Rosa, Rose, Rosenbaum, K. Rossi, Sale, Schmidt, Schubert, Shore, Stone, Summers, Swearingen, Tomaso, Valigursky, Vernam, Waterhouse, Whitney, York. Paid circulation, 1961: 317,771; 1963: 280,647.

SALVO   '57 JAN   #3 '57 APR   3+

SAVAGE ADVENTURE   #1 '60 OCT   #4 '61 MAY   4+
Matclif Publications. Cover art: Norm Eastman, Mawa. Interior art: Arneson, Brucie, Correa, Donnermacher, Doore, Frank, Lewin, Keane, Tony Miccarelli, Poppe, Waldman.

SAVAGE ADVENTURES FOR MEN   #7 '59 MAY   #8 '59 SEP   2+
Cape Magazine. Formerly titled *Brave* magazine.

SCOOP   v.1#3 '42 DEC
Picture
Picture Scoop, Inc. published this oversize wartime magazine which announced it was "pledged to Victory!" Issue three had the nasty sadistic Nazi whipping the blonde American housewife's face.

SEE FOR MEN   v16#1 '57 JAN   v21#10 '64 JUL   40–44+
Literary Ent., Excellent, Par Publications. Painted action and some photo covers. 1/61 has unusual military painting of German soldiers being shot at by a plane while walking through snow. 3/63 cover painting has Berlin wall with commie Vopo chasing a couple. Earlier issues were news/photo type magazine. Cover art: Abbett, Gross, C. Smith, M. Thomas, G. Wilson. Interior art: Abbett, Aviano, Baumgartner, Bear, Beck, Beecham, Carboe, Correa, Darden, OeSoto, Garrido, Gross, Hantman, Hess, Howard, Isip, Keane, Kidder, Kiehl, Lupo, Mays, Meese, Tony Micarelli, Minnie, J. Mitchell, Mott, Osterling, Rader, Ritter, Rosa, Saunders, Savitt, C. Smith, Summers, Superior, M. Thomas, G. Wilson. Paid circulation, 1961: 250,000; 1963: 129,397.

SENSATION   v2#4 '58 OCT   '59 APR
Skye Publishing. Becomes *Exposé for Men* with 6/59 issue. There is an early 1940s mag titled *Sensation* as well.

SHOWDOWN FOR MEN   #2 '56   2+

SIR!   v7#1 '51 OCT   v19#5 '63 FEB   113–116+
Published by Volitant Publishing. Was in the adventure genre during the '50s and early '60s. Alternated formats between pin-up, scandal and adventure frequently during the '50s. Nazi cover painting on 11/61 cover. Switched to a "pin-up" format in 1963. Continued into the early '80s. Cover art: Norm Eastman, Mark Schneider. Interior art: Dominguez, Jon Laurell, Ed Moritz, Nicolai, Schneider.

SOUTH SEA STORIES   #3 '61 JAN   v5#2 '64 NOV   26+
Published by Counterpoint, Inc. Wild 9/63 cover has girl tied up on an anthill while a guy on an elephant shoots at the guy torturing the girl! Cover art: Mark Schneider. Interior art: Carty, R. Gifford, Powell, Schneider, Shores, "IZ." Paid circulation, 1963: 86,191.

SPIES CONFIDENTIAL   #1 '60
H.S. Publishing. By the editors of *Confidential* magazine. Probably a one-shot special. All photos, more exposé than adventure. No art, news photos.

SPORT ADVENTURE   v1#1 '57 JUN
(see *ACE*)

SPORT LIFE   v1#4 '54 OCT   '57 MAR   3+
Select Publications, an Atlas publication. Cover art: Tom Ryan. Interior art: Vic Dowd, Mort Künstler, Leone, Bob Moore, Tom Ryan.

SPORTSMAN   v1#2 '53 AUG   '68 FEB   120+?
Male Publishing, a part of the Atlas/Diamond group. Cover paintings featured safari, jungle and hostile natives. Many stories were reprinted from earlier Atlas mags. Cover art: Jim Bentley, Mort Künstler. Interior art: Bama, Bolle, Copeland, DeSoto, Doares, Emsh, Hantman, Ray Johnson, Künstler, McCann, Minney, Nappi, Paul, Pollen, Powell, Prezio, Rader, Saunders, Stanley, Sternberg, Stirnweis. Paid circulation, 1960: 81,699.

SPORT TRAILS   v1#1 '56 SUM   v1#2 '56 FALL   2+?

SPUR   v2#5 '59 APR   v2#8 '59 SEP   4–5
Stanley Publications. Formerly *Rugged Men*. 4/59 has a Western cover

painting. *Spur* changed back to *Rugged Men* with v2#9 dated '60 OCT. V2#4 could be either *Rugged Men* or *Spur*. Who knows? Cover art: Vic Prezio. Interior art: Bob Correa, Emile Ferrari, Ed Franklin, Hugh Hirtle.

SPY   v2#1 '67
Hewfred Pubs.

STAG   #1 '50 MAR   v27#2 '76 FEB   314+
STAG ANNUAL   #1 '64   #18 '75   18+
By Official Comics (3/51), Official Magazine (2/52–3/58), Atlas (7/58–10/68), Magazine Management (12/70-) and others, part of the Atlas/Diamond group. *Stag* had an earlier incarnation as an *Esquire* competitor. Title was revived in 1950 in a large-size format, at least through #5; #7 is "regular" size. Long-running title, great painted covers throughout the run. Military, western and adventure themes. Photo covers start in '69; becomes a girlie/sex mag, lasting to 6/92 or later. *Stag Annual* #1 has excerpt from James Bond novel by Fleming. Cover art: Cohen, DeSoto, Kaye, Künstler, Maguire, Mott, Norem, Schulz, Shaare, Singer. Interior art: Ackerman, Ames, Bama, Beck, J. Bentley, Block, Cohen, Copeland, Crair, David, DeSoto, Englert, Gross, Holloway, Houlihan, Jesse, Kaye, Keller, Künstler, Larkin, Lavin, Little, Lynch, McIntosh, Meese, Minney, Mooney (Pussycat), Nappi, Norem, Pollen, Popp, Pezio, Al Rossi, Rubek, Ryan, Schaare, Schulz, Shelton, Soltesz, Stanley, Bill Ward (Pussycat). Paid circulation, 1960: 471,702; 1966: 352,839; 1967: 368,087; 1970: 303,111; 1975: 245,483.

TARGET   v1#1 '61 OCT   #2 '61 DEC   2+
VIP Productions.

THRILLING ADVENTURE '70 SEP (Yearbook)

TRUE   '37 FEB   v56#454 '75 MAR   454+
Published by Fawcett, and Petersen Publishing: "The Man's Magazine." Issues from early '40s had color photos of women in bondage or in danger. Numerous adventure cover paintings and interior color illustrations during the '50s. Photo covers from late '50s on. *True* probably had the largest circulation of all the adventure type mags, at over two million copies per month in the early '60s. Cover art: Bob Abbett, Stan Galli, Tom Lovell, Fred Ludekens. Interior art: Abbett, Adams, Baumgartner, Bingham, Bomberger, Candy, Clymer, F. Davis, Glanzman, Grohe, Gross, Helck, Hunter, Hurst, Justis, Kuhn, Künstler, Linscott, Lovell, Ludekens, Mayan, McGinnis, Meyers, Monroe, Price, Reusswig, Alex Ross, Schmidt, Siebel, W. Smith, R. Stein, Sugarman, James Triggs. Paid circulation, 1972: 1,130,333.

TRUE ACTION   v4#1 '59 JAN   v20#2 '76 APR   90+
Published by Official (1/59–11/67), Magazine Management (4/74-) as part of the Atlas/Diamond group. Cover paintings through '67, girl photo covers in later years. Cover art: Borack, Cohen, Copeland, Künstler. Interior art: Bama, Cohen, Copeland, Emsh, Ray Johnson. Kaye, Künstler, Minney, Norem, Paul, Pike, Pollen, Prezio, Rickard, Al Rossi, Schaare, Stanley. Paid circulation, 1973: 83,933, 1974: 76,142.

TRUE ADVENTURES v23#1 '56 JAN   v39#6 '70 OCT   90+
New Publications. Likely a continuation of the numbering of *Detective Stories* pulp. Many western and other non-military cover paintings. 8/68 has "Dream Girl for GIs" photo cover. Cover art: DeSoto, Gogos, Gross, Little, Pollen. Interior art: Bettencourt, Bolivar, Copeland, Dallasta, Dekuh, L.S.G., Gogos, Lesser, Minney, Nelson, Newquist, Pollen, Popp, Prezio, Ramus, Roberts, Rosenbaum, Al Rossi, Saunders, Shane, Sorrentino, Spanfeller, Stevens, J. Triggs, Valigursky, Walters. Paid circulation, 1961: 156,221, 1963: 131,399, 1965: 104,119.

TRUE BATTLES OF WORLD WAR II v1#2 '64 FEB   v3#4 '66 JUN   12+
Stanley Magazine Corp. No art, all photos, all war stories.

TRUE DANGER (see MAN'S TRUE DANGER)

TRUE MEN STORIES #1 '56 OCT   v14#8 '73 FEB   108+
Feature Publications (-11/65), Stanley Publications (6/66-). Nice cover paintings on early numbers. Interior art: Clarence Doore. Paid circulation, 1963: 145,224, 1964: 100,111

TRUE PRIZE-WINNING WAR STORIES '63 SPR
Macfadden-Bartell Corp. Most likely a one-shot, produced by the editors of *Saga*. Painted cover by Stan Borack.

TRUE SPY AND WAR STORIES '66 SEP   '67 FEB   2+

Jalart House. Reprints from earlier mags. Cover painting. Interior art: Stan Borack, Mel Crair, Hal DuBose, H.W. Johnson.

TRUE STRANGE   #1 '56 OCT   v2#1 '58 FEB   6+
Weider Periodicals. "Incredible Weird and Factual" Bizarre covers. Cover art: Tom Beecham. Interior art: Baumann, Lou Cole, Harrison, D. Kammit, S. Kammet, Kimball, Lambert, Bob Lewis, Manning.

TRUE WAR   v1#1 '56 OCT   v2#5 '58 JUL   5+
Magnum Magazines. Painted covers. Cover art: Mal Singer. Interior art: S. Giglio, Micarelli, Santo Sorrentino.

TRUE WAR   #5 '75 AUG   5+
Countrywide Pubs. True WWII stories, all photos, Hitler on cover.

TRUE WEIRD   v1#1 '55 NOV   #3 '56 MAY   3+
Weider Publications. Companion to *True Strange*.

TRUE WEST   1953   CURRENT
Wild West magazine originally published by Joe "Hosstail" Small in Austin, Texas, and sold to several other owners beginning in 1974. A limited fannish partnership from Arizona rehabilitated the magazine in October 1999, along with *Old West* and *Frontier Times* magazines.

TRUE WORLD   #2 '56 FEB

UNTAMED   #1 '59 FEB '60 JAN   3+
Magnum Publications.

VALOR   v1#1 '57 JUN   v3#3 '59 OCT   15+
VALOR ANNUAL   '60
Skye Publishing. Jungle and military covers. Cover art: Mel Crair, Marchetti. Interior art: Budd, Howell Dodd, H.W. Johnson, Lopshire, Ed Smalle.

WAR   v1#1 64
Male Publ., Atlas/Diamond group. Cover says "by the editors of *Male* and *Stag*." Reprints? Künstler cover. All photos inside and one Gil Cohen illo.

WAR CRIMINALS v1#1 '61 AUG   v3#9 '66 JUL   20–33+
Normandy Associates. Nazi tortures in the background with portraits of Eichmann, Heydrich, Goebbels, etc. in these painted covers. Issue numbering is inconsistent. Interior art: Norm Eastman, Basil Gogos.

WAR STORIES   '63 SPR   '64 SUM   5+
WAR STORY   v1#3 '58 JAN   '59 FEB   6+
Charlton Publications. Painted cover.

WILD   '57 DEC
Exotica decapitation cover. One only?

WILDCAT ADVENTURES   #2 '59 AUG   v5#4 '64 AUG   22–30
Candar Publishing. Great action covers and inside art of Nazis, torture, plane crashes, juvenile delinquents. Changed format to a pin-up type mag with v5#5 '65 JAN. Interior art: Duillo, Victor Olson, Bill Ward (cartoons).

WOMEN-IN-WAR   '59 JAN   v2#2 '64 FEB   3+
Normandy Associates. Three known issues.

WORLD OF MEN   #2 '63 MAR   v10#4 '72 JUL   58+
EmTee Publications. Great Nazi bondage and torture covers. 12/64 has infamous Nazi rat torture cover painting. Inside art: Norm Eastman.

WWW.FERALHOUSE.COM

VOLUPTUOUS PANIC
THE EROTIC WORLD OF WEIMAR BERLIN
Mel Gordon

"The Encyclopedia Britannica of Weimar smut."—Stephen Lemons, *Salon.com*
"Like a Fodor's guide published by Taschen—but hipper—*Voluptuous Panic* is divine decadence."—Max Buda, *Flaunt*
"The sexiest—and strangest—book of the season."—*Talk Magazine*
"*Voluptuous Panic* is simultaneously appalling and thrilling, repellent and seductive, grotesque and gorgeous—not a typical coffee table book."—Gary Meyer, *Cleansheets*

Deluxe full-color paper on board • 8 1/2 x 11 • lavishly illustrated • 267 pages • ISBN: 0-922915-58-X • $29.95

THE HOT GIRLS OF WEIMAR BERLIN
Edited by Barbara Ulrich, Introduction by Jerry Stahl

"Even as Death, smiling like a sadistic Domina, lowers her high-heeled boot on your face, you can smile, and grind, and know that, for one tragic and ecstatic moment, release is yours. And you can forget about the obliteration to come. *The Hot Girls of Weimar Berlin* could make anybody forget."
—Jerry Stahl

Feral House's second full-color investigation into the sexual culture of pre-Nazi Germany this time focuses on women, their fetishistic ascendance over men and legionary consumption of drugs. Fashion, Sapphic cults and psychiatric case studies fill the pages.

Over 140 paintings, illustrations and photos • 8 x 11 • 120 pages • in full color • ISBN 0-922915-76-8 • $19.95

MUERTE!
DEATH IN MEXICAN POPULAR CULTURE
Edited by Harvey Bennett Stafford

Muerte! explores blood-obsessed tabloids like *Alarma!* and their huge influence in Mexican popular culture. Editor's Choice: "A magnificent investigation..."—*Journal of Forensic Medicine and Toxicology*. Extremely graphic.

10 x 8 • 114 pages • full color • ISBN 0-922915-59-8 • $16.95

To order from Feral House: domestic orders add $4.50 shipping for first item, $2.00 each additional item. Amex, MasterCard, Visa, checks and money orders are accepted. (CA state residents add 8.25% tax.) Canadian orders add $9 shipping for first item, $6 each additional item. Other countries add $11 shipping for first item, $9 each additional item. Non-U.S. originated orders must be international money order or check drawn on a U.S. Bank only.
Send orders to: Feral House, P.O. Box 13067, Los Angeles, CA 90013.
For a free full-color catalogue, send an S.A.S.E. to the Feral House address.